NON SANZ DROICT.

THE
Taming of the Shrew.

Decorative headband and title of the earliest authoritative
edition, in the First Folio (1623)

William Shakespeare

The Taming of the Shrew

With New and Updated
Critical Essays
and a Revised Bibliography

Edited by Robert B. Heilman

THE SIGNET CLASSICS SHAKESPEARE
General Editor: Sylvan Barnet

SIGNET CLASSICS

SIGNET CLASSICS
Published by New American Library, a division of
Penguin Group (USA) Inc., 375 Hudson Street,
New York, New York 10014, USA
Penguin Group (Canada), 90 Eglinton Avenue East, Suite 700, Toronto,
Ontario M4P 2Y3, Canada (a division of Pearson Penguin Canada Inc.)
Penguin Books Ltd., 80 Strand, London WC2R 0RL, England
Penguin Ireland, 25 St. Stephen's Green, Dublin 2,
Ireland (a division of Penguin Books Ltd.)
Penguin Group (Australia), 250 Camberwell Road, Camberwell, Victoria 3124,
Australia (a division of Pearson Australia Group Pty. Ltd.)
Penguin Books India Pvt. Ltd., 11 Community Centre, Panchsheel Park,
New Delhi - 110 017, India
Penguin Group (NZ), 67 Apollo Drive, Rosedale, North Shore 0632,
New Zealand (a division of Pearson New Zealand Ltd.)
Penguin Books (South Africa) (Pty.) Ltd., 24 Sturdee Avenue,
Rosebank, Johannesburg 2196, South Africa

Penguin Books Ltd., Registered Offices:
80 Strand, London WC2R 0RL, England

Published by Signet Classics, an imprint of New American Library, a division
of Penguin Group (USA) Inc. The Signet Classics edition of *The Taming of
the Shrew* was first published in 1966, and an updated edition was published
in 1986.

First Signet Classics Printing (Second Revised Edition), April 1999
40 39 38 37

Copyright © Robert B. Heilman, 1966, 1986
Copyright © Sylvan Barnet, 1966, 1987, 1998
All rights reserved

Ⓒ REGISTERED TRADEMARK—MARCA REGISTRADA

Printed in the United States of America

Contents

Shakespeare: An Overview

Biographical Sketch

Between the record of his baptism in Stratford on 26 April 1564 and the record of his burial in Stratford on 25 April 1616, some forty official documents name Shakespeare, and many others name his parents, his children, and his grandchildren. Further, there are at least fifty literary references to him in the works of his contemporaries. More facts are known about William Shakespeare than about any other playwright of the period except Ben Jonson. The facts should, however, be distinguished from the legends. The latter, inevitably more engaging and better known, tell us that the Stratford boy killed a calf in high style, poached deer and rabbits, and was forced to flee to London, where he held horses outside a playhouse. These traditions are only traditions; they may be true, but no evidence supports them, and it is well to stick to the facts.

Mary Arden, the dramatist's mother, was the daughter of a substantial landowner; about 1557 she married John Shakespeare, a tanner, glove-maker, and trader in wool, grain, and other farm commodities. In 1557 John Shakespeare was a member of the council (the governing body of Stratford), in 1558 a constable of the borough, in 1561 one of the two town chamberlains, in 1565 an alderman (entitling him to the appellation of "Mr."), in 1568 high bailiff— the town's highest political office, equivalent to mayor. After 1577, for an unknown reason he drops out of local politics. What *is* known is that he had to mortgage his wife's property, and that he was involved in serious litigation.

The birthday of William Shakespeare, the third child and the eldest son of this locally prominent man, is unrecorded, but the Stratford parish register records that the infant was baptized on 26 April 1564. (It is quite possible that he was born on 23 April, but this date has probably been assigned by tradition because it is the date on which, fifty-two years later, he died, and perhaps because it is the feast day of St. George, patron saint of England.) The attendance records of the Stratford grammar school of the period are not extant, but it is reasonable to assume that the son of a prominent local official attended the free school—it had been established for the purpose of educating males precisely of his class—and received substantial training in Latin. The masters of the school from Shakespeare's seventh to fifteenth years held Oxford degrees; the Elizabethan curriculum excluded mathematics and the natural sciences but taught a good deal of Latin rhetoric, logic, and literature, including plays by Plautus, Terence, and Seneca.

On 27 November 1582 a marriage license was issued for the marriage of Shakespeare and Anne Hathaway, eight years his senior. The couple had a daughter, Susanna, in May 1583. Perhaps the marriage was necessary, but perhaps the couple had earlier engaged, in the presence of witnesses, in a formal "troth plight" which would render their children legitimate even if no further ceremony were performed. In February 1585, Anne Hathaway bore Shakespeare twins, Hamnet and Judith.

That Shakespeare was born is excellent; that he married and had children is pleasant; but that we know nothing about his departure from Stratford to London or about the beginning of his theatrical career is lamentable and must be admitted. We would gladly sacrifice details about his children's baptism for details about his earliest days in the theater. Perhaps the poaching episode is true (but it is first reported almost a century after Shakespeare's death), or perhaps he left Stratford to be a schoolmaster, as another tradition holds; perhaps he was moved (like Petruchio in *The Taming of the Shrew*) by

> Such wind as scatters young men through the world,
> To seek their fortunes farther than at home
> Where small experience grows.   (1.2.49–51)

In 1592, thanks to the cantankerousness of Robert Greene, we have our first reference, a snarling one, to Shakespeare as an actor and playwright. Greene, a graduate of St. John's College, Cambridge, had become a playwright and a pamphleteer in London, and in one of his pamphlets he warns three university-educated playwrights against an actor who has presumed to turn playwright:

> There is an upstart crow, beautified with our feathers, that with his *tiger's heart wrapped in a player's hide* supposes he is as well able to bombast out a blank verse as the best of you, and being an absolute Johannes-factotum [i.e., jack-of-all-trades] is in his own conceit the only Shake-scene in a country.

The reference to the player, as well as the allusion to Aesop's crow (who strutted in borrowed plumage, as an actor struts in fine words not his own), makes it clear that by this date Shakespeare had both acted and written. That Shakespeare is meant is indicated not only by *Shake-scene* but also by the parody of a line from one of Shakespeare's plays, *3 Henry VI*: "O, tiger's heart wrapped in a woman's hide" (1.4.137). If in 1592 Shakespeare was prominent enough to be attacked by an envious dramatist, he probably had served an apprenticeship in the theater for at least a few years.

In any case, although there are no extant references to Shakespeare between the record of the baptism of his twins in 1585 and Greene's hostile comment about "Shake-scene" in 1592, it is evident that during some of these "dark years" or "lost years" Shakespeare had acted and written. There are a number of subsequent references to him as an actor. Documents indicate that in 1598 he is a "principal comedian," in 1603 a "principal tragedian," in 1608 he is one of the "men players." (We do not have, however, any solid information about which roles he may have played; later traditions say he played Adam in *As You Like It* and the ghost in *Hamlet*, but nothing supports the assertions. Probably his role as dramatist came to supersede his role as actor.) The profession of actor was not for a gentleman, and it occasionally drew the scorn of university men like Greene who resented writing speeches for persons less educated than themselves, but it was respectable enough; players, if prosperous, were in effect members of the bourgeoisie, and there is nothing to suggest that Stratford considered William Shakespeare less than a solid citizen. When, in 1596, the Shakespeares were granted a coat of arms—i.e., the right to be considered gentlemen—the grant was made to Shakespeare's father, but probably William Shakespeare had arranged the matter on his own behalf. In subsequent transactions he is occasionally styled a gentleman.

Although in 1593 and 1594 Shakespeare published two narrative poems dedicated to the Earl of Southampton, *Venus and Adonis* and *The Rape of Lucrece*, and may well have written most or all of his sonnets in the middle nineties, Shakespeare's literary activity seems to have been almost entirely devoted to the theater. (It may be significant that the two narrative poems were written in years when the plague closed the theaters for several months.) In 1594 he was a charter member of a theatrical company called the Chamberlain's Men, which in 1603 became the royal company, the King's Men, making Shakespeare the king's playwright. Until he retired to Stratford (about 1611, apparently), he was with this remarkably stable company. From 1599 the company acted primarily at the Globe theater, in which Shakespeare held a one-tenth interest. Other Elizabethan dramatists are known to have acted, but no other is known also to have been entitled to a share of the profits.

Shakespeare's first eight published plays did not have his name on them, but this is not remarkable; the most popular play of the period, Thomas Kyd's *The Spanish Tragedy*, went through many editions without naming Kyd, and Kyd's authorship is known only because a book on the profession of acting happens to quote (and attribute to Kyd) some lines on the interest of Roman emperors in the drama. What is remarkable is that after 1598 Shakespeare's name commonly appears on printed plays—some of which are not his. Presumably his name was a drawing card, and publishers used it to attract potential buyers. Another indication of his popularity comes from Francis Meres, author of *Palladis Tamia: Wit's Treasury* (1598). In this anthology of snippets accompanied by an essay on literature, many playwrights are mentioned, but Shakespeare's name occurs more often than any other, and Shakespeare is the only playwright whose plays are listed.

From his acting, his play writing, and his share in a playhouse, Shakespeare seems to have made considerable money. He put it to work, making substantial investments in Stratford real estate. As early as 1597 he bought New Place, the second-largest house in Stratford. His family moved in soon afterward, and the house remained in the family until a granddaughter died in 1670. When Shakespeare made his will in 1616, less than a month before he died, he sought to leave his property intact to his descendants. Of small bequests to relatives and to friends (including three actors, Richard Burbage, John Heminges, and Henry Condell), that to his wife of the second-best bed has provoked the most comment. It has sometimes been taken as a sign of an unhappy marriage (other supposed signs are the apparently hasty marriage, his wife's seniority of eight years, and his residence in London without his family). Perhaps the second-best bed was the bed the couple had slept in, the best bed being reserved for visitors. In any case, had Shakespeare not excepted it, the bed would have gone (with the rest of his household possessions) to his daughter and her husband.

On 25 April 1616 Shakespeare was buried within the chancel of the church at Stratford. An unattractive monument to his memory, placed on a wall near the grave, says that he died on 23 April. Over the grave itself are the lines, perhaps by Shakespeare, that (more than his literary fame) have kept his bones undisturbed in the crowded burial ground where old bones were often dislodged to make way for new:

> Good friend, for Jesus' sake forbear
> To dig the dust enclosed here.
> Blessed be the man that spares these stones
> And cursed be he that moves my bones.

A Note on the Anti-Stratfordians, Especially Baconians and Oxfordians

Not until 1769—more than a hundred and fifty years after Shakespeare's death—is there any record of anyone expressing doubt about Shakespeare's authorship of the plays and poems. In 1769, however, Herbert Lawrence nominated Francis Bacon (1561–1626) in *The Life and Adventures of Common Sense*. Since then, at least two dozen other nominees have been offered, including Christopher Marlowe, Sir Walter Raleigh, Queen Elizabeth I, and Edward de Vere, 17th earl of Oxford. The impulse behind all anti-Stratfordian movements is the scarcely concealed snobbish opinion that "the man from Stratford" simply could not have written the plays because he was a country fellow without a university education and without access to high society. Anyone, the argument goes, who used so many legal terms, medical terms, nautical terms, and so forth, and who showed some familiarity with classical writing, must have attended a university, and anyone who knew so much about courtly elegance and courtly deceit must himself have moved among courtiers. The plays do indeed reveal an author whose interests were exceptionally broad, but specialists in any given field—law, medicine, arms and armor, and so on—soon find that the plays do not reveal deep knowledge in specialized matters; indeed, the playwright often gets technical details wrong.

The claim on behalf of Bacon, forgotten almost as soon as it was put forth in 1769, was independently reasserted by Joseph C. Hart in 1848. In 1856 it was reaffirmed by W. H. Smith in a book, and also by Delia Bacon in an article; in 1857 Delia Bacon published a book, arguing that Francis Bacon had directed a group of intellectuals who wrote the plays.

Francis Bacon's claim has largely faded, perhaps because it was advanced with such evident craziness by Ignatius Donnelly, who in *The Great Cryptogram* (1888) claimed to break a code in the plays that proved Bacon had written not only the plays attributed to Shakespeare but also other Renaissance works, for instance the plays of Christopher Marlowe and the essays of Montaigne.

Consider the last two lines of the Epilogue in *The Tempest*:

As you from crimes would pardoned be,
Let your indulgence set me free.

What was Shakespeare—sorry, Francis Bacon, Baron Verulam—*really* saying in these two lines? According to Baconians, the lines are an anagram reading, "Tempest of Francis Bacon, Lord Verulam; do ye ne'er divulge me, ye words." Ingenious, and it is a pity that in the quotation the letter *a* appears only twice in the cryptogram, whereas in the deciphered message it appears three times. Oh, no problem; just alter "Verulam" to "Verul'm" and it works out very nicely.

Most people understand that with sufficient ingenuity one can torture any text and find in it what one wishes. For instance: Did Shakespeare have a hand in the King James Version of the Bible? It was nearing completion in 1610, when Shakespeare was forty-six years old. If you look at the 46th Psalm and count forward for forty-six words, you will find the word *shake*. Now if you go to the end of the psalm and count backward forty-six words, you will find the word *spear*. Clear evidence, according to some, that Shakespeare slyly left his mark in the book.

Bacon's candidacy has largely been replaced in the twentieth century by the candidacy of Edward de Vere (1550–1604), 17th earl of Oxford. The basic ideas behind the Oxford theory, advanced at greatest length by Dorothy and Charlton Ogburn in *This Star of England* (1952, rev. 1955), a book of 1297 pages, and by Charlton Ogburn in *The Mysterious William Shakespeare* (1984), a book of 892 pages, are these: (1) The man from Stratford could not possibly have had the mental equipment and the experience to have written the plays—only a courtier could have written them; (2) Oxford had the requisite background (social position, education, years at Queen Elizabeth's court); (3) Oxford did not wish his authorship to be known for two basic reasons: writing for the public theater was a vulgar pursuit, and the plays show so much courtly and royal disreputable behavior that they would have compromised Oxford's position at court. Oxfordians offer countless details to support the claim. For example, Hamlet's phrase "that ever I was born to set it right" (1.5.89) barely conceals "E. Ver, I was born to set it right," an unambiguous announcement of de Vere's authorship, according to *This Star of England* (p. 654). A second example: Consider Ben

xiv   SHAKESPEARE: AN OVERVIEW

Jonson's poem entitled "To the Memory of My Beloved Master William Shakespeare," prefixed to the first collected edition of Shakespeare's plays in 1623. According to Oxfordians, when Jonson in this poem speaks of the author of the plays as the "swan of Avon," he is alluding not to William Shakespeare, who was born and died in Stratford-on-Avon and who throughout his adult life owned property there; rather, he is alluding to Oxford, who, the Ogburns say, used "William Shakespeare" as his pen name, and whose manor at Bilton was on the Avon River. Oxfordians do not offer any evidence that Oxford took a pen name, and they do not mention that Oxford had sold the manor in 1581, forty-two years before Jonson wrote his poem. Surely a reference to the Shakespeare who was born in Stratford, who had returned to Stratford, and who had died there only seven years before Jonson wrote the poem is more plausible. And exactly why Jonson, who elsewhere also spoke of Shakespeare as a playwright, and why Heminges and Condell, who had acted with Shakespeare for about twenty years, should speak of Shakespeare as the author in their dedication in the 1623 volume of collected plays is never adequately explained by Oxfordians. Either Jonson, Heminges and Condell, and numerous others were in on the conspiracy, or they were all duped—equally unlikely alternatives. Another difficulty in the Oxford theory is that Oxford died in 1604, and some of the plays are clearly indebted to works and events later than 1604. Among the Oxfordian responses are: At his death Oxford left some plays, and in later years these were touched up by hacks, who added the material that points to later dates. *The Tempest*, almost universally regarded as one of Shakespeare's greatest plays and pretty clearly dated to 1611, does indeed date from a period after the death of Oxford, but it is a crude piece of work that should not be included in the canon of works by Oxford.

The anti-Stratfordians, in addition to assuming that the author must have been a man of rank and a university man, usually assume two conspiracies: (1) a conspiracy in Elizabethan and Jacobean times, in which a surprisingly large number of persons connected with the theater knew that the actor Shakespeare did not write the plays attributed to him but for some reason or other pretended that he did; (2) a conspiracy of today's Stratfordians, the professors who teach Shakespeare in the colleges and universities, who are said to have a vested interest in preserving Shakespeare as the author of the plays they teach. In fact, (1) it is inconceivable that the secret of Shakespeare's non-authorship could have been preserved by all of the people who supposedly were in on the conspiracy, and (2) academic fame awaits any scholar today who can disprove Shakespeare's authorship.

The Stratfordian case is convincing not only because hundreds or even thousands of anti-Stratford arguments—of the sort that say "ever I was born" has the secret double meaning "E. Ver, I was born"—add up to nothing at all but also because irrefutable evidence connects the man from Stratford with the London theater and with the authorship of particular plays. The anti-Stratfordians do not seem to understand that it is not enough to dismiss the Stratford case by saying that a fellow from the provinces simply couldn't have written the plays. Nor do they understand that it is not enough to dismiss all of the evidence connecting Shakespeare with the plays by asserting that it is perjured.

The Shakespeare Canon

We return to William Shakespeare. Thirty-seven plays as well as some nondramatic poems are generally held to constitute the Shakespeare canon, the body of authentic works. The exact dates of composition of most of the works are highly uncertain, but evidence of a starting point and/or of a final limiting point often provides a framework for informed guessing. For example, _Richard II_ cannot be earlier than 1595, the publication date of some material to which it is indebted; _The Merchant of Venice_ cannot be later than 1598, the year Francis Meres mentioned it. Sometimes arguments for a date hang on an alleged topical allusion, such as the lines about the unseasonable weather in _A Midsummer Night's Dream_, 2.1.81–117, but such an allusion, if indeed it is an allusion to an event in the real world, can be variously interpreted, and in any case there is always the possibility that a topical allusion was inserted years later, to bring the play up to date. (The issue of alterations in a text between the time that Shakespeare drafted it and the time that it was printed—alterations due to censorship or playhouse practice or Shakespeare's own second thoughts—will be discussed in "The Play Text as a Collaboration" later in this overview.) Dates are often attributed on the basis of style, and although conjectures about style usually rest on other conjectures (such as Shakespeare's development as a playwright, or the appropriateness of lines to character), sooner or later one must rely on one's literary sense. There is no documentary proof, for example, that *Othello* is not as early as *Romeo and Juliet*, but one feels that *Othello* is a later, more mature work, and because the first record of its performance is 1604, one is glad enough to set its composition at that date and not push it back into Shakespeare's early years. (*Romeo and Juliet* was first published in 1597, but evidence suggests that it was written a little earlier.) The following chronology, then, is indebted not only to facts but also to informed guesswork and sensitivity. The dates, necessarily imprecise for some works, indicate something like a scholarly consensus concerning the time of original composition. Some plays show evidence of later revision.

Plays. The first collected edition of Shakespeare, published in 1623, included thirty-six plays. These are all accepted as Shakespeare's, though for one of them, *Henry VIII*, he is thought to have had a collaborator. A thirty-seventh play, *Pericles*, published in 1609 and attributed to Shakespeare on the title page, is also widely accepted as being partly by Shakespeare even though it is not included in the 1623 volume. Still another play not in the 1623 volume, *The Two Noble Kinsmen*, was first published in 1634, with a title page attributing it to John Fletcher and Shakespeare. Probably most students of the subject now believe that Shakespeare did indeed have a hand in it. Of the remaining plays attributed at one time or another to Shakespeare, only one, *Edward III*, anonymously published in 1596, is now regarded by some scholars as a serious candidate. The prevailing opinion, however, is that this rather simpleminded play is not Shakespeare's; at most he may have revised some passages, chiefly scenes with the Countess of

Salisbury. We include *The Two Noble Kinsmen* but do not include *Edward III* in the following list.

1588–94	*The Comedy of Errors*
1588–94	*Love's Labor's Lost*
1589–91	*2 Henry VI*
1590–91	*3 Henry VI*
1589–92	*1 Henry VI*
1592–93	*Richard III*
1589–94	*Titus Andronicus*
1593–94	*The Taming of the Shrew*
1592–94	*The Two Gentlemen of Verona*
1594–96	*Romeo and Juliet*
1595	*Richard II*
1595–96	*A Midsummer Night's Dream*
1596–97	*King John*
1594–96	*The Merchant of Venice*
1596–97	*1 Henry IV*
1597	*The Merry Wives of Windsor*
1597–98	*2 Henry IV*
1598–99	*Much Ado About Nothing*
1598–99	*Henry V*
1599	*Julius Caesar*
1599–1600	*As You Like It*
1599–1600	*Twelfth Night*
1600–1601	*Hamlet*
1601–1602	*Troilus and Cressida*
1602–1604	*All's Well That Ends Well*
1603–1604	*Othello*
1604	*Measure for Measure*
1605–1606	*King Lear*
1605–1606	*Macbeth*
1606–1607	*Antony and Cleopatra*
1605–1608	*Timon of Athens*
1607–1608	*Coriolanus*
1607–1608	*Pericles*
1609–10	*Cymbeline*
1610–11	*The Winter's Tale*
1611	*The Tempest*

| 1612–13 | *Henry VIII* |
| 1613 | *The Two Noble Kinsmen* |

Poems. In 1989 Donald W. Foster published a book in which he argued that "A Funeral Elegy for Master William Peter," published in 1612, ascribed only to the initials W.S., *may* be by Shakespeare. Foster later published an article in a scholarly journal, *PMLA* 111 (1996), in which he asserted the claim more positively. The evidence begins with the initials, and includes the fact that the publisher and the printer of the elegy had published Shakespeare's *Sonnets* in 1609. But such facts add up to rather little, especially because no one has found any connection between Shakespeare and William Peter (an Oxford graduate about whom little is known, who was murdered at the age of twenty-nine). The argument is based chiefly on statistical examinations of word patterns, which are said to correlate with Shakespeare's known work. Despite such correlations, however, many readers feel that the poem does not sound like Shakespeare. True, Shakespeare has a great range of styles, but his work is consistently imaginative and interesting. Many readers find neither of these qualities in "A Funeral Elegy."

1592–93	*Venus and Adonis*
1593–94	*The Rape of Lucrece*
1593–1600	*Sonnets*
1600–1601	*The Phoenix and the Turtle*

Shakespeare's English

1. Spelling and Pronunciation. From the philologist's point of view, Shakespeare's English is modern English. It requires footnotes, but the inexperienced reader can comprehend substantial passages with very little help, whereas for the same reader Chaucer's Middle English is a foreign language. By the beginning of the fifteenth century the chief grammatical changes in English had taken place, and the final unaccented *-e* of Middle English had been lost (though it survives even today in spelling, as in *name*); during the fifteenth century the dialect of London, the commercial and political center, gradually displaced the provincial dialects, at least in writing; by the end of the century, printing had helped to regularize and stabilize the language, especially spelling. Elizabethan spelling may seem erratic to us (there were dozens of spellings of *Shakespeare*, and a simple word like *been* was also spelled *beene* and *bin*), but it had much in common with our spelling. Elizabethan spelling was conservative in that for the most part it reflected an older pronunciation (Middle English) rather than the sound of the language as it was then spoken, just as our spelling continues to reflect medieval pronunciation—most obviously in the now silent but formerly pronounced letters in a word such as *knight*. Elizabethan pronunciation, though not identical with ours, was much closer to ours than to that of the Middle Ages. Incidentally, though no one can be certain about what Elizabethan English sounded like, specialists tend to believe it was rather like the speech of a modern stage Irishman (*time* apparently was pronounced *toime*, *old* pronounced *awld*, *day* pronounced *die*, and *join* pronounced *jine*) and not at all like the Oxford speech that most of us think it was.

An awareness of the difference between our pronunciation and Shakespeare's is crucial in three areas—in accent, or number of syllables (many metrically regular lines may look irregular to us); in rhymes (which may not look like rhymes); and in puns (which may not look like puns). Examples will be useful. Some words that were at least on occasion stressed differently from today are *aspèct*, *còmplete*, *fòrlorn*, *revènue*, and *sepùlcher*. Words that sometimes had an additional syllable are *emp[e]ress*, *Hen[e]ry*, *mon[e]th*, and *villain* (three syllables, *vil-lay-in*). An additional syllable is often found in possessives, like *moon*'s (pronounced *moones*) and in words ending in *-tion* or *-sion*. Words that had one less syllable than they now have are *needle* (pronounced *neel*) and *violet* (pronounced *vilet*). Among rhymes now lost are *one* with *loan*, *love* with *prove*, *beast* with *jest*, *eat* with *great*. (In reading, trust your sense of metrics and your ear, more than your eye.) An example of a pun that has become obliterated by a change in pronunciation is Falstaff's reply to Prince Hal's "Come, tell us your reason" in *1 Henry IV*: "Give you a reason on compulsion? If reasons were as plentiful as blackberries, I would give no man a reason upon compulsion, I" (2.4.237–40). The *ea* in *reason* was pronounced rather like a long *a,* like the *ai* in *raisin,* hence the comparison with blackberries.

Puns are not merely attempts to be funny; like metaphors they often involve bringing into a meaningful relationship areas of experience normally seen as remote. In *2 Henry IV,* when Feeble is conscripted, he stoically says, "I care not. A man can die but once. We owe God a death" (3.2.242–43), punning on *debt,* which was the way *death* was pronounced. Here an enormously significant fact of life is put into simple commercial imagery, suggesting its commonplace quality. Shakespeare used the same pun earlier in *1 Henry IV,* when Prince Hal says to Falstaff, "Why, thou owest God a death," and Falstaff replies, " 'Tis not due yet: I would be loath to pay him before his day. What need I be so forward with him that calls not on me?" (5.1.126–29).

Sometimes the puns reveal a delightful playfulness; sometimes they reveal aggressiveness, as when, replying to Claudius's "But now, my cousin Hamlet, and my son," Hamlet says, "A little more than kin, and less than kind!" (1.2.64–65). These are Hamlet's first words in the play, and we already hear him warring verbally against Claudius. Hamlet's "less than kind" probably means (1) Hamlet is not of Claudius's family or nature, *kind* having the sense it still has in our word *mankind*; (2) Hamlet is not kindly (affectionately) disposed toward Claudius; (3) Claudius is not naturally (but rather unnaturally, in a legal sense incestuously) Hamlet's father. The puns evidently were not put in as sops to the groundlings; they are an important way of communicating a complex meaning.

2. *Vocabulary.* A conspicuous difficulty in reading Shakespeare is rooted in the fact that some of his words are no longer in common use—for example, words concerned with armor, astrology, clothing, coinage, hawking, horsemanship, law, medicine, sailing, and war. Shakespeare had a large vocabulary—something near thirty thousand words— but it was not so much a vocabulary of big words as a vocabulary drawn from a wide range of life, and it is partly

his ability to call upon a great body of concrete language that gives his plays the sense of being in close contact with life. When the right word did not already exist, he made it up. Among words thought to be his coinages are *accommodation, all-knowing, amazement, bare-faced, countless, dexterously, dislocate, dwindle, fancy-free, frugal, indistinguishable, lackluster, laughable, overawe, premeditated, sea change, star-crossed.* Among those that have not survived are the verb *convive,* meaning to feast together, and *smilet,* a little smile.

Less overtly troublesome than the technical words but more treacherous are the words that seem readily intelligible to us but whose Elizabethan meanings differ from their modern ones. When Horatio describes the Ghost as an "erring spirit," he is saying not that the ghost has sinned or made an error but that it is wandering. Here is a short list of some of the most common words in Shakespeare's plays that often (but not always) have a meaning other than their most usual modern meaning:

'a	he
abuse	deceive
accident	occurrence
advertise	inform
an, and	if
annoy	harm
appeal	accuse
artificial	skillful
brave	fine, splendid
censure	opinion
cheer	(1) face (2) frame of mind
chorus	a single person who comments on the events
closet	small private room
competitor	partner
conceit	idea, imagination
cousin	kinsman
cunning	skillful
disaster	evil astrological influence
doom	judgment
entertain	receive into service

envy	malice
event	outcome
excrement	outgrowth (of hair)
fact	evil deed
fancy	(1) love (2) imagination
fell	cruel
fellow	(1) companion (2) low person (often an insulting term if addressed to someone of approximately equal rank)
fond	foolish
free	(1) innocent (2) generous
glass	mirror
hap, haply	chance, by chance
head	army
humor	(1) mood (2) bodily fluid thought to control one's psychology
imp	child
intelligence	news
kind	natural, acting according to nature
let	hinder
lewd	base
mere(ly)	utter(ly)
modern	commonplace
natural	a fool, an idiot
naughty	(1) wicked (2) worthless
next	nearest
nice	(1) trivial (2) fussy
noise	music
policy	(1) prudence (2) stratagem
presently	immediately
prevent	anticipate
proper	handsome
prove	test
quick	alive
sad	serious
saw	proverb
secure	without care, incautious
silly	innocent

sensible	capable of being perceived by the senses
shrewd	sharp
so	provided that
starve	die
still	always
success	that which follows
tall	brave
tell	count
tonight	last night
wanton	playful, careless
watch	keep awake
will	lust
wink	close both eyes
wit	mind, intelligence

All glosses, of course, are mere approximations; sometimes one of Shakespeare's words may hover between an older meaning and a modern one, and as we have seen, his words often have multiple meanings.

3. Grammar. A few matters of grammar may be surveyed, though it should be noted at the outset that Shakespeare sometimes made up his own grammar. As E.A. Abbott says in *A Shakespearian Grammar,* "Almost any part of speech can be used as any other part of speech": a noun as a verb ("he childed as I fathered"); a verb as a noun ("She hath made compare"); or an adverb as an adjective ("a seldom pleasure"). There are hundreds, perhaps thousands, of such instances in the plays, many of which at first glance would not seem at all irregular and would trouble only a pedant. Here are a few broad matters.

Nouns: The Elizabethans thought the *-s* genitive ending for nouns (as in *man's*) derived from *his*; thus the line " 'gainst the count his galleys I did some service," for "the count's galleys."

Adjectives: By Shakespeare's time adjectives had lost the endings that once indicated gender, number, and case. About the only difference between Shakespeare's adjectives and ours is the use of the now redundant *more* or *most* with the comparative ("some more fitter place") or superlative

("This was the most unkindest cut of all"). Like double comparatives and double superlatives, double negatives were acceptable; Mercutio "will not budge for no man's pleasure."

Pronouns: The greatest change was in pronouns. In Middle English *thou, thy,* and *thee* were used among familiars and in speaking to children and inferiors; *ye, your,* and *you* were used in speaking to superiors (servants to masters, nobles to the king) or to equals with whom the speaker was not familiar. Increasingly the "polite" forms were used in all direct address, regardless of rank, and the accusative *you* displaced the nominative *ye.* Shakespeare sometimes uses *ye* instead of *you,* but even in Shakespeare's day *ye* was archaic, and it occurs mostly in rhetorical appeals.

Thou, thy, and *thee* were not completely displaced, however, and Shakespeare occasionally makes significant use of them, sometimes to connote familiarity or intimacy and sometimes to connote contempt. In *Twelfth Night* Sir Toby advises Sir Andrew to insult Cesario by addressing him as *thou:* "If thou thou'st him some thrice, it shall not be amiss" (3.2.46–47). In *Othello* when Brabantio is addressing an unidentified voice in the dark he says, "What are you?" (1.1.91), but when the voice identifies itself as the foolish suitor Roderigo, Brabantio uses the contemptuous form, saying, "I have charged thee not to haunt about my doors" (93). He uses this form for a while, but later in the scene, when he comes to regard Roderigo as an ally, he shifts back to the polite *you,* beginning in line 163, "What said she to you?" and on to the end of the scene. For reasons not yet satisfactorily explained, Elizabethans used *thou* in addresses to God—"O God, thy arm was here," the king says in *Henry V* (4.8.108)—and to supernatural characters such as ghosts and witches. A subtle variation occurs in *Hamlet.* When Hamlet first talks with the Ghost in 1.5, he uses *thou,* but when he sees the Ghost in his mother's room, in 3.4, he uses *you,* presumably because he is now convinced that the Ghost is not a counterfeit but is his father.

Perhaps the most unusual use of pronouns, from our point of view, is the neuter singular. In place of our *its, his* was often used, as in "How far that little candle throws *his* beams." But the use of a masculine pronoun for a neuter noun came to seem unnatural, and so *it* was used for the possessive as well as the nominative: "The hedge-sparrow fed the cuckoo so long / That it had it head bit off by it young." In the late sixteenth century the possessive form *its* developed, apparently by analogy with the *-s* ending used to indicate a genitive noun, as in *book*'s, but *its* was not yet common usage in Shakespeare's day. He seems to have used *its* only ten times, mostly in his later plays. Other usages, such as "you have seen Cassio and she together" or the substitution of *who* for *whom,* cause little problem even when noticed.

Verbs, Adverbs, and Prepositions: Verbs cause almost no difficulty: The third person singular present form commonly ends in *-s,* as in modern English (e.g., "He blesses"), but sometimes in *-eth* (Portia explains to Shylock that mercy "blesseth him that gives and him that takes"). Broadly speaking, the *-eth* ending was old-fashioned or dignified or "literary" rather than colloquial, except for the words *doth, hath,* and *saith.* The *-eth* ending (regularly used in the King James Bible, 1611) is very rare in Shakespeare's dramatic prose, though not surprisingly it occurs twice in the rather formal prose summary of the narrative poem *Lucrece.* Sometimes a plural subject, especially if it has collective force, takes a verb ending in *-s,* as in "My old bones aches." Some of our strong or irregular preterites (such as *broke*) have a different form in Shakespeare (*brake*); some verbs that now have a weak or regular preterite (such as *helped*) in Shakespeare have a strong or irregular preterite (*holp*). Some adverbs that today end in *-ly* were not inflected: "grievous sick," "wondrous strange." Finally, prepositions often are not the ones we expect: "We are such stuff as dreams are made on," "I have a king here to my flatterer."

Again, none of the differences (except meanings that have substantially changed or been lost) will cause much difficulty. But it must be confessed that for some elliptical passages there is no widespread agreement on meaning. Wise editors resist saying more than they know, and when they are uncertain they add a question mark to their gloss.

Shakespeare's Theater

In Shakespeare's infancy, Elizabethan actors performed wherever they could—in great halls, at court, in the courtyards of inns. These venues implied not only different audiences but also different playing conditions. The innyards must have made rather unsatisfactory theaters: on some days they were unavailable because carters bringing goods to London used them as depots; when available, they had to be rented from the innkeeper. In 1567, presumably to avoid such difficulties, and also to avoid regulation by the Common Council of London, which was not well disposed toward theatricals, one John Brayne, brother-in-law of the carpenter turned actor James Burbage, built the Red Lion in an eastern suburb of London. We know nothing about its shape or its capacity; we can say only that it may have been the first building in Europe constructed for the purpose of giving plays since the end of antiquity, a thousand years earlier. Even after the building of the Red Lion theatrical activity continued in London in makeshift circumstances, in marketplaces and inns, and always uneasily. In 1574 the Common Council required that plays and playing places in London be licensed because

> sundry great disorders and inconveniences have been found to ensue to this city by the inordinate haunting of great multitudes of people, specially youth, to plays, interludes, and shows, namely occasion of frays and quarrels, evil practices of incontinency in great inns having chambers and secret places adjoining to their open stages and galleries.

The Common Council ordered that innkeepers who wished licenses to hold performance put up a bond and make contributions to the poor.

The requirement that plays and innyard theaters be licensed, along with the other drawbacks of playing at inns and presumably along with the success of the Red Lion, led James Burbage to rent a plot of land northeast of the city walls, on property outside the jurisdiction of the city. Here he built England's second playhouse, called simply the Theatre. About all that is known of its construction is that it was wood. It soon had imitators, the most famous being the Globe (1599), essentially an amphitheater built across the Thames (again outside the city's jurisdiction), constructed with timbers of the Theatre, which had been dismantled when Burbage's lease ran out.

Admission to the theater was one penny, which allowed spectators to stand at the sides and front of the stage that jutted into the yard. An additional penny bought a seat in a covered part of the theater, and a third penny bought a more comfortable seat and a better location. It is notoriously difficult to translate prices into today's money, since some things that are inexpensive today would have been expensive in the past and vice versa—a pipeful of tobacco (imported, of course) cost a lot of money, about three pennies, and an orange (also imported) cost two or three times what a chicken cost—but perhaps we can get some idea of the low cost of the penny admission when we realize that a penny could also buy a pot of ale. An unskilled laborer made about five or sixpence a day, an artisan about twelve pence a day, and the hired actors (as opposed to the sharers in the company, such as Shakespeare) made about ten pence a performance. A printed play cost five or sixpence. Of course a visit to the theater (like a visit to a baseball game today) usually cost more than the admission since the spectator probably would also buy food and drink. Still, the low entrance fee meant that the theater was available to all except the very poorest people, rather as movies and most athletic events are today. Evidence indicates that the audience ranged from apprentices who somehow managed to scrape together the minimum entrance fee and to escape from their masters for a few hours, to prosperous members of the middle class and aristocrats who paid the additional fee for admission to the galleries. The exact proportion of men to women cannot be determined, but women of all classes certainly were present. Theaters were open every afternoon but Sundays for much of the year, except in times of plague, when they were closed because of fear of infection. By the way, no evidence suggests the presence of toilet facilities. Presumably the patrons relieved themselves by making a quick trip to the fields surrounding the playhouses.

There are four important sources of information about the

structure of Elizabethan public playhouses—drawings, a contract, recent excavations, and stage directions in the plays. Of drawings, only the so-called de Witt drawing (c. 1596) of the Swan—really his friend Aernout van Buchell's copy of Johannes de Witt's drawing—is of much significance. The drawing, the only extant representation of the interior of an Elizabethan theater, shows an amphitheater of three tiers, with a stage jutting from a wall into the yard or

Johannes de Witt, a Continental visitor to London, made a drawing of the Swan theater in about the year 1596. The original drawing is lost; this is Aernout van Buchell's copy of it.

center of the building. The tiers are roofed, and part of the stage is covered by a roof that projects from the rear and is supported at its front on two posts, but the groundlings, who paid a penny to stand in front of the stage or at its sides, were exposed to the sky. (Performances in such a playhouse were held only in the daytime; artificial illumination was not used.) At the rear of the stage are two massive doors; above the stage is a gallery.

The second major source of information, the contract for the Fortune (built in 1600), specifies that although the Globe (built in 1599) is to be the model, the Fortune is to be square, eighty feet outside and fifty-five inside. The stage is to be forty-three feet broad, and is to extend into the middle of the yard, i.e., it is twenty-seven and a half feet deep.

The third source of information, the 1989 excavations of the Rose (built in 1587), indicate that the Rose was fourteen-sided, about seventy-two feet in diameter with an inner yard almost fifty feet in diameter. The stage at the Rose was about sixteen feet deep, thirty-seven feet wide at the rear, and twenty-seven feet wide downstage. The relatively small dimensions and the tapering stage, in contrast to the rectangular stage in the Swan drawing, surprised theater historians and have made them more cautious in generalizing about the Elizabethan theater. Excavations at the Globe have not yielded much information, though some historians believe that the fragmentary evidence suggests a larger theater, perhaps one hundred feet in diameter.

From the fourth chief source, stage directions in the plays, one learns that entrance to the stage was by the doors at the rear (*"Enter one citizen at one door, and another at the other"*). A curtain hanging across the doorway—or a curtain hanging between the two doorways—could provide a place where a character could conceal himself, as Polonius does, when he wishes to overhear the conversation between Hamlet and Gertrude. Similarly, withdrawing a curtain from the doorway could "discover" (reveal) a character or two. Such discovery scenes are very rare in Elizabethan drama, but a good example occurs in *The Tempest* (5.1.171), where a stage direction tells us, *"Here Prospero discovers Ferdinand and Miranda playing at chess."* There was also some sort of playing space "aloft" or "above" to represent, for instance, the top of a city's walls or a room above the street. Doubtless each theater had its own peculiarities, but perhaps we can talk about a "typical" Elizabethan theater if we realize that no theater need exactly fit the description, just as no mother is the average mother with 2.7 children.

This hypothetical theater is wooden, round, or polygonal (in *Henry V* Shakespeare calls it a "wooden *O*") capable of holding some eight hundred spectators who stood in the yard around the projecting elevated stage—these spectators were the "groundlings"—and some fifteen hundred additional spectators who sat in the three roofed galleries. The stage, protected by a "shadow" or "heavens" or roof, is entered from two doors; behind the doors is the "tiring house" (attiring house, i.e., dressing room), and above the stage is some sort of gallery that may sometimes hold spectators but can be used (for example) as the bedroom from which Romeo—according to a stage direction in one text—"goeth down." Some evidence suggests that a throne can be lowered onto the platform stage, perhaps from the "shadow"; certainly characters can descend from the stage through a trap or traps into the cellar or "hell." Sometimes this space beneath the stage accommodates a sound-effects man or musician (in *Antony and Cleopatra "music of the hautboys* [oboes] *is under the stage"*) or an actor (in *Hamlet* the *"Ghost cries under the stage"*). Most characters simply walk on and off through the doors, but because there is no curtain in front of the platform, corpses will have to be carried off (Hamlet obligingly clears the stage of Polonius's corpse, when he says, "I'll lug the guts into the neighbor room"). Other characters may have fallen at the rear, where a curtain on a doorway could be drawn to conceal them.

Such may have been the "public theater," so called because its inexpensive admission made it available to a wide range of the populace. Another kind of theater has been called the "private theater" because its much greater admission charge (sixpence versus the penny for general admission at the public theater) limited its audience to the wealthy or the prodigal. The private theater was basically a large room, entirely roofed and therefore artificially illuminated, with a stage at one end. The theaters thus were distinct in two ways: One was essentially an amphitheater that catered to the general public; the other was a hall that catered to the wealthy. In 1576 a hall theater was established in Blackfriars, a Dominican priory in London that had been suppressed in 1538 and confiscated by the Crown and thus was not under the city's jurisdiction. All the actors in this Blackfriars theater were boys about eight to thirteen years old (in the public theaters similar boys played female parts; a boy Lady Macbeth played to a man Macbeth). Near the end of this section on Shakespeare's theater we will talk at some length about possible implications in this convention of using boys to play female roles, but for the moment we should say that it doubtless accounts for the relative lack of female roles in Elizabethan drama. Thus, in *A Midsummer Night's Dream*, out of twenty-one named roles, only four are female; in *Hamlet*, out of twenty-four, only two (Gertrude and Ophelia) are female. Many of Shakespeare's characters have fathers but no mothers—for instance, King Lear's daughters. We need not bring in Freud to explain the disparity; a dramatic company had only a few boys in it.

To return to the private theaters, in some of which all of the performers were children—the "eyrie of . . . little eyases" (nest of unfledged hawks—2.2.347–48) which Rosencrantz mentions when he and Guildenstern talk with Hamlet. The theater in Blackfriars had a precarious existence, and ceased operations in 1584. In 1596 James Burbage, who had already made theatrical history by building the Theatre, began to construct a second Blackfriars theater. He died in 1597, and for several years this second Blackfriars theater was used by a troupe of boys, but in 1608 two of Burbage's sons and five other actors (including Shakespeare) became joint operators of the theater, using it in the winter when the open-air Globe was unsuitable. Perhaps such a smaller theater, roofed, artificially illuminated, and with a tradition of a wealthy audience, exerted an influence in Shakespeare's late plays.

Performances in the private theaters may well have had intermissions during which music was played, but in the public theaters the action was probably uninterrupted, flowing from scene to scene almost without a break. Actors would enter, speak, exit, and others would immediately enter and establish (if necessary) the new locale by a few properties and by words and gestures. To indicate that the scene took place at night, a player or two would carry a torch. Here are some samples of Shakespeare establishing the scene:

This is Illyria, lady.   (*Twelfth Night,* 1.2.2)

Well, this is the Forest of Arden.   (*As You Like It,* 2.4.14)

This castle has a pleasant seat; the air
Nimbly and sweetly recommends itself
Unto our gentle senses.   (*Macbeth,* 1.6.1–3)

The west yet glimmers with some streaks of day.
                                          (*Macbeth,* 3.3.5)

Sometimes a speech will go far beyond evoking the minimal setting of place and time, and will, so to speak, evoke the social world in which the characters move. For instance, early in the first scene of *The Merchant of Venice* Salerio suggests an explanation for Antonio's melancholy. (In the following passage, *pageants* are decorated wagons, floats, and *cursy* is the verb "to curtsy," or "to bow.")

Your mind is tossing on the ocean,
There where your argosies with portly sail—
Like signiors and rich burghers on the flood,
Or as it were the pageants of the sea—
Do overpeer the petty traffickers
That cursy to them, do them reverence,
As they fly by them with their woven wings.   (1.1.8–14)

Late in the nineteenth century, when Henry Irving produced the play with elaborate illusionistic sets, the first scene showed a ship moored in the harbor, with fruit vendors and dock laborers, in an effort to evoke the bustling and exotic life of Venice. But Shakespeare's words give us this exotic, rich world of commerce in his highly descriptive language when Salerio speaks of "argosies with portly sail" that fly with "woven wings"; equally important, through Salerio Shakespeare conveys a sense of the orderly, hierarchical society in which the lesser ships, "the petty traffickers," curtsy and thereby "do . . . reverence" to their superiors, the merchant prince's ships, which are "Like signiors and rich burghers."

On the other hand, it is a mistake to think that except for verbal pictures the Elizabethan stage was bare. Although Shakespeare's Chorus in *Henry V* calls the stage an "unworthy scaffold" (Prologue 1.10) and urges the spectators to "eke out our performance with your mind" (Prologue 3.35), there was considerable spectacle. The last act of *Macbeth,* for instance, has five stage directions calling for *"drum and colors, "* and another sort of appeal to the eye is indicated by the stage direction *"Enter Macduff, with Macbeth's head."* Some scenery and properties may have been substantial; doubtless a throne was used, but the pillars supporting the roof would have served for the trees on which Orlando pins his poems in *As You Like It.*

Having talked about the public theater—"this wooden *O*"—at some length, we should mention again that Shakespeare's plays were performed also in other locales. Alvin Kernan, in *Shakespeare, the King's Playwright: Theater in the Stuart Court 1603–1613* (1995) points out that "several of [Shakespeare's] plays contain brief theatrical performances, set always in a court or some noble house. When Shakespeare portrayed a theater, he did not, except for the choruses in *Henry V*, imagine a public theater" (p. 195). (Examples include episodes in *The Taming of the Shrew*, *A Midsummer Night's Dream*, *Hamlet*, and *The Tempest*.)

A Note on the Use of Boy Actors in Female Roles

Until fairly recently, scholars were content to mention that the convention existed; they sometimes also mentioned that it continued the medieval practice of using males in female roles, and that other theaters, notably in ancient Greece and in China and Japan, also used males in female roles. (In classical Noh drama in Japan, males still play the female roles.) Prudery may have been at the root of the academic failure to talk much about the use of boy actors, or maybe there really is not much more to say than that it was a convention of a male-centered culture (Stephen Greenblatt's view, in *Shakespearean Negotiations* [1988]). Further, the very nature of a convention is that it is not thought about: Hamlet is a Dane and Julius Caesar is a Roman, but in Shakespeare's plays they speak English, and we in the audience never give this odd fact a thought. Similarly, a character may speak in the presence of others and we understand, again without thinking about it, that he or she is not heard by the figures on the stage (the aside); a character alone on the stage may speak (the soliloquy), and we do not take the character to be unhinged; in a realistic (box) set, the fourth wall, which allows us to see what is going on, is miraculously missing. The no-nonsense view, then, is that the boy actor was an accepted convention, accepted unthinkingly—just as today we know that Kenneth Branagh is not Hamlet, Al Pacino is not Richard III, and Denzel Washington is not the Prince of Aragon. In this view, the audience takes the performer for the role, and that is that; such is the argument we now make for race-free casting, in which African-Americans and Asians can play roles of persons who lived in medieval Denmark and ancient Rome. But gender perhaps is different, at least today. It is a matter of abundant academic study: The Elizabethan theater is now sometimes called a transvestite theater, and we hear much about cross-dressing.

Shakespeare himself in a very few passages calls attention to the use of boys in female roles. At the end of *As You Like It* the boy who played Rosalind addresses the audience, and says, "O men, . . . if I were a woman, I would kiss as many of you as had beards that pleased me." But this is in the Epilogue; the plot is over, and the actor is stepping out of the play and into the audience's everyday world. A second reference to the practice of boys playing female roles occurs in *Antony and Cleopatra*, when Cleopatra imagines that she and Antony will be the subject of crude plays, her role being performed by a boy:

> The quick comedians
> Extemporally will stage us, and present
> Our Alexandrian revels: Antony
> Shall be brought drunken forth, and I shall see
> Some squeaking Cleopatra boy my greatness. (5.2.216–20)

In a few other passages, Shakespeare is more indirect. For instance, in *Twelfth Night* Viola, played of course by a boy, disguises herself as a young man and seeks service in the house of a lord. She enlists the help of a Captain, and (by way of explaining away her voice and her beardlessness) says,

> I'll serve this duke
> Thou shalt present me as an eunuch to him.　　(1.2.55–56)

In *Hamlet*, when the players arrive in 2.2, Hamlet jokes with the boy who plays a female role. The boy has grown since Hamlet last saw him: "By'r Lady, your ladyship is nearer to heaven than when I saw you last by the altitude of a chopine" (a lady's thick-soled shoe). He goes on: "Pray God your voice . . . be not cracked" (434–38).

Exactly how sexual, how erotic, this material was and is, is now much disputed. Again, the use of boys may have been unnoticed, or rather not thought about—an unexamined convention—by most or all spectators most of the time, perhaps *all* of the time, except when Shakespeare calls the convention to the attention of the audience, as in the passages just quoted. Still, an occasional bit seems to invite erotic thoughts. The clearest example is the name that Rosalind takes in *As You Like It*, Ganymede—the beautiful youth whom Zeus abducted. Did boys dressed to play female roles carry homoerotic appeal for straight men (Lisa Jardine's view, in *Still Harping on Daughters* [1983]), or for gay men, or for some or all women in the audience? Further, when the boy actor played a woman who (for the purposes of the plot) disguised herself as a male, as Rosalind, Viola, and Portia do—so we get a boy playing a woman playing a man—what sort of appeal was generated, and for what sort of spectator?

Some scholars have argued that the convention empowered women by letting female characters display a freedom unavailable in Renaissance patriarchal society; the convention, it is said, undermined rigid gender distinctions. In this view, the convention (along with plots in which female characters for a while disguised themselves as young men) allowed Shakespeare to say what some modern gender

critics say: Gender is a constructed role rather than a bio-
logical given, something we make, rather than a fixed binary
opposition of male and female (see Juliet Dusinberre, in
Shakespeare and the Nature of Women [1975]). On the other
hand, some scholars have maintained that the male disguise
assumed by some female characters serves only to reaffirm
traditional social distinctions since female characters who
don male garb (notably Portia in *The Merchant of Venice*
and Rosalind in *As You Like It*) return to their female garb
and at least implicitly (these critics say) reaffirm the status
quo. (For this last view, see Clara Claiborne Park, in an
essay in *The Woman's Part*, ed. Carolyn Ruth Swift Lenz et
al. [1980].) Perhaps no one answer is right for all plays; in
As You Like It cross-dressing empowers Rosalind, but in
Twelfth Night cross-dressing comically traps Viola.

Shakespeare's Dramatic Language: Costumes, Gestures and Silences; Prose and Poetry

Because Shakespeare was a dramatist, not merely a poet,
he worked not only with language but also with costume,
sound effects, gestures, and even silences. We have already
discussed some kinds of spectacle in the preceding section,
and now we will begin with other aspects of visual language;
a theater, after all, is literally a "place for seeing." Consider
the opening stage direction in *The Tempest*, the first play in
the first published collection of Shakespeare's plays: "*A
tempestuous noise of thunder and Lightning heard: Enter a
Ship-master, and a Boteswain.*"

Costumes: What did that shipmaster and that boatswain
wear? Doubtless they wore something that identified them
as men of the sea. Not much is known about the costumes
that Elizabethan actors wore, but at least three points are
clear: (1) many of the costumes were splendid versions of
contemporary Elizabethan dress; (2) some attempts were
made to approximate the dress of certain occupations and of
antique or exotic characters such as Romans, Turks, and
Jews; (3) some costumes indicated that the wearer was

supernatural. Evidence for elaborate Elizabethan clothing can be found in the plays themselves and in contemporary comments about the "sumptuous" players who wore the discarded clothing of noblemen, as well as in account books that itemize such things as "a scarlet cloak with two broad gold laces, with gold buttons down the sides."

The attempts at approximation of the dress of certain occupations and nationalities also can be documented from the plays themselves, and it derives additional confirmation from a drawing of the first scene of Shakespeare's *Titus Andronicus*—the only extant Elizabethan picture of an identifiable episode in a play. (See pp. xxxviii–xxxix.) The drawing, probably done in 1594 or 1595, shows Queen Tamora pleading for mercy. She wears a somewhat medieval-looking robe and a crown; Titus wears a toga and a wreath, but two soldiers behind him wear costumes fairly close to Elizabethan dress. We do not know, however, if the drawing represents an actual stage production in the public theater, or perhaps a private production, or maybe only a reader's visualization of an episode. Further, there is some conflicting evidence: In *Julius Caesar* a reference is made to Caesar's doublet (a close-fitting jacket), which, if taken literally, suggests that even the protagonist did not wear Roman clothing; and certainly the lesser characters, who are said to wear hats, did not wear Roman garb.

It should be mentioned, too, that even ordinary clothing can be symbolic: Hamlet's "inky cloak," for example, sets him apart from the brightly dressed members of Claudius's court and symbolizes his mourning; the fresh clothes that are put on King Lear partly symbolize his return to sanity. Consider, too, the removal of disguises near the end of some plays. For instance, Rosalind in *As You Like It* and Portia and Nerissa in *The Merchant of Venice* remove their male attire, thus again becoming fully themselves.

Gestures and Silences: Gestures are an important part of a dramatist's language. King Lear kneels before his daughter Cordelia for a benediction (4.7.57–59), an act of humility that contrasts with his earlier speeches banishing her and that contrasts also with a comparable gesture, his ironic

kneeling before Regan (2.4.153–55). Northumberland's failure to kneel before King Richard II (3.3.71–72) speaks volumes. As for silences, consider a moment in *Coriolanus*: Before the protagonist yields to his mother's entreaties (5.3.182), there is this stage direction: *"Holds her by the hand, silent."* Another example of "speech in dumbness" occurs in *Macbeth*, when Macduff learns that his wife and children have been murdered. He is silent at first, as Malcolm's speech indicates: "What, man! Ne'er pull your hat upon your brows. Give sorrow words" (4.3.208–09). (For a discussion of such moments, see Philip C. McGuire's *Speechless Dialect: Shakespeare's Open Silences* [1985].)

Of course when we think of Shakespeare's work, we think primarily of his language, both the poetry and the prose.

Prose: Although two of his plays (*Richard II* and *King John*) have no prose at all, about half the others have at least one quarter of the dialogue in prose, and some have notably more: *1 Henry IV* and *2 Henry IV*, about half; *As You Like It*

and *Twelfth Night*, a little more than half; *Much Ado About Nothing*, more than three quarters; and *The Merry Wives of Windsor*, a little more than five sixths. We should remember that despite Molière's joke about M. Jourdain, who was amazed to learn that he spoke prose, most of us do not speak prose. Rather, we normally utter repetitive, shapeless, and often ungrammatical torrents; prose is something very different—a sort of literary imitation of speech at its most coherent.

Today we may think of prose as "natural" for drama; or even if we think that poetry is appropriate for high tragedy we may still think that prose is the right medium for comedy. Greek, Roman, and early English comedies, however, were written in verse. In fact, prose was not generally considered a literary medium in England until the late fifteenth century; Chaucer tells even his bawdy stories in verse. By the end of the 1580s, however, prose had established itself on the English comic stage. In tragedy, Marlowe made some use of prose, not simply in the speeches of clownish servants but even in the speech of a tragic hero, Doctor Faustus. Still, before Shakespeare, prose normally was used in the theater only for special circumstances: (1) letters and proclamations, to set them off from the poetic dialogue; (2) mad characters, to indicate that normal thinking has become disordered; and (3) low comedy, or speeches uttered by clowns even when they are not being comic. Shakespeare made use of these conventions, but he also went far beyond them. Sometimes he begins a scene in prose and then shifts into verse as the emotion is heightened; or conversely, he may shift from verse to prose when a speaker is lowering the emotional level, as when Brutus speaks in the Forum.

Shakespeare's prose usually is not prosaic. Hamlet's prose includes not only small talk with Rosencrantz and Guildenstern but also princely reflections on "What a piece of work is a man" (2.2.312). In conversation with Ophelia, he shifts from light talk in verse to a passionate prose denunciation of women (3.1.103), though the shift to prose here is perhaps also intended to suggest the possibility of madness. (Consult Brian Vickers, *The Artistry of Shakespeare's Prose* [1968].)

Poetry: Drama in rhyme in England goes back to the Middle Ages, but by Shakespeare's day rhyme no longer dominated poetic drama; a finer medium, blank verse (strictly speaking, unrhymed lines of ten syllables, with the stress on every second syllable) had been adopted. But before looking at unrhymed poetry, a few things should be said about the chief uses of rhyme in Shakespeare's plays. (1) A couplet (a pair of rhyming lines) is sometimes used to convey emotional heightening at the end of a blank verse speech; (2) characters sometimes speak a couplet as they leave the stage, suggesting closure; (3) except in the latest plays, scenes fairly often conclude with a couplet, and sometimes, as in *Richard II*, 2.1.145–46, the entrance of a new character within a scene is preceded by a couplet, which wraps up the earlier portion of that scene; (4) speeches of two characters occasionally are linked by rhyme, most notably in *Romeo and Juliet*, 1.5.95–108, where the lovers speak a sonnet between them; elsewhere a taunting reply occasionally rhymes with the previous speaker's last line; (5) speeches with sententious or gnomic remarks are sometimes in rhyme, as in the duke's speech in *Othello* (1.3.199–206); (6) speeches of sardonic mockery are sometimes in rhyme—for example, Iago's speech on women in *Othello* (2.1.146–58)—and they sometimes conclude with an emphatic couplet, as in Bolingbroke's speech on comforting words in *Richard II* (1.3.301–2); (7) some characters are associated with rhyme, such as the fairies in *A Midsummer Night's Dream*; (8) in the early plays, especially *The Comedy of Errors* and *The Taming of the Shrew*, comic scenes that in later plays would be in prose are in jingling rhymes; (9) prologues, choruses, plays-within-the-play, inscriptions, vows, epilogues, and so on are often in rhyme, and the songs in the plays are rhymed.

Neither prose nor rhyme immediately comes to mind when we first think of Shakespeare's medium: It is blank verse, unrhymed iambic pentameter. (In a mechanically exact line there are five iambic feet. An iambic foot consists of two syllables, the second accented, as in *away*; five feet make a pentameter line. Thus, a strict line of iambic pentameter contains ten syllables, the even syllables being stressed more heavily than the odd syllables. Fortunately, Shakespeare usually varies the line somewhat.) The first speech in *A Midsummer Night's Dream*, spoken by Duke Theseus to his betrothed, is an example of blank verse:

> Now, fair Hippolyta, our nuptial hour
> Draws on apace. Four happy days bring in
> Another moon; but, O, methinks, how slow
> This old moon wanes! She lingers my desires,
> Like to a stepdame, or a dowager,
> Long withering out a young man's revenue.   (1.1.1–6)

As this passage shows, Shakespeare's blank verse is not mechanically unvarying. Though the predominant foot is the iamb (as in *apace* or *desires*), there are numerous variations. In the first line the stress can be placed on "fair," as the regular metrical pattern suggests, but it is likely that "Now" gets almost as much emphasis; probably in the second line "Draws" is more heavily emphasized than "on," giving us a trochee (a stressed syllable followed by an unstressed one); and in the fourth line each word in the phrase "This old moon wanes" is probably stressed fairly heavily, conveying by two spondees (two feet, each of two stresses) the oppressive tedium that Theseus feels.

In Shakespeare's early plays much of the blank verse is end-stopped (that is, it has a heavy pause at the end of each line), but he later developed the ability to write iambic pentameter verse paragraphs (rather than lines) that give the illusion of speech. His chief techniques are (1) enjambing, i.e., running the thought beyond the single line, as in the first three lines of the speech just quoted; (2) occasionally replacing an iamb with another foot; (3) varying the position of the chief pause (the caesura) within a line; (4) adding an occasional unstressed syllable at the end of a line, traditionally called a feminine ending; (5) and beginning or ending a speech with a half line.

Shakespeare's mature blank verse has much of the rhythmic flexibility of his prose; both the language, though richly figurative and sometimes dense, and the syntax seem natural. It is also often highly appropriate to a particular character. Consider, for instance, this speech from *Hamlet*, in which Claudius, King of Denmark ("the Dane"), speaks to Laertes:

> And now, Laertes, what's the news with you?
> You told us of some suit. What is't, Laertes?
> You cannot speak of reason to the Dane
> And lose your voice. What wouldst thou beg, Laertes,
> That shall not be my offer, not thy asking?   (1.2.42–46)

Notice the short sentences and the repetition of the name "Laertes," to whom the speech is addressed. Notice, too, the shift from the royal "us" in the second line to the more intimate "my" in the last line, and from "you" in the first three lines to the more intimate "thou" and "thy" in the last two lines. Claudius knows how to ingratiate himself with Laertes.

For a second example of the flexibility of Shakespeare's blank verse, consider a passage from *Macbeth*. Distressed by the doctor's inability to cure Lady Macbeth and by the imminent battle, Macbeth addresses some of his remarks to the doctor and others to the servant who is arming him. The entire speech, with its pauses, interruptions, and irresolution (in "Pull't off, I say," Macbeth orders the servant to remove the armor that the servant has been putting on him), catches Macbeth's disintegration. (In the first line, *physic* means "medicine," and in the fourth and fifth lines, *cast the water* means "analyze the urine.")

> Throw physic to the dogs, I'll none of it.
> Come, put mine armor on. Give me my staff.
> Seyton, send out.—Doctor, the thanes fly from me.—
> Come, sir, dispatch. If thou couldst, doctor, cast
> The water of my land, find her disease
> And purge it to a sound and pristine health,
> I would applaud thee to the very echo,
> That should applaud again.—Pull't off, I say.—
> What rhubarb, senna, or what purgative drug,
> Would scour these English hence? Hear'st thou of them?
>
> (5.3.47–56)

Blank verse, then, can be much more than unrhymed iambic pentameter, and even within a single play Shakespeare's blank verse often consists of several styles, depending on the speaker and on the speaker's emotion at the moment.

The Play Text as a Collaboration

Shakespeare's fellow dramatist Ben Jonson reported that the actors said of Shakespeare, "In his writing, whatsoever he penned, he never blotted out line," i.e., never crossed out material and revised his work while composing. None of Shakespeare's plays survives in manuscript (with the possible exception of a scene in *Sir Thomas More*), so we cannot fully evaluate the comment, but in a few instances the published work clearly shows that he revised his manuscript. Consider the following passage (shown here in facsimile) from the best early text of *Romeo and Juliet*, the Second Quarto (1599):

Ro. Would I were sleepe and peace so sweet to rest
The grey eyde morne smiles on the frowning night,
Checkring the Easterne Clouds with streaks of light,
And darknesse fleckted like a drunkard reeles,
From forth daies pathway, made by *Tytans* wheeles.
Hence will I to my ghostly Friers close cell,
His helpe to craue, and my deare hap to tell.

Exit.

Enter Frier alone with a basket.   (night,
Fri. The grey-eyed morne smiles on the frowning
Checking the Easterne clowdes with streaks of light:
And fleckeld darknesse like a drunkard reeles,
From forth daies path, and *Titans* burning wheeles:
Now erethe sun aduance his burning eie,

Romeo rather elaborately tells us that the sun at dawn is dispelling the night (morning is smiling, the eastern clouds are checked with light, and the sun's chariot—Titan's wheels—advances), and he will seek out his spiritual father, the Friar. He exits and, oddly, the Friar enters and says pretty much the same thing about the sun. Both speakers say that "the gray-eyed morn smiles on the frowning night," but there are small differences, perhaps having more to do with the business of printing the book than with the author's composition: For Romeo's "checkring," "fleckted," and "pathway," we get the Friar's "checking," "fleckeld," and "path." (Notice, by the way, the inconsistency in Elizabethan spelling: Romeo's "clouds" become the Friar's "clowdes.")

Both versions must have been in the printer's copy, and it seems safe to assume that both were in Shakespeare's manuscript. He must have written one version—let's say he first wrote Romeo's closing lines for this scene—and then he decided, no, it's better to give this lyrical passage to the Friar, as the opening of a new scene, but he neglected to delete the first version. Editors must make a choice, and they may feel that the reasonable thing to do is to print the text as Shakespeare intended it. But how can we know what he intended? Almost all modern editors delete the lines from

Romeo's speech, and retain the Friar's lines. They don't do this because they know Shakespeare's intention, however. They give the lines to the Friar because the first published version (1597) of *Romeo and Juliet* gives only the Friar's version, and this text (though in many ways inferior to the 1599 text) is thought to derive from the memory of some act's, that is, it is thought to represent a performance, not a script. Maybe during the course of rehearsals Shakespeare—an actor as well as an author—unilaterally decided that the Friar should speak the lines; if so (remember that we don't know this to be a fact) his final intention was to give the speech to the Friar. Maybe, however, the actors talked it over and settled on the Friar, with or without Shakespeare's approval. On the other hand, despite the 1597 version, one might argue (if only weakly) on behalf of giving the lines to Romeo rather than to the Friar, thus: (1) Romeo's comment on the coming of the daylight emphasizes his separation from Juliet, and (2) the figurative language seems more appropriate to Romeo than to the Friar. Having said this, in the Signet edition we have decided in this instance to draw on the evidence provided by earlier text and to give the lines to the Friar, on the grounds that since Q1 reflects a production, in the theater (at least on one occasion) the lines were spoken by the Friar.

A playwright sold a script to a theatrical company. The script thus belonged to the company, not the author, and author and company alike must have regarded this script not as a literary work but as the basis for a play that the actors would create on the stage. We speak of Shakespeare as the author of the plays, but readers should bear in mind that the texts they read, even when derived from a single text, such as the First Folio (1623), are inevitably the collaborative work not simply of Shakespeare with his company—doubtless during rehearsals the actors would suggest alterations—but also with other forces of the age. One force was governmental censorship. In 1606 parliament passed "an Act to restrain abuses of players," prohibiting the utterance of oaths and the name of God. So where the earliest text of *Othello* gives us "By heaven" (3.3.106), the first Folio gives "Alas," presumably reflecting the compliance of stage practice with the law. Similarly, the 1623 version of *King Lear* omits the oath "Fut" (probably from "By God's foot") at 1.2.142, again presumably reflecting the line as it was spoken on the stage. Editors who seek to give the reader the play that Shakespeare initially conceived—the "authentic" play conceived by the solitary Shakespeare—probably will restore the missing oaths and references to God. Other editors, who see the play as a collaborative work, a construction made not only by Shakespeare but also by actors and compositors and even government censors, may claim that what counts is the play as it was actually performed. Such editors regard the censored text as legitimate, since it is the play that was (presumably) finally put on. A performed text, they argue, has more historical reality than a text produced by an editor who has sought to get at what Shakespeare initially wrote. In this view, the text of a play is rather like the script of a film; the script is not the film, and the play text is not the performed play. Even if we want to talk about the play that Shakespeare "intended," we will find ourselves talking about a script that he handed over to a company with the intention that it be implemented by actors. The "intended" play is the one that the actors—we might almost say "society"—would help to construct.

Further, it is now widely held that a play is also the work of readers and spectators, who do not simply receive meaning, but who create it when they respond to the play. This idea is fully in accord with contemporary post-structuralist critical thinking, notably Roland Barthes's "The Death of the Author," in *Image-Music-Text* (1977) and Michel Foucault's "What Is an Author?," in *The Foucault Reader* (1984). The gist of the idea is that an author is not an isolated genius; rather, authors are subject to the politics and other social structures of their age. A dramatist especially is a worker in a collaborative project, working most obviously with actors—parts may be written for particular actors—but working also with the audience. Consider the words of Samuel Johnson, written to be spoken by the actor David Garrick at the opening of a theater in 1747:

> The stage but echoes back the public voice;
> The drama's laws, the drama's patrons give,
> For we that live to please, must please to live.

The audience—the public taste as understood by the playwright—helps to determine what the play is. Moreover, even members of the public who are not part of the playwright's immediate audience may exert an influence through censorship. We have already glanced at governmental censorship, but there are also other kinds. Take one of Shakespeare's most beloved characters, Falstaff, who appears in three of Shakespeare's plays, the two parts of *Henry IV* and *The Merry Wives of Windsor*. He appears with this name in the earliest printed version of the first of these plays, *1 Henry IV*, but we know that Shakespeare originally called him (after an historical figure) Sir John Oldcastle. Oldcastle appears in Shakespeare's source (partly reprinted in the Signet edition of *1 Henry IV*), and a trace of the name survives in Shakespeare's play, 1.2.43–44, where Prince Hal punningly addresses Falstaff as "my old lad of the castle." But for some reason—perhaps because the family of the historical Oldcastle complained—Shakespeare had to change the name. In short, the play as we have it was (at least in this detail) subject to some sort of censorship. If we think that a text should present what we take to be the author's intention, we probably will want to replace *Falstaff* with *Oldcastle*. But if we recognize that a play is a collaboration, we may welcome the change, even if it was forced on Shakespeare. Somehow *Falstaff*, with its hint of *false-staff*, i.e., inadequate prop, seems just right for this fat knight who, to our delight, entertains the young prince with untruths. We can go as far as saying that, at least so far as a play is concerned, an insistence on the author's original intention (even if we could know it) can sometimes impoverish the text.

The tiny example of Falstaff's name illustrates the point that the text we read is inevitably only a version—something in effect produced by the collaboration of the playwright with his actors, audiences, compositors, and editors—of a fluid text that Shakespeare once wrote, just as the *Hamlet* that we see on the screen starring Kenneth Branagh is not the *Hamlet* that Shakespeare saw in an open-air playhouse starring Richard Burbage. *Hamlet* itself, as we shall note in a moment, also exists in several versions. It is not surprising that there is now much talk about the *instability* of Shakespeare's texts.

Because he was not only a playwright but was also an actor and a shareholder in a theatrical company, Shakespeare probably was much involved with the translation of the play from a manuscript to a stage production. He may or may not have done some rewriting during rehearsals, and he may or may not have been happy with cuts that were made. Some plays, notably *Hamlet* and *King Lear*, are so long that it is most unlikely that the texts we read were acted in their entirety. Further, for both of these plays we have more than one early text that demands consideration. In *Hamlet*, the Second Quarto (1604) includes some two hundred lines not found in the Folio (1623). Among the passages missing from the Folio are two of Hamlet's reflective speeches, the "dram of evil" speech (1.4.13–38) and "How all occasions do inform against me" (4.4.32–66). Since the Folio has more numerous and often fuller stage directions, it certainly looks as though in the Folio we get a theatrical version of the play, a text whose cuts were probably made—this is only a hunch, of course—not because Shakespeare was changing his conception of Hamlet but because the playhouse demanded a modified play. (The problem is complicated, since the Folio not only cuts some of the Quarto but adds some material. Various explanations have been offered.)

Or take an example from *King Lear*. In the First and Second Quarto (1608, 1619), the final speech of the play is given to Albany, Lear's surviving son-in-law, but in the First Folio version (1623), the speech is given to Edgar. The Quarto version is in accord with tradition—usually the highest-ranking character in a tragedy speaks the final words. Why does the Folio give the speech to Edgar? One possible answer is this: The Folio version omits some of Albany's speeches in earlier scenes, so perhaps it was decided (by Shakespeare? by the players?) not to give the final lines to so pale a character. In fact, the discrepancies are so many between the two texts, that some scholars argue we do not simply have texts showing different theatrical productions. Rather, these scholars say, Shakespeare substantially revised the play, and we really have two versions of *King Lear* (and of *Othello* also, say some)—two different plays—not simply two texts, each of which is in some ways imperfect.

In this view, the 1608 version of *Lear* may derive from Shakespeare's manuscript, and the 1623 version may derive from his later revision. The Quartos have almost three hundred lines not in the Folio, and the Folio has about a hundred lines not in the Quartos. It used to be held that all the texts were imperfect in various ways and from various causes—some passages in the Quartos were thought to have been set from a manuscript that was not entirely legible, other passages were thought to have been set by a compositor who was new to setting plays, and still other passages were thought to have been provided by an actor who misremembered some of the lines. This traditional view held that an editor must draw on the Quartos and the Folio in order to get Shakespeare's "real" play. The new argument holds (although not without considerable strain) that we have two authentic plays, Shakespeare's early version (in the Quarto) and Shakespeare's—or his theatrical company's—revised version (in the Folio). Not only theatrical demands but also Shakespeare's own artistic sense, it is argued, called for extensive revisions. Even the titles vary: Q1 is called *True Chronicle Historie of the life and death of King Lear and his three Daughters*, whereas the Folio text is called *The Tragedie of King Lear*. To combine the two texts in order to produce what the editor thinks is the play that Shakespeare intended to write is, according to this view, to produce a text that is false to the history of the play. If the new view is correct, and we do have texts of two distinct versions of *Lear* rather than two imperfect versions of one play, it supports in a textual way the poststructuralist view that we cannot possibly have an unmediated vision of (in this case) a play by Shakespeare; we can only recognize a plurality of visions.

Editing Texts

Though eighteen of his plays were published during his lifetime, Shakespeare seems never to have supervised their publication. There is nothing unusual here; when a playwright sold a play to a theatrical company he surrendered his ownership to it. Normally a company would not publish the play, because to publish it meant to allow competitors to acquire the piece. Some plays did get published: Apparently hard-up actors sometimes pieced together a play for a publisher; sometimes a company in need of money sold a play; and sometimes a company allowed publication of a play that no longer drew audiences. That Shakespeare did not concern himself with publication is not remarkable; of his contemporaries, only Ben Jonson carefully supervised the publication of his own plays.

In 1623, seven years after Shakespeare's death, John Heminges and Henry Condell (two senior members of Shakespeare's company, who had worked with him for about twenty years) collected his plays—published and unpublished—into a large volume, of a kind called a folio. (A folio is a volume consisting of large sheets that have been folded once, each sheet thus making two leaves, or four pages. The size of the page of course depends on the size of the sheet—a folio can range in height from twelve to sixteen inches, and in width from eight to eleven; the pages in the 1623 edition of Shakespeare, commonly called the First Folio, are approximately thirteen inches tall and eight inches wide.) The eighteen plays published during Shakespeare's lifetime had been issued one play per volume in small formats called quartos. (Each sheet in a quarto has been folded twice, making four leaves, or eight pages, each page being about nine inches tall and seven inches wide, roughly the size of a large paperback.)

Heminges and Condell suggest in an address "To the great variety of readers" that the republished plays are presented in better form than in the quartos:

> Before you were abused with diverse stolen and surreptitious copies, maimed and deformed by the frauds and stealths of injurious impostors that exposed them; even those, are now offered to your view cured and perfect of their limbs, and all the rest absolute in their numbers, as he [i.e., Shakespeare] conceived them.

There is a good deal of truth to this statement, but some of the quarto versions are better than others; some are in fact preferable to the Folio text.

Whoever was assigned to prepare the texts for publication

in the first Folio seems to have taken the job seriously and yet not to have performed it with uniform care. The sources of the texts seem to have been, in general, good unpublished copies or the best published copies. The first play in the collection, *The Tempest*, is divided into acts and scenes, has unusually full stage directions and descriptions of spectacle, and concludes with a list of the characters, but the editor was not able (or willing) to present all of the succeeding texts so fully dressed. Later texts occasionally show signs of carelessness: in one scene of *Much Ado About Nothing* the names of actors, instead of characters, appear as speech prefixes, as they had in the Quarto, which the Folio reprints; proofreading throughout the Folio is spotty and apparently was done without reference to the printer's copy; the pagination of *Hamlet* jumps from 156 to 257. Further, the proofreading was done while the presses continued to print, so that each play in each volume contains a mix of corrected and uncorrected pages.

Modern editors of Shakespeare must first select their copy; no problem if the play exists only in the Folio, but a considerable problem if the relationship between a Quarto and the Folio—or an early Quarto and a later one—is unclear. In the case of *Romeo and Juliet*, the First Quarto (Q1), published in 1597, is vastly inferior to the Second (Q2), published in 1599. The basis of Q1 apparently is a version put together from memory by some actors. Not surprisingly, it garbles many passages and is much shorter than Q2. On the other hand, occasionally Q1 makes better sense than Q2. For instance, near the end of the play, when the parents have assembled and learned of the deaths of Romeo and Juliet, in Q2 the Prince says (5.3.208–9),

> Come, *Montague;* for thou art early vp
> To see thy sonne and heire, now earling downe.

The last three words of this speech surely do not make sense, and many editors turn to Q1, which instead of "now earling downe" has "more early downe." Some modern editors take only "early" from Q1, and print "now early down"; others take "more early," and print "more early down." Further, Q1 (though, again, quite clearly a garbled and abbreviated text) includes some stage directions that are not found in Q2, and today many editors who base their text on Q2 are glad to add these stage directions, because the directions help to give us a sense of what the play looked like on Shakespeare's stage. Thus, in 4.3.58, after Juliet drinks the potion, Q1 gives us this stage direction, not in Q2: *"She falls upon her bed within the curtains."*

In short, an editor's decisions do not end with the choice of a single copy text. First of all, editors must reckon with Elizabethan spelling. If they are not producing a facsimile, they probably modernize the spelling, but ought they to preserve the old forms of words that apparently were pronounced quite unlike their modern forms—*lanthorn, alablaster*? If they preserve these forms are they really preserving Shakespeare's forms or perhaps those of a compositor in the printing house? What is one to do when one finds *lanthorn* and *lantern* in adjacent lines? (The editors of this series in general, but not invariably, assume that words should be spelled in their modern form, unless, for instance, a rhyme is involved.) Elizabethan punctuation, too, presents problems. For example, in the First Folio, the only text for the play, Macbeth rejects his wife's idea that he can wash the blood from his hand (2.2.60–62):

> No: this my Hand will rather
> The multitudinous Seas incarnadine,
> Making the Greene one, Red.

Obviously an editor will remove the superfluous capitals, and will probably alter the spelling to "incarnadine," but what about the comma before "Red"? If we retain the comma, Macbeth is calling the sea "the green one." If we drop the comma, Macbeth is saying that his bloody hand will make the sea ("the Green") *uniformly* red.

An editor will sometimes have to change more than spelling and punctuation. Macbeth says to his wife (1.7.46–47):

> I dare do all that may become a man,
> Who dares no more, is none.

For two centuries editors have agreed that the second line is unsatisfactory, and have emended "no" to "do": "Who dares do more is none." But when in the same play (4.2.21–22) Ross says that fearful persons

> Floate vpon a wilde and violent Sea
> Each way, and moue,

need we emend the passage? On the assumption that the compositor misread the manuscript, some editors emend "each way, and move" to "and move each way"; others emend "move" to "none" (i.e., "Each way and none"). Other editors, however, let the passage stand as in the original. The editors of the Signet Classic Shakespeare have restrained themselves from making abundant emendations. In their minds they hear Samuel Johnson on the dangers of emendation: "I have adopted the Roman sentiment, that it is more honorable to save a citizen than to kill an enemy." Some departures (in addition to spelling, punctuation, and lineation) from the copy text have of course been made, but the original readings are listed in a note following the play, so that readers can evaluate the changes for themselves.

Following tradition, the editors of the Signet Classic Shakespeare have prefaced each play with a list of characters, and throughout the play have regularized the names of the speakers. Thus, in our text of *Romeo and Juliet*, all speeches by Juliet's mother are prefixed "Lady Capulet," although the 1599 Quarto of the play, which provides our copy text, uses at various points seven speech tags for this one character: *Capu. Wi.* (i.e., Capulet's wife), *Ca. Wi., Wi., Wife, Old La.* (i.e., Old Lady), *La.,* and *Mo.* (i.e., Mother). Similarly, in *All's Well That Ends Well*, the character whom we regularly call "Countess" is in the Folio (the copy text) variously identified as *Mother, Countess, Old Countess, Lady,* and *Old Lady*. Admittedly there is some loss in regularizing, since the various prefixes may give us a hint of the way Shakespeare (or a scribe who copied Shakespeare's manuscript) was thinking of the character in a particular scene—for instance, as a mother, or as an old lady. But too much can be made of these differing prefixes, since the social relationships implied are *not* always relevant to the given scene.

We have also added line numbers and in many cases act and scene divisions as well as indications of locale at the beginning of scenes. The Folio divided most of the plays into acts and some into scenes. Early eighteenth-century editors increased the divisions. These divisions, which provide a convenient way of referring to passages in the plays, have been retained, but when not in the text chosen as the basis for the Signet Classic text they are enclosed within square brackets, [ ], to indicate that they are editorial additions. Similarly, though no play of Shakespeare's was equipped with indications of the locale at the heads of scene divisions, locales have here been added in square brackets for the convenience of readers, who lack the information that costumes, properties, gestures, and scenery afford to spectators. Spectators can tell at a glance they are in the throne room, but without an editorial indication the reader may be puzzled for a while. It should be mentioned, incidentally, that there are a few authentic stage directions—perhaps Shakespeare's, perhaps a prompter's—that suggest locales, such as *"Enter Brutus in his orchard,"* and *"They go up into the Senate house."* It is hoped that the bracketed additions in the Signet text will provide readers with the sort of help provided by these two authentic directions, but it is equally hoped that the reader will remember that the stage was not loaded with scenery.

Shakespeare on the Stage

Each volume in the Signet Classic Shakespeare includes a brief stage (and sometimes film) history of the play. When we read about earlier productions, we are likely to find them eccentric, obviously wrongheaded—for instance, Nahum Tate's version of *King Lear*, with a happy ending, which held the stage for about a century and a half, from the late seventeenth century until the end of the first quarter of the nineteenth. We see engravings of David Garrick, the greatest actor of the eighteenth century, in eighteenth-century garb as King Lear, and we smile, thinking how absurd the production must have been. If we are more thoughtful, we say, with the English novelist L. P. Hartley, "The past is a foreign country: they do things differently there." But if the eighteenth-century staging is a foreign country, what of the plays of the late sixteenth and seventeenth centuries? A foreign language, a foreign theater, a foreign audience.

Probably all viewers of Shakespeare's plays, beginning with Shakespeare himself, at times have been unhappy with the plays on the stage. Consider three comments about production that we find in the plays themselves, which suggest Shakespeare's concerns. The Chorus in *Henry V* complains that the heroic story cannot possibly be adequately staged:

> But pardon, gentles all,
> The flat unraisèd spirits that hath dared
> On this unworthy scaffold to bring forth
> So great an object. Can this cockpit hold
> The vasty fields of France? Or may we cram
> Within this wooden *O* the very casques
> That did affright the air at Agincourt?
>
> . . . .
> Piece out our imperfections with your thoughts.
>
> (Prologue 1.8–14,23)

Second, here are a few sentences (which may or may not represent Shakespeare's own views) from Hamlet's longish lecture to the players:

> Speak the speech, I pray you, as I pronounced it to you, trippingly on the tongue. But if you mouth it, as many of our players do, I had as lief the town crier spoke my lines. . . . O, it offends me to the soul to hear a robustious periwig-pated fellow tear a passion to tatters, to very rags, to split the ears of the groundlings. . . . And let those that play your clowns speak no more than is set down for them, for there be of them that will themselves laugh, to set on some quantity of barren spectators to laugh too, though in the meantime some necessary question of the play be then to be considered. That's villainous and shows a most pitiful ambition in the fool that uses it. (3.2.1–47)

Finally, we can quote again from the passage cited earlier in this introduction, concerning the boy actors who played the female roles. Cleopatra imagines with horror a theatrical version of her activities with Antony:

> The quick comedians
> Extemporally will stage us, and present
> Our Alexandrian revels: Antony
> Shall be brought drunken forth, and I shall see
> Some squeaking Cleopatra boy my greatness
> I' th' posture of a whore.
>
> (5.2.216–21)

It is impossible to know how much weight to put on such passages—perhaps Shakespeare was just being modest about his theater's abilities—but it is easy enough to think that he was unhappy with some aspects of Elizabethan production. Probably no production can fully satisfy a playwright, and for that matter, few productions can fully satisfy *us;* we regret this or that cut, this or that way of costuming the play, this or that bit of business.

One's first thought may be this: Why don't they just do "authentic" Shakespeare, "straight" Shakespeare, the play as Shakespeare wrote it? But as we read the plays—words written to be performed—it sometimes becomes clear that we do not know *how* to perform them. For instance, in *Antony and Cleopatra* Antony, the Roman general who has succumbed to Cleopatra and to Egyptian ways, says, "The nobleness of life / Is to do thus" (1.1.36–37). But what is "thus"? Does Antony at this point embrace Cleopatra? Does he embrace and kiss her? (There are, by the way, very few scenes of kissing on Shakespeare's stage, possibly because boys played the female roles.) Or does he make a sweeping gesture, indicating the Egyptian way of life?

This is not an isolated example; the plays are filled with lines that call for gestures, but we are not sure what the gestures should be. *Interpretation* is inevitable. Consider a passage in *Hamlet*. In 3.1, Polonius persuades his daughter, Ophelia, to talk to Hamlet while Polonius and Claudius eavesdrop. The two men conceal themselves, and Hamlet encounters Ophelia. At 3.1.131 Hamlet suddenly says to her, "Where's your father?" Why does Hamlet, apparently out of nowhere—they have not been talking about Polonius—ask this question? Is this an example of the "antic disposition" (fantastic behavior) that Hamlet earlier (1.5.172) had told Horatio and others—including us—he would display? That is, is the question about the whereabouts of her father a seemingly irrational one, like his earlier question (3.1.103) to Ophelia, "Ha, ha! Are you honest?" Or, on the other hand, has Hamlet (as in many productions) suddenly glimpsed Polonius's foot protruding from beneath a drapery at the rear? That is, does Hamlet ask the question because he has suddenly seen something suspicious and now is testing Ophelia? (By the way, in productions that do give Hamlet a physical cue, it is almost always Polonius rather than Claudius who provides the clue. This itself is an act of interpretation on the part of the director.) Or (a third possibility) does Hamlet get a clue from Ophelia, who inadvertently betrays the spies by nervously glancing at their place of hiding? This is the interpretation used in the BBC television version, where Ophelia glances in fear toward the hiding place just after Hamlet says "Why wouldst thou be a breeder of sinners?" (121–22). Hamlet, realizing that he is being observed, glances here and there *before* he asks "Where's your father?" The question thus is a climax to what he has been doing while speaking the preceding lines. Or (a fourth interpretation) does Hamlet suddenly, without the aid of any clue whatsoever, intuitively (insightfully, mysteriously, wonderfully) sense that someone is spying? Directors must decide, of course—and so must readers.

Recall, too, the preceding discussion of the texts of the plays, which argued that the texts—though they seem to be before us in permanent black on white—are unstable. The Signet text of *Hamlet*, which draws on the Second Quarto (1604) and the First Folio (1623) is considerably longer than any version staged in Shakespeare's time. Our version, even if spoken very briskly and played without any intermission, would take close to four hours, far beyond "the two hours' traffic of our stage" mentioned in the Prologue to *Romeo and Juliet*. (There are a few contemporary references to the duration of a play, but none mentions more than three hours.) Of Shakespeare's plays, only *The Comedy of Errors*, *Macbeth*, and *The Tempest* can be done in less than three hours without cutting. And even if we take a play that exists only in a short text, *Macbeth*, we cannot claim that we are experiencing the very play that Shakespeare conceived, partly because some of the Witches' songs almost surely are non-Shakespearean additions, and partly because we are not willing to watch the play performed without an intermission and with boys in the female roles.

Further, as the earlier discussion of costumes mentioned, the plays apparently were given chiefly in contemporary, that is, in Elizabethan dress. If today we give them in the costumes that Shakespeare probably saw, the plays seem not contemporary but curiously dated. Yet if we use our own dress, we find lines of dialogue that are at odds with what we see; we may feel that the language, so clearly not our own, is inappropriate coming out of people in today's dress. A common solution, incidentally, has been to set the plays in the nineteenth century, on the grounds that this attractively distances the plays (gives them a degree of foreignness, allowing for interesting costumes) and yet doesn't put them into a museum world of Elizabethan England.

Inevitably our productions are adaptations, *our* adaptations, and inevitably they will look dated, not in a century but in twenty years, or perhaps even in a decade. Still, we cannot escape from our own conceptions. As the director Peter Brook has said, in *The Empty Space* (1968):

> It is not only the hair-styles, costumes and make-ups that look dated. All the different elements of staging—the shorthands of behavior that stand for emotions; gestures, gesticulations and tones of voice—are all fluctuating on an invisible stock exchange all the time. . . . A living theatre that thinks it can stand aloof from anything as trivial as fashion will wilt. (p. 16)

As Brook indicates, it is through today's hairstyles, costumes, makeup, gestures, gesticulations, tones of voice—this includes our *conception* of earlier hairstyles, costumes, and so forth if we stage the play in a period other than our own—that we inevitably stage the plays.

It is a truism that every age invents its own Shakespeare, just as, for instance, every age has invented its own classical world. Our view of ancient Greece, a slave-holding society in which even free Athenian women were severely circum-scribed, does not much resemble the Victorians' view of ancient Greece as a glorious democracy, just as, perhaps, our view of Victorianism itself does not much resemble theirs. We cannot claim that the Shakespeare on our stage is the true Shakespeare, but in our stage productions we find a Shakespeare that speaks to us, a Shakespeare that our ances-tors doubtless did not know but one that seems to us to be the true Shakespeare—at least for a while.

Our age is remarkable for the wide variety of kinds of staging that it uses for Shakespeare, but one development deserves special mention. This is the now common practice of race-blind or color-blind or nontraditional casting, which allows persons who are not white to play in Shakespeare. Previously blacks performing in Shakespeare were limited to a mere three roles, Othello, Aaron (in *Titus Andronicus*), and the Prince of Morocco (in *The Merchant of Venice*), and there were no roles at all for Asians. Indeed, African-Americans rarely could play even one of these three roles, since they were not welcome in white companies. Ira Aldridge (c.1806–1867), a black actor of undoubted talent, was forced to make his living by performing Shakespeare in England and in Europe, where he could play not only Othello but also—in whiteface—other tragic roles such as King Lear. Paul Robeson (1898–1976) made theatrical his-tory when he played Othello in London in 1930, and there was some talk about bringing the production to the United States, but there was more talk about whether American audiences would tolerate the sight of a black man—a real black man, not a white man in blackface—kissing and then killing a white woman. The idea was tried out in summer stock in 1942, the reviews were enthusiastic, and in the fol-lowing year Robeson opened on Broadway in a production that ran an astounding 296 performances. An occasional all-black company sometimes performed Shakespeare's plays, but otherwise blacks (and other minority members) were in effect shut out from performing Shakespeare. Only since about 1970 has it been common for nonwhites to play major roles along with whites. Thus, in a 1996–97 production of *Antony and Cleopatra*, a white Cleopatra, Vanessa Red-grave, played opposite a black Antony, David Harewood.

Multiracial casting is now especially common at the New York Shakespeare Festival, founded in 1954 by Joseph Papp, and in England, where even siblings such as Claudio and Isabella in *Measure for Measure* or Lear's three daughters may be of different races. Probably most viewers today soon stop worrying about the lack of realism, and move beyond the color of the performers' skin to the quality of the performance.

Nontraditional casting is not only a matter of color or race; it includes sex. In the past, occasionally a distinguished woman of the theater has taken on a male role—Sarah Bernhardt (1844–1923) as Hamlet is perhaps the most famous example—but such performances were widely regarded as eccentric. Although today there have been some performances involving cross-dressing (a drag *As You Like It* staged by the National Theatre in England in 1966 and in the United States in 1974 has achieved considerable fame in the annals of stage history), what is more interesting is the casting of women in roles that traditionally are male but that need not be. Thus, a 1993–94 English production of *Henry V* used a woman—*not* cross-dressed—in the role of the governor of Harfleur. According to Peter Holland, who reviewed the production in *Shakespeare Survey* 48 (1995), "having a female Governor of Harfleur feminized the city and provided a direct response to the horrendous threat of rape and murder that Henry had offered, his language and her body in direct connection and opposition" (p. 210). Ten years from now the device may not play so effectively, but today it speaks to us. Shakespeare, born in the Elizabethan Age, has been dead nearly four hundred years, yet he is, as Ben Jonson said, "not of an age but for all time." We must understand, however, that he is "for all time" precisely because each age finds in his abundance something for itself and something of itself.

And here we come back to two issues discussed earlier in this introduction—the instability of the text and, curiously, the Bacon/Oxford heresy concerning the authorship of the plays. *Of course* Shakespeare wrote the plays, and we should daily fall on our knees to thank him for them—and yet there is something to the idea that he is not their only author. Every editor, every director and actor, and every reader to some degree shapes them, too, for when we edit, direct, act, or read, we inevitably become Shakespeare's collaborator and re-create the plays. The plays, one might say, are so cunningly contrived that they guide our responses, tell us how we ought to feel, and make a mark on us, but (for better or for worse) we also make a mark on them.

—SYLVAN BARNET
Tufts University

Introduction

At a number of points critics of *The Taming of the Shrew* are in general agreement. No one doubts that Christopher Sly is skillfully characterized—in his coarseness, his liveliness, his unaffectedness, his candor, his partial yielding to illusion, his incongruous mixture of two styles of life, his difficulty in acting the gentleman and attending to even a rather popular brand of theatrical fare. No one doubts that Petruchio and Kate are made, if not altogether well-rounded characters, at least human beings of vitality and imaginativeness, so that they have an interest and plausibility that stereotypes would not have. Each first acts in a way that suggests a rather single-ply, rigid nature, and then reveals a capacity for crucial action of another quality and value. No one doubts that the Bianca plot is of secondary interest, that it turns on a conventional love story, that it has in it more of intrigue than of the romantic intensity that Shakespeare would later develop in his lovers, and that despite its manifest limitations, Shakespeare had pumped theatrical life into it by the multiplication of candidates for Bianca's hand and by a brisk representation of their schemes and styles. No one doubts that the suitors are effectively distinguished from each other—Gremio, the clownish overage lover; Tranio, the virtuoso quasi-competitor who loves to play the gentleman; Hortensio, who can settle for an unromantic down-to-earth arrangement like a sensible man in Restoration comedy; and Lucentio, the straight man and winner. No one doubts that the lesser characters are, in brief space, endowed with much individuality and substance—Baptista, the worried and well-meaning father; Grumio, the spirited servant who finds histrionic pleasure in opposite roles, whether taking it from Petruchio or dishing it out to other servants; Biondello, the lively-talking aide-de-camp in the war of love; the conscientious and frustrated Tailor; the earnest Pedant, grimly determined to succeed in his role as Lucentio's helpful father; the actual Vincentio, driven into a temper by successive experiences of being put upon.

No one doubts, finally, that all these materials from diverse sources (see A Note on the Sources, p. 115) have been combined with so much ingenuity that the play has a convincing air of unity. The play within a play is an old device: no one feels any hiatus between the audience (Sly and the Lord's household) and the performers of a play (the actors presenting the two love affairs). The taming plot and the relatively straight love plot are brought together mechanically by the fact that the two women are sisters and that the marriage of one depends on that of the other; by the fact that Bianca's suitors collaborate in finding a suitor for Kate and, even more than that, in assisting him in his suit; by the fact that Petruchio first aids Hortensio and that Hortensio later plays along with Petruchio's game as wife-tamer; and by the fact that the final wedding celebration is a joint affair. The two ac-tions are held together organically by the fact that the women wooed, the wooers, and their methods of wooing are in contrast, not only aesthetically but, by implication, morally; and by the still more striking fact that the apparent contrast, which seems so obvious at first, is reversed in the final act. When Kate and Bianca undergo a partial change of roles at the end, we see them, not simply as ending parallel plots, but as ironically revealing different aspects of one fundamental situation—the relations of husbands and wives.

In recent years critics have begun to detect a still subtler form of unity, one that considerably raises the aesthetic status of the play. This is "the unity of 'supposes.'" When Lucentio is made to use the phrase "counterfeit supposes" (5.1.115), Shakespeare is alluding,* it is assumed, to his

---

*There is a similar allusion in Tranio's decision that "supposed Lucentio / Must get a father, called 'supposed Vincentio'" (2.1.400–01).

source, Gascoigne's play *Supposes*; in this title Gascoigne is Englishing the title of his source play, Ariosto's *I Suppositi*. The idea behind these words is that of "posing," of assuming identities other than one's own. From Gascoigne Shakespeare got the Bianca plot, which is of course full of assumed or "supposed" identities: Hortensio as Litio, Lucentio as Cambio, Tranio as Lucentio, and the Pedant as Vincentio; and then the true Vincentio is accused of being someone else posing as Vincentio. But recent criticism has observed that "supposes" are not limited either to physical identity or to the Bianca plot. Within the Bianca plot, Bianca and the widow are both "supposed" to be agreeable women who will be accommodating wives. That is, the dramatic treatment encourages us to see that beyond the mere putting on of a false name and a false social or professional identity may lie the putting on of a personality or moral identity (whether as a long-lasting habit or as a short-term device to secure a given end).

Once given such hints, the reader sees quickly a new and closer tie between the Bianca plot and the Sly plot (the induction): in each, the basic mechanism is the use of "supposed" identities. The Lord and members of his household pretend to be Sly's servants and his wife. But we have hardly noted this when we see, also, that the mainspring of the induction is a subtler alteration of identity: Sly is persuaded, or at least half-persuaded, that he is a Lord. The Lord and his men have voluntarily changed identity in order to cause Sly involuntarily to change identity (just as Bianca's lovers, so to speak, have voluntarily changed identity in order to cause Bianca to accept them). From here it is only a quick step to the remarkable kinship that the main Petruchio-Kate plot has with the other two: Petruchio voluntarily assumes an identity ("poses" as a contrary, willful, autocratic, irrational man, a "shrew") in order to cause Kate involuntarily to change identity, to give up shrewishness and become a charming, cooperative wife. In three plots a "supposition" or impersonation is the means of inducing a person to act in a certain way: a man accepts a "wife" and two women accept husbands. "Acting" is the means of moving people toward a desired feeling and role; in this sense *The Taming* anticipates the much-quoted line in *As You Like It*, "All the world's a stage. . . ."

But there is a still subtler element in the functional identity of parts which creates the unity of the play. The "supposed" servants of Sly not only tell him he is a Lord but hold before him verbal pictures—of omnipotence, luxury, pleasures—that move him in their own way toward imaginative acceptance of his high role. At least he accepts the external circumstances in which he finds himself; perhaps he even accepts the idea of a lordly personality in himself. The further he goes in this direction, the more fully the induction anticipates the taming plot. For a part of Petruchio's method (by no means all of it) is to hold before Kate a picture of what she potentially is and may become if she will but cease resisting it—a "most patient, sweet, and virtuous wife" (3.2.195). It is possible to assume that she imaginatively accepts this picture of herself and, under the stimulus of Petruchio's love, makes it come true. If this interpretation is valid, then the play—not only one of Shakespeare's earliest but a farcical one—has advanced remarkably, at least to the edge of a philosophical realm. For it induces us to reflect on the belief in the primacy of the idea, on the creative powers of the imagination, on the view that, in Hamlet's phrase, which has become a cliché, "Thinking makes it so." Hence *The Taming*, never thought one of Shakespeare's high achievements, moves up into the company of the truly Shakespearean, in which, however stereotyped the exterior and however obvious the popular appeal, there is a heart of profound meaningfulness and hence enduring excellence. It is possible that a once underrated play may be in danger of being overrated.

So far we have been summarizing the main grounds of agreement among critics, especially the grounds on which *The Taming* has been praised. However, the argument for unity depends somewhat on how we understand the change in Kate—transformation, acceptance of discipline, discovery of true nature, rejection of an assumed role? This is not so demonstrable as is the tight interweaving of plots at the level of overt action. When it is asserted that the play uncovers Bianca as the real shrew and reveals that Kate is not a shrew at all or else was only pretending to be a shrew to serve her own ends, surely we come into the realm of the arguable. There is something of the arguable about *The Taming*; indeed there has been, alongside the areas of unanimity, considerable difference of opinion about it. We can profitably change our course, then, and approach the play from the other side—in terms of the disagreements, or at least the changes of opinion, about it.

One argument grows out of sheer factual uncertainty: did Shakespeare, or did he not, keep Sly in the play for occasional comments in the later acts, and for an epilogue completing the dramatic "frame"? In *The Taming of a Shrew*, a play related to this one (see A Note on the Sources), Sly stayed on. Hence, what about *The Shrew*? There are various opinions: (1) Shakespeare forgot about Sly; (2) Shakespeare originally wrote a Sly epilogue, but it dropped out; (3) the loss of Sly, though not a major blot, is unfortunate; (4) the loss of Sly is fortunate, and shows Shakespeare's artistry. If Shakespeare did originally give Sly the closing lines, and if these did disappear—from an acting script and hence from the printer's copy—the only compelling reason for this (in the opinion of the present editor) was not aesthetic but practical: it simplified production problems such as size of cast. There is no merit in the argument that the elimination of Sly prevented an anticlimax, for this begs the question whether a Sly epilogue would inevitably be anticlimactic. There is likewise little merit in the argument that the Sly story comes to its logical end when Sly takes himself for a Lord and thus in anticipation parallels Kate's transformation into a lady. For, while Kate can, with effort, retain her new moral identity, Sly cannot, with any amount of effort, retain his new social identity. Hence it is possible to visualize a very effective Sly epilogue which would work by contrast, making us note the discrepancy between an imaginable change of being and a temporary change of status, between a hypnotism for the therapy of the subject and the imposition of a dream for the fun of the observers. We can imagine, also, the use of Sly for a cynical irony such as we know in "black comedy": the end of his new lordship might hint the diminution of Kate's new ladyship. Or, in a lighter vein, Sly might entertain, as he does in *A Shrew*, visions of being a wife-tamer, and thus introduce an implicit contrast between those who can pull off such an exploit and those who cannot. Well, the imagining of alternative endings serves only one purpose: showing that the present one is not necessarily ideal. Surely most readers feel spontaneously that, in the treatment of Sly in *The Shrew*, something is left uncomfortably hanging, and many stage directors borrow additional Sly materials from *A Shrew*.

While Petruchio and Kate, as we have noted, are admired as lively and charming creatures, forerunners of Benedick and Beatrice in *Much Ado About Nothing*, there is lack of agreement on their natures and on the nature of the transactions between them. No one doubts, of course, that they come to love each other; the problem is what they bring to that love and how they exercise it. The older view was that Petruchio was a very skillful psychologist, one who really knew how to handle a difficult woman. On the other hand, many commentators, especially in the nineteenth century, tended to feel that Petruchio's methods were not civilized and that though they may once have been countenanced, they would never do in modern life. That sense of real life, or what it is and should be, which repeatedly infiltrates literary judgments, appears in estimates of Petruchio: There have been editors who get on the bandwagon and declare him out of date and yet rather wistfully intimate that it is too bad he has gone out of date while the world still has need of him. But in repudiating Petruchio's methods, critics have had to find ways of redeeming Petruchio, since the play obviously does not make him an intolerable man. So it has been said that he is not so much "taming" Kate as leading her to a needed discipline; that in no essential does he pass the bounds of gentlemanliness; that he simply offers Kate a picture of male strength that can elicit the respect without which she cannot love; that the heart of his method is a love which begets love. Here we have Petruchio transmuted from the relentless and mechanical task-master, required by a monstrous female, into a remarkably gifted gentleman-lover who simply brings out the best in an extraordinary woman—a best that, as it comes out, totally displaces a worst that had once seemed pretty much the whole story. This view is much more in tune with modern views of the right relations between men and women. But this interpretation too, if not utterly replaced, has been given a new twist and all but turned upside down by a still more "modern" view. In this reading of the play, Petruchio, far from "taming" or subtly having a beneficent influence on a woman, is in reality tamed by her. While having the illusion of conquering, he is conquered by her; when she says what he wants to hear, she is being ironic, undermining him with a show of acquiescence and virtually a wink to the audience. In this view, Shakespeare wrote *What Every Woman Knows* over three hundred years before Barrie.

Kate, of course, has been done over in the same way. Once, she was naturally and unquestionably taken to be a shrew, that is, a type of woman widely known in life and constantly represented in song and story. Then critics began to contend that Kate differed from the stereotype: that instead of being simply aggressive and contentious, she was ripe for love, wanted love, and really suffered from the fact that, inside the family and out, Bianca more readily attracted affection. Here is the move toward seeing Kate, not as an allegorical abstraction, a figure of shrewishness, but as an actual human being with impulses and motives experienced by all of us. This move goes still further. In one modern view (that of Nevill Coghill and the late Professor Goddard), Kate's disagreeableness of manner is not a primary fact of personality but is caused by lack of affection at home: Baptista, a "family tyrant," has petted and spoiled Bianca, and Kate is the unhappy byproduct of parental irresponsibility and stupidity ("gross partiality" toward Bianca). In this view, Kate is very much like a modern problem child. But the distinguished director of Shakespeare, Margaret Webster, offers us a still different Kate. To Miss Webster, Kate is a strong, intelligent, independent woman who is stuck in a stuffy household, "despises" her father and her "horrid little sister," thinks the local boys "beneath contempt," and finds in her fresh and vehement style the only available outlet for the talents and energy of a superior woman. Here we have the feminist's Kate, the modern woman whom it is perilous to hold back from self-expression and leadership—a far cry from the nagging Xanthippe that every now and then, from the beginning of time, would afflict a husband doomed, unless he took strong measures, to be ridiculed for his misfortune. But Goddard and Miss Webster agree in one thing: it is really Kate who takes over Petruchio, takes him over by simulating an obedience that is a paradoxical mastery. Her last long speech, then, is only a prolonged ironic commentary on the subordination of wives, and could be taken literally only by naïve believers in male supremacy.

As might be expected, critics differ on where Shakespeare stood. The most widely held assumption is that Shakespeare believed in the subordination of wives, and that in his age he could hardly do otherwise. While some readers accept this as calmly as most people accept what has happened long ago, others regret that Shakespeare was so little in accord with modern views; as early as 1897, even G. B. Shaw could insist that "the last scene is altogether disgusting to modern sensibility." The reader with a severe case of "modern sensibility" can either join Shaw in slapping Shakespeare's wrist or else go him one better by arguing that Shakespeare was really a modern at heart. The unspoken assumption here is that the "divine Shakespeare" could not possibly disagree with our answers to fundamental problems, especially those we have come to more recently. So various commentators say flatly that Shakespeare did *not* believe in the subordination of wives. Of Kate's long speech on the duty of wives (5.2.136–79), Goddard, amazed at three centuries of acceptance, exclaims, "as if Shakespeare could ever have meant it!"

But only Miss Webster faced the fact that to make Shakespeare a modern, one had to do something better with the wifely duty speech than ignore it or just assert that though the longest speech in the play, it doesn't count. So she went whole-hog and treated the speech as Kate's choicest joke of all on Petruchio, who from now on, we judge, will be simply a complacent husband, happy in the laughable illusion that he has an obedient wife.

It is doubtful that we can know "what Shakespeare thought," and in a sense it does not matter; what is important is how the play is to be taken (it is by no means impossible that the play "believes" something other than what Shakespeare as a man may have "believed"). All the aspects of it that have been taken now in one way, now in another, come together pretty well in the issue of what the play is to be called. By many critics it is called a "farce" and is discussed as a farce; yet there are those who deny vigorously that it is a farce. This difference of opinion is caused by a loose use of the term *farce*. Some people take farce as simply hurly-burly theater, with much slapstick, roughhouse (Petruchio with a whip, in the older productions), pratfalls, general confusion, trickery, uproar, gags, and so on. Yet such characteristics, which do appear generally in farce, are surface manifestations. What we need to identify is the "spirit of farce" that lies behind them. We may then be able to get away from insisting either that *The Shrew* is farce or that it is not farce, and to get on to seeing what it does with the genre of farce.

A genre is a conventionalized way of dealing with actuality, and different genres represent different habits of the human mind or minister to the capacity for finding pleasure in different styles of representation. "Romance," for instance, is the genre that conceives of obstacles, dangers, and threats, especially those of an unusual or spectacular kind, as yielding to human ingenuity, spirit, or just good luck. On the other hand, "naturalism," as a literary mode, conceives of man as overcome by the pressure of outer forces, especially those of a dull, glacier-like, grinding persistence. The essential procedure of farce is to deal with people as if they lack, largely or totally, the physical, emotional, intellectual, and moral sensitivity that we think of as "normal." The enormous popularity of farce for several thousand years indicates that, though "farce" is often a term of disparagement, a great many people, no doubt all of us at times, take pleasure in seeing human beings acting as if they were very limited human beings. Farce offers a spectacle that resembles daily actuality but lets us participate without feeling the responsibilities and liabilities that the situation would normally evoke. Perhaps we feel superior to the diminished men and women in the plot; perhaps we harmlessly work off aggressions (since verbal and physical assaults are frequent in farce). Participation in farce is easy on us; in it we escape the full complexity of our own natures and cut up without physical or moral penalties. Farce is the realm without pain or conscience. Farce offers a holiday from vulnerability, consequences, costs. It is the opposite of all the dramas of disaster in which a man's fate is too much for him. It carries out our desire to simplify life by a selective anesthetizing of the whole person; man retains all his energy yet never gets really hurt. The give-and-take of life becomes a brisk skirmishing in which one needs neither health insurance nor liability insurance; when one is on the receiving end and has to take it, it's possible to bounce back up resiliently, and when one dishes it out, the pleasure in conquest is never undercut by the guilt of inflicting injury.

In farce, the human personality is without depth. Hence action is not slowed down by thought or by the friction of competing motives. Everything goes at high speed, with dash, variety, never a pause for stocktaking, and ever an athlete's quick glance ahead at the action coming up next. No sooner do the players come in than the Lord plans a show to help bamboozle Sly. As soon as Baptista appears with his daughters and announces the marriage priority, other lovers plan to find a man for Kate, Lucentio falls in love with Bianca and hits on an approach in disguise, Petruchio plans to go for Kate, Bianca's lovers promise him support, Petruchio begins his suit and introduces Hortensio into the scramble of disguised lovers. Petruchio rushes through the preliminary business with Baptista and they act just as quickly and unambiguously as if someone had pressed a control button. Farce simplifies life by making it painless and automatic; indeed the two qualities come together in the concept of man as machine. (The true opposite of farce is Capek's *R.U.R.*, in which manlike robots actually begin to feel.) There is a sense in which we might legitimately call the age of computers a farcical one, for it lets us feel that basic choices are made without mental struggle or will or anxiety, and as speedily and inevitably as a series of human ninepins falling down one after another on the stage when each is bumped by the one next to it. "Belike you mean," says Kate to Petruchio, "to make a puppet of me" (4.3.103). It is what farce does to all characters. Now the least obvious illustration of the farcical view of life lies, not in some of the peripheral goings-on that we have been observing, but in the title action itself: the taming of the shrew. Fundamentally—we will come shortly to the necessary qualifications—Kate is conceived of as responding automatically to a certain kind of calculated treatment, as automatically as an animal to the devices of a skilled trainer. Petruchio not only uses the word *tame* more than once, but openly compares his method to that used in training falcons (4.1.184ff.). There is no reason whatever to suppose that this was not meant quite literally. Petruchio is not making a great jest or developing a paradoxical figure but describing a process taken at face value. He tells exactly what he has done and is doing—withholding food and sleep until the absolute need of them brings assent. (We hardly note that up to a point the assumptions are those of the "third degree" and of the more rigorous "cures" of bad habits: making it more unprofitable to assert one's will or one's bad habits than to act differently.) Before he sees Kate, he announces his method: he will assert as true the opposite of whatever she says and does and is, that is to say, will frustrate the manifestations of her will and establish the dominance of his own. Without naming them, he takes other steps that we know to be important in animal training. From the beginning he shows that he will stop at nothing to achieve his end, that he will not hesitate for a second to do anything necessary—to discard all dignity, or carry out any indecorous act or any outrageousness that will serve. He creates an image of utter invincibility, of having no weakness through which he can be appealed to. He does not use a literal whip, such as stage Petruchios were once addicted to, but he unmistakably uses a symbolic whip. Like a good trainer, however, he uses the carrot, too—not only marriage, but a new life, a happier personality for Kate. Above all, he offers love; in the end, the trainer succeeds best who makes the trainee feel the presence of something warmer than technique, rigor, and invincibility. Not that Petruchio fakes love, but that love has its part, ironically, in a process that is farcically conceived and that never wholly loses the markings of farce.

Only in farce could we conceive of the occurrence, almost in a flash, of that transformation of personality which, as known only too well in modern experience, normally requires a long, gradual, painstaking application of psychotherapy. True, conversion is believable and does happen, but even as a secular experience it requires a prior development of readiness, or an extraordinary revelatory shock, or both. (In the romantic form of this psychic event, an old hag, upon marriage to the knight, suddenly turns into a beautiful maiden.) Kate is presented initially as a very troubled woman; aggressiveness and tantrums are her way of feeling a sense of power. Though very modern, the argument that we see in her the results of paternal unkindness is not very impressive. For one thing, recent research on infants—if we may risk applying heavy science to light farce—suggests that basic personality traits precede, and perhaps influence, parental attitudes to children. More important, the text simply does not present Baptista as the overbearing and tyrannical father that he is sometimes said to be. Kate has made him almost as unhappy as she is and driven him toward Bianca; nevertheless, when he heavily handicaps Bianca in the matrimonial sweepstakes, he is trying to even things up for the daughter that he naturally thinks is a poor runner. Nor is he willing to marry her off to Petruchio simply to get rid of her; "her love," he says, "is all in all." On her wedding day he says, kindly enough,

"I cannot blame thee now to weep," and at the risk of losing husbands for both daughters he rebukes Petruchio (3.2.97ff.). (The Baptista that some commentators describe would surely have said nothing but "What do you expect, you bitch?") We cannot blacken Baptista to save Kate. Shakespeare presents her binding and beating Bianca (2.1.1ff.) to show that he is really committed to a shrew; such episodes make it hard to defend the view that she is an innocent victim or is posing as a shrew out of general disgust. To sum up: in real life her disposition would be difficult to alter permanently, but farce secures its pleasurable effect by assuming a ready and total change in response to the stimuli applied by Petruchio, as if he were going through an established and proved routine. On the other hand, only farce makes it possible for Petruchio to be so skillful a tamer, that is, so unerring, so undeviating, so mechanical an enforcer of the rules for training in falconry. If Petruchio were by nature the disciplinarian that he acts for a while, he would hardly change after receiving compliance; and if he were, in real life, the charming and affectionate gentleman that he becomes in the play, he would find it impossible so rigorously to play the falcon-tamer, to outbully the bully, especially when the bully lies bleeding on the ground, for this role would simply run afoul of too much of his personality. The point here is not that the play is "unrealistic" (this would be a wholly irrelevant criticism) but that we can understand how a given genre works by testing it against the best sense of reality that we can bring to bear. It is the farcical view of life that makes possible the treatment of both Kate and Petruchio.

But this picture, of course, is incomplete; for the sake of clarity we have been stressing the purely generic in *The Shrew* and gliding over the specific variations. Like any genre, farce is a convention, not a straitjacket; it is a fashion, capable of many variations. Genre provides a perspective, which in the individual work can be used narrowly or inclusively: comedy of manners, for instance, can move toward the character studies of James's novels or toward the superficial entertainments of Terence Rattigan. Shakespeare hardly ever uses a genre constrictively. In both *The Comedy of Errors* and *The Taming of the Shrew,* the resemblances between which are well known, Shakespeare moves away from the limited conception of personality that we find in "basic farce," such as that of Plautus, who influences both these plays. True, he protects both main characters in *The Shrew* against the expectable liabilities that would make one a less perfect reformer and the other less than a model reformee, but he is unwilling to leave them automatons, textbook types of reformer and reformee. So he equips both with a good deal of intelligence and feeling that they would not have in elementary farce. Take sex, for instance. In basic farce, sex is purely a mechanical response, with no more overtones of feeling than ordinary hunger and thirst; the normal "love affair" is an intrigue with a courtesan. Like virtually all Renaissance lovers, Petruchio tells Kate candidly that he proposes to keep warm "in thy bed" (2.1.260). But there is no doubt that Petruchio, in addition to wanting a good financial bargain and enjoying the challenge of the shrew, develops real warmth of feeling for Kate as an individual—a warmth that makes him strive to bring out the best in her, to keep the training in a tone of jesting, well-meant fantasy, to provide Kate with face-saving devices (she is "curst . . . for policy" and only "in company"—285, 298), to praise her for her virtues (whether she has them or not) rather than blame her for her vices, to never fall into boorishness, to repeatedly protest his affection for her, and by asking a kiss at a time she thinks unsuitable, to show that he really wants it. Here farce expands toward comedy of character by using a fuller range of personality. Likewise with Kate. The fact that she is a shrew does not mean that she cannot have hurt feelings, as it would in a plainer farce; indeed a shrew may be defined—once she develops beyond a mere stereotype—as a person who has an excess of hurt feelings and is taking revenge on the world for them. We do not, because we dislike the revenge, deny the painful feelings that may lie behind. Shakespeare has chosen to show some of those feelings, not making Kate an insentient virago on the one hand, or a pathetic victim on the other. She is jealous of Bianca and her lovers, she accuses Baptista of favoritism (in the opinion of the present editor, without justification); on her wedding day she suffers real anguish rather than simply an automatic, conventionally furious resolve for retaliation. The painful emotions take her way beyond the limitations of the essentially pain-free personality of basic farce. Further, she is witty, though, truth to tell, the first verbal battle between her and Petruchio, like various other such scenes, hardly goes beyond verbal farce, in which words are mechanical jokes or blows rather than an artistic game that delights by its quality, and in which all the speed of the short lines hardly conceals the heavy labors of the dutiful but uninspired punster (the best jokes are the bawdy ones). Kate has imagination. It shows first in a new human sympathy when she defends the servants against Petruchio (4.1.150, 162–63). Then it develops into a gay, inspired gamesomeness that rivals Petruchio's own. When he insists, "It shall be what o'clock I say it is" (4.3.193) and "[The sun] shall be moon or star or what I list" (4.5.7), he is at one level saying again that he will stop at nothing, at no irrationality, as tamer; but here he moves the power game into a realm of fancy in which his apparent willfulness becomes the acting of the creative imagination. He is a poet, and he asks her, in effect, less to kiss the rod than to join in the game of playfully transforming ordinary reality. It is the final step in transforming herself. The point here is that, instead of not catching on or simply sulking, Kate has the dash and verve to join in the fun, and to do it with skill and some real touches of originality.

This scene on the road to Padua (4.5) is the high point of the play. From here on, it tends to move back closer to the boundaries of ordinary farce. When Petruchio asks a kiss, we do have human beings with feelings, not robots; but the key line in the scene, which is sometimes missed, is Petruchio's "Why, then let's home again. Come sirrah, let's away" (5.1.146). Here Petruchio is again making the same threat that he made at 4.5.8–9, that is, not playing an imaginative game but hinting the symbolic whip, even though the end is a compliance that she is inwardly glad to give. The whole wager scene, as we have already noted, falls essentially within the realm of farce: the responses are largely mechanical, as is their symmetry. Kate's final long speech on the obligations and fitting style of wives we can think of as a more or less automatic statement of a generally held doctrine. The easiest way to deal with it is to say that we no longer believe in it, just as we no longer believe in the divine right of kings, which is an important dramatic element in many Shakespeare plays. But to some interpreters, Kate has become such a charming heroine that they cannot stand her being anything less than a modern feminist. Hence the claim that she is speaking ironically. There are two arguments against this interpretation. One is that a careful reading of the lines will show that most of them have to be taken literally; only the last seven or eight lines can be read with ironic overtones, but this means, at most, a return to the imaginative gamesomeness of 4.5, rather than a denial of the doctrine formally asserted. The second is that forty-five lines of straight irony would be too much to be borne; it would be inconsistent with the straightforwardness of most of the play, and it would really turn Kate back into a hidden shrew whose new technique was sarcastic indirection, side-mouthing at the audience while her not very intelligent husband, bamboozled, cheered her on. It would be a poor triumph. If one has to modernize the speech of the obedient wife, a better way to do it is to develop a hint of Professor Goddard's: that behind a passé doctrine lies a continuing truth. That truth is that there are real differences between the sexes, and that they are to be kept in mind. That view at least does not strain the spirit of Kate's speech.

The Katolatry which has developed in recent years reveals the romantic tendency to create heroes and heroines by denying the existence of flaws in them and by imputing all sorts of flaws to their families and other associates. We have already seen how the effort to save Kate at the beginning has resulted in an untenable effort to make Baptista into a villainous, punitive father and Bianca into a calculating little devil whose inner shrewishness slowly comes out. But it is hard to see why, if we are to admire Kate's spirit of open defiance at the beginning and her alleged ironic defiance at the end, we should not likewise admire the spirit of Bianca and Hortensio's widow at the end. It is equally hard to see why we should admire Kate's quiet, ironic, what-every-woman-knows victory, as some would have it, over an attractive man at the end, but should not admire Petruchio's open victory over a very unattractive woman earlier. In fact, it is a little difficult to know just what Kate's supposed victory consists in. The play gives no evidence that from now on she will be twisting her husband around her finger. The evidence is rather that she will win peace and quiet and contentment by giving in to his wishes, and that her willingness will entirely eliminate unreasonable and autocratic wishes in him. But after all, the unreasonable and the autocratic are his strategy, not his nature; he gives up an assumed vice, while Kate gives up a real one. The truth is that Kate's great victory is, with Petruchio's help, over herself; she has come to accept herself as having enough merits so that she can be content without having the last word and scaring everybody off. To see this means to acknowledge that she was originally a shrew, whatever virtues may also have been latent in her personality.

What Shakespeare has done is to take an old, popular farcical situation and turn it into a well-organized, somewhat complex, fast-moving farce of his own. He has worked with the basic conceptions of farce—mainly that of a somewhat limited personality that acts and responds in a mechanical way and hence moves toward a given end with a perfection not likely if all the elements in human nature were really at work. So the tamer never fails in his technique, and the shrew responds just as she should. Now this situation might have tempted the dramatist to let his main characters be flat automatons—he a dull and rough whipwielder, and she a stubborn intransigent until beaten into insensibility (as in the ballad that was perhaps a Shakespearean source). Shakespeare, however, makes a gentleman and lady of his central pair. As tamer, Petruchio is a gay and witty and precocious artist and, beyond that, an affectionate man; and hence, a remarkable therapist. In Kate, Shakespeare has imagined, not merely a harridan who is incurable or a moral stepchild driven into a misconduct by mistreatment, but a difficult woman—a shrew, indeed—who combines willfulness with feelings that elicit sympathy, with imagination, and with a latent cooperativeness that can bring this war of the sexes to an honorable settlement. To have started with farce, to have stuck to the main lines of farce, and yet to have got so much of the supra-farcical into farce—this is the achievement of *The Taming of the Shrew* and the source of the pleasure that it has always given.

—ROBERT B. HEILMAN
University of Washington

The Taming of the Shrew

The Taming of the Shrew

[INDUCTION]

Scene 1. [*Outside rural alehouse.*]

Enter Hostess and Beggar, Christophero Sly.

Sly. I'll pheeze°¹ you, in faith.

Hostess. A pair of stocks,° you rogue!

Sly. Y'are a baggage, the Slys are no rogues. Look in
the chronicles: we came in with Richard° Con-
queror. Therefore, *paucas pallabris;*° let the world   5
slide.° Sessa!°

Hostess. You will not pay for the glasses you have
burst?

Sly. No, not a denier.° Go, by St. Jeronimy,° go to
thy cold bed and warm thee.   10

Hostess. I know my remedy: I must go fetch the
thirdborough.°   [*Exit.*]

Sly. Third or fourth or fifth borough, I'll answer him
by law. I'll not budge an inch, boy;° let him come
and kindly.°   *Falls asleep.*   15

---

¹ The degree sign (°) indicates a footnote, which is keyed to the text by
line number. Text references are printed in **boldface**; the annotation follows in roman type.
Ind.1.1 **pheeze** do for (cf. *faze*) 2 **stocks** (threatened punishment)
4 **Richard** (he means William) 5 **paucas pallabris** few words (Spanish
pocas palabras) 6 **slide** go by (proverb; cf. Ind.2.143) 6 **Sessa** scram (?)
shut up (?) 9 **denier** very small coin (cf. "a copper") 9 **Jeronimy** (Sly's
oath inaccurately reflects a line in Kyd's *Spanish Tragedy*) 12 **thirdborough** constable 14 **boy** wretch 15 **kindly** by all means

3

Wind° horns. Enter a Lord from hunting,
with his train.

Lord. Huntsman, I charge thee, tender° well my
    hounds.
    Broach° Merriman—the poor cur is embossed°—
    And couple Clowder with the deep-mouthed brach.°
    Saw'st thou not, boy, how Silver made it good
20   At the hedge-corner in the coldest fault?°
    I would not lose the dog for twenty pound.

First Huntsman. Why, Bellman is as good as he, my
    lord;
    He cried upon it at the merest loss°
    And twice today picked out the dullest scent.
25   Trust me, I take him for the better dog.

Lord. Thou art a fool. If Echo were as fleet,
    I would esteem him worth a dozen such.
    But sup them well and look unto them all.
    Tomorrow I intend to hunt again.

30 *First Huntsman.* I will, my lord.

Lord. What's here? One dead or drunk? See, doth
    he breathe?

Second Huntsman. He breathes, my lord. Were he not
    warmed with ale,
    This were a bed but cold to sleep so soundly.

Lord. O monstrous beast, how like a swine he lies!
35   Grim death, how foul and loathsome is thine image!
    Sirs, I will practice on° this drunken man.
    What think you, if he were conveyed to bed,
    Wrapped in sweet clothes, rings put upon his fin-
    gers,
    A most delicious banquet by his bed,

15.s.d. **Wind** blow   16 **tender** look after   17 **Broach** bleed, i.e., medi-
cate (some editors emend to *Breathe*)   17 **embossed** foaming at the
mouth   18 **brach** hunting bitch   20 **fault** lost ("cold") scent   23 **cried
. . . loss** gave cry despite complete loss (of scent)   36 **practice on** play a
trick on

And brave° attendants near him when he wakes—   40
Would not the beggar then forget himself?

First Huntsman. Believe me, lord, I think he cannot
 choose.

Second Huntsman. It would seem strange unto him
 when he waked.

Lord. Even as a flatt'ring dream or worthless fancy.
 Then take him up and manage well the jest.   45
 Carry him gently to my fairest chamber
 And hang it round with all my wanton° pictures;
 Balm° his foul head in warm distillèd waters
 And burn sweet wood to make the lodging sweet.
 Procure me music ready when he wakes   50
 To make a dulcet° and a heavenly sound;
 And if he chance to speak, be ready straight°
 And with a low submissive reverence
 Say, "What is it your honor will command?"
 Let one attend him with a silver basin   55
 Full of rose water and bestrewed with flowers;
 Another bear the ewer, the third a diaper,°
 And say, "Will't please your lordship cool your
  hands?"
 Some one be ready with a costly suit
 And ask him what apparel he will wear,   60
 Another tell him of his hounds and horse
 And that his lady mourns at his disease.
 Persuade him that he hath been lunatic,
 And when he says he is,° say that he dreams,
 For he is nothing but a mighty lord.   65
 This do, and do it kindly,° gentle sirs.
 It will be pastime passing excellent
 If it be husbanded with modesty.°

First Huntsman. My lord, I warrant you we will play
 our part

40 **brave** well dressed   47 **wanton** gay   48 **Balm** bathe   51 **dulcet**
sweet   52 **straight** without delay   57 **diaper** towel   64 **is** i.e., is "lunatic" now   66 **kindly** naturally   68 **husbanded with modesty** carried
out with moderation

70   As° he shall think by our true diligence
      He is no less than what we say he is.

Lord. Take him up gently and to bed with him,
      And each one to his office° when he wakes.
                [*Sly is carried out.*] *Sound trumpets.*
      Sirrah,° go see what trumpet 'tis that sounds.
                       [*Exit Servingman.*]
75   Belike° some noble gentleman that means,
      Traveling some journey, to repose him here.

Enter Servingman.

How now? Who is it?

Servingman.   An't° please your honor, players
      That offer service to your lordship.

Enter Players.

Lord. Bid them come near.
                Now, fellows, you are welcome.
80 *Players.* We thank your honor.

Lord. Do you intend to stay with me tonight?

A Player. So please your lordship to accept our duty.°

Lord. With all my heart. This fellow I remember
      Since once he played a farmer's eldest son;
85   'Twas where you wooed the gentlewoman so well.
      I have forgot your name, but sure that part
      Was aptly fitted° and naturally performed.

Second Player. I think 'twas Soto° that your honor
      means.

Lord. 'Tis very true; thou didst it excellent.
90   Well, you are come to me in happy° time,
      The rather for° I have some sport in hand

---

70 **As** so that   73 **office** assignment   74 **Sirrah** (term of address used to inferiors)   75 **Belike** likely   77 **An't** if it   82 **duty** respectful greeting 87 **aptly fitted** well suited (to you)   88 **Soto** (in John Fletcher's *Women Pleased,* 1620; reference possibly inserted here later)   90 **in happy** at the right   91 **The rather for** especially because

Wherein your cunning° can assist me much.
There is a lord will hear you play tonight.
But I am doubtful of your modesties,°
Lest over-eyeing° of his odd behavior—   95
For yet his honor never heard a play—
You break into some merry passion°
And so offend him, for I tell you, sirs,
If you should smile he grows impatient.

A Player. Fear not, my lord, we can contain ourselves   100
Were he the veriest antic° in the world.

Lord. Go, sirrah, take them to the buttery°
And give them friendly welcome every one.
Let them want° nothing that my house affords.
                           Exit one with the Players.
Sirrah, go you to Barthol'mew my page   105
And see him dressed in all suits° like a lady.
That done, conduct him to the drunkard's chamber
And call him "madam"; do him obeisance.
Tell him from me—as he will° win my love—
He bear himself with honorable action   110
Such as he hath observed in noble ladies
Unto their lords, by them accomplishèd.°
Such duty to the drunkard let him do
With soft low tongue and lowly courtesy,
And say, "What is't your honor will command   115
Wherein your lady and your humble wife
May show her duty and make known her love?"
And then, with kind embracements, tempting kisses,
And with declining head into his bosom,
Bid him shed tears, as being overjoyed   120
To see her noble lord restored to health
Who for this seven years hath esteemèd him
No better than a poor and loathsome beggar.
And if the boy have not a woman's gift

92 **cunning** talent   94 **modesties** self-restraint   95 **over-eyeing** seeing
97 **merry passion** fit of merriment   101 **antic** odd person   102 **buttery** liquor pantry, bar   104 **want** lack   106 **suits** respects (with pun)
109 **as he will** if he wishes to   112 **by them accomplishèd** i.e., as carried out by the ladies

125   To rain a shower of commanded tears,
An onion will do well for such a shift,°
Which in a napkin° being close conveyed°
Shall in despite° enforce a watery eye.
See this dispatched with all the haste thou canst;
130   Anon° I'll give thee more instructions.

Exit a Servingman.

I know the boy will well usurp° the grace,
Voice, gait, and action of a gentlewoman.
I long to hear him call the drunkard husband,
And how my men will stay themselves from laughter
135   When they do homage to this simple peasant.
I'll in to counsel them; haply° my presence
May well abate the over-merry spleen°
Which otherwise would grow into extremes.

[Exeunt.]

[Scene 2. *Bedroom in the Lord's house.*]

*Enter aloft° the Drunkard [Sly] with Attendants—
some with apparel, basin and ewer, and
other appurtenances—and Lord.*

Sly. For God's sake, a pot of small° ale!

First Servingman. Will't please your lordship drink a
cup of sack?°

Second Servingman. Will't please your honor taste of
these conserves?°

Third Servingman. What raiment will your honor
wear today?

126 **shift** purpose   127 **napkin** handkerchief   127 **close conveyed** secretly carried   128 **Shall in despite** can't fail to   130 **Anon** then   131 **usurp** take on   Ind.2.s.d. **aloft** (on balcony above stage at back)   1 **small** thin, diluted (inexpensive)   2 **sack** imported sherry (costly)   3 **conserves** i.e., of fruit

Sly. I am Christophero Sly; call not me "honor" nor   5
"lordship." I ne'er drank sack in my life, and if you
give me any conserves, give me conserves of beef.°
Ne'er ask me what raiment I'll wear, for I have no
more doublets° than backs, no more stockings than
legs nor no more shoes than feet—nay, sometime   10
more feet than shoes or such shoes as my toes look
through the overleather.

Lord. Heaven cease this idle humor° in your honor!
O that a mighty man of such descent,
Of such possessions and so high esteem,   15
Should be infusèd with so foul a spirit!

Sly. What, would you make me mad? Am not I Christopher Sly, old Sly's son of Burton-heath,° by birth
a peddler, by education a cardmaker,° by transmu-
tation a bearherd,° and now by present profession   20
a tinker? Ask Marian Hacket, the fat ale-wife of
Wincot,° if she know me not. If she say I am not
fourteen pence on the score° for sheer ale,° score
me up for the lying'st knave in Christendom. What,
I am not bestraught!° Here's—   25

Third Servingman. O, this it is that makes your lady
    mourn.

Second Servingman. O, this is it that makes your ser-
    vants droop.

Lord. Hence comes it that your kindred shuns your
    house
As beaten hence by your strange lunacy.
O noble lord, bethink thee of thy birth,   30
Call home thy ancient thoughts° from banishment

---

7 **conserves of beef** salt beef   9 **doublets** close-fitting jackets   13 **idle
humor** unreasonable fantasy   18 **Burton-heath** (probably Barton-
on-the-Heath, south of Stratford)   19 **cardmaker** maker of cards, or
combs, for arranging wool fibers before spinning   20 **bearherd** leader
of a tame bear   22 **Wincot** village near Stratford (some Hackets lived
there)   23 **score** charge account   23 **sheer ale** ale alone (?) undiluted
ale (?)   25 **bestraught** distraught, crazy   31 **ancient thoughts** original
sanity

And banish hence these abject lowly dreams.
Look how thy servants do attend on thee,
Each in his office ready at thy beck.
35 Wilt thou have music? Hark, Apollo° plays, *Music.*
And twenty cagèd nightingales do sing.
Or wilt thou sleep? We'll have thee to a couch
Softer and sweeter than the lustful bed
On purpose trimmed up for Semiramis.°
40 Say thou wilt walk, we will bestrow° the ground.
Or wilt thou ride? Thy horses shall be trapped,°
Their harness studded all with gold and pearl.
Dost thou love hawking? Thou hast hawks will soar
Above the morning lark. Or wilt thou hunt?
45 Thy hounds shall make the welkin° answer them
And fetch shrill echoes from the hollow earth.

First Servingman. Say thou wilt course,° thy grey-
          hounds are as swift
As breathèd° stags, ay, fleeter than the roe.°

Second Servingman. Dost thou love pictures? We will
          fetch thee straight
50 Adonis° painted by a running brook
And Cytherea all in sedges° hid,
Which seem to move and wanton° with her breath
Even as the waving sedges play with wind.

Lord. We'll show thee Io° as she was a maid
55 And how she was beguilèd and surprised,
As lively° painted as the deed was done.

Third Servingman. Or Daphne° roaming through a
          thorny wood,

---

35 **Apollo** here, god of music   39 **Semiramis** mythical Assyrian queen,
noted for beauty and sexuality (cf. *Titus Andronicus,* 2.1.22, 2.3.118)
40 **bestrow** cover   41 **trapped** decorated   45 **welkin** sky   47 **course**
hunt hares   48 **breathèd** having good wind   48 **roe** small deer
50 **Adonis** young hunter loved by Venus (Cytherea) and killed by wild
boar   51 **sedges** grasslike plant growing in marshy places   52 **wanton**
sway sinuously   54 **Io** mortal loved by Zeus and changed into a heifer
56 **lively** lifelike   57 **Daphne** nymph loved by Apollo and changed into
laurel to evade him

Scratching her legs that one shall swear she bleeds,
And at that sight shall sad Apollo weep,
So workmanly the blood and tears are drawn.   60

Lord. Thou art a lord and nothing but a lord.
Thou hast a lady far more beautiful
Than any woman in this waning° age.

First Servingman. And till the tears that she hath shed
    for thee
Like envious floods o'errun her lovely face,   65
She was the fairest creature in the world,
And yet° she is inferior to none.

Sly. Am I a lord, and have I such a lady?
Or do I dream? Or have I dreamed till now?
I do not sleep: I see, I hear, I speak,   70
I smell sweet savors and I feel soft things.
Upon my life, I am a lord indeed
And not a tinker nor Christopher Sly.
Well, bring our lady hither to our sight,
And once again a pot o' th' smallest° ale.   75

Second Servingman. Will't please your mightiness to
    wash your hands?
O, how we joy to see your wit° restored!
O, that once more you knew but what you are!
These fifteen years you have been in a dream,
Or when you waked so waked as if you slept.   80

Sly. These fifteen years! By my fay,° a goodly nap.
But did I never speak of° all that time?

First Servingman. O yes, my lord, but very idle words,
For though you lay here in this goodly chamber,
Yet would you say ye were beaten out of door   85
And rail upon the hostess of the house°
And say you would present her at the leet°

---

63 **waning** decadent   67 **yet** now, still   75 **smallest** weakest   77 **wit**
mind   81 **fay** faith   82 **of** in   86 **house** inn   87 **present her at the**
leet accuse her at the court under lord of a manor

Because she brought stone jugs and no sealed°
    quarts.
Sometimes you would call out for Cicely Hacket.

90 *Sly.* Ay, the woman's maid of the house.

Third Servingman. Why, sir, you know no house nor
    no such maid
Nor no such men as you have reckoned up,
As Stephen Sly° and old John Naps of Greece,°
And Peter Turph and Henry Pimpernell,
95 And twenty more such names and men as these
Which never were nor no man ever saw.

Sly. Now, Lord be thankèd for my good amends!°

All. Amen.

  Enter [the Page, as a] Lady, with Attendants.

Sly. I thank thee; thou shalt not lose by it.

100 *Page.* How fares my noble lord?

Sly. Marry,° I fare well, for here is cheer enough.
    Where is my wife?

Page. Here, noble lord. What is thy will with her?

Sly. Are you my wife and will not call me husband?
    My men should call me "lord"; I am your good
105   man.°

Page. My husband and my lord, my lord and husband,
    I am your wife in all obedience.

Sly. I know it well. What must I call her?

Lord. Madam.

110 *Sly.* Al'ce madam or Joan madam?

Lord. Madam and nothing else. So lords call ladies.

---

88 **sealed** marked by a seal guaranteeing quantity   93 **Stephen Sly** Stratford man (Naps, etc., may also be names of real persons)   93 **Greece** the Green (?) Greet, hamlet not far from Stratford (?)   97 **amends** recovery   101 **Marry** in truth (originally, [by St.] Mary)   105 **goodman** husband

Sly. Madam wife, they say that I have dreamed
    And slept above some fifteen year or more.

Page. Ay, and the time seems thirty unto me,
    Being all this time abandoned° from your bed.   *115*

Sly. 'Tis much. Servants, leave me and her alone.
    Madam, undress you and come now to bed.

Page. Thrice noble lord, let me entreat of you
    To pardon me yet for a night or two
    Or, if not so, until the sun be set.   *120*
    For your physicians have expressly charged,
    In peril to incur° your former malady,
    That I should yet absent me from your bed.
    I hope this reason stands for my excuse.

Sly. Ay, it stands so° that I may hardly tarry so long,   *125*
    but I would be loath to fall into my dreams again. I
    will therefore tarry in despite of the flesh and the
    blood.

Enter a Messenger.

Messenger. Your Honor's players, hearing your
    amendment,
    Are come to play a pleasant comedy.   *130*
    For so your doctors hold it very meet,
    Seeing too much sadness hath congealed your blood,
    And melancholy is the nurse of frenzy.°
    Therefore they thought it good you hear a play
    And frame your mind to mirth and merriment,   *135*
    Which bars a thousand harms and lengthens life.

Sly. Marry, I will let them play it. Is not a comontie°
    a Christmas gambold° or a tumbling trick?

Page. No, my good lord, it is more pleasing stuff.

---

115 **abandoned** excluded   122 **In peril to incur** because of the danger
of a return of   125 **stands so** will do (with phallic pun, playing on
"reason," which was pronounced much like "raising")   133 **frenzy**
mental illness   137 **comontie** comedy (as pronounced by Sly)   138 **gam-
bold** gambol (game, dance, frolic)

140 *Sly.* What, household stuff?°

    Page. It is a kind of history.

    Sly. Well, we'll see't. Come, madam wife, sit by my
        side
    And let the world slip.° We shall ne'er be younger.

---

140 **stuff** (with sexual innuendo; see Eric Partridge, *Shakespeare's Bawdy*)   143 **slip** go by

[ACT 1

Scene 1. *Padua. A street.*]

Flourish.° Enter Lucentio and his man° Tranio.

Lucentio. Tranio, since for the great desire I had
  To see fair Padua,° nursery of arts,
  I am arrived for fruitful Lombardy,
  The pleasant garden of great Italy,
  And by my father's love and leave am armed   5
  With his good will and thy good company,
  My trusty servant well approved° in all,
  Here let us breathe and haply institute
  A course of learning and ingenious° studies.
  Pisa, renownèd for grave citizens,   10
  Gave me my being and my father first,°
  A merchant of great traffic° through the world,
  Vincentio, come of the Bentivolii.
  Vincentio's son, brought up in Florence,
  It shall become to serve° all hopes conceived,   15
  To deck his fortune with his virtuous deeds;
  And therefore, Tranio, for the time I study,
  Virtue and that part of philosophy
  Will I apply° that treats of happiness
  By virtue specially to be achieved.   20
  Tell me thy mind, for I have Pisa left
  And am to Padua come, as he that leaves

1.1.s.d. **Flourish** fanfare of trumpets   s.d. **man** servant   2 **Padua** (noted for its university)   7 **approved** proved, found reliable   9 **ingenious** mind-training   11 **first** i.e., before that   12 **traffic** business   15 **serve** work for   19 **apply** apply myself to

A shallow plash° to plunge him in the deep
And with satiety seeks to quench his thirst.

25 *Tranio.* Mi perdonato,° gentle master mine,
I am in all affected° as yourself,
Glad that you thus continue your resolve
To suck the sweets of sweet philosophy.
Only, good master, while we do admire
30 This virtue and this moral discipline,
Let's be no stoics nor no stocks,° I pray,
Or so devote° to Aristotle's checks°
As° Ovid° be an outcast quite abjured.
Balk logic° with acquaintance that you have
35 And practice rhetoric in your common talk.
Music and poesy use to quicken° you.
The mathematics and the metaphysics,
Fall to them as you find your stomach° serves you.
No profit grows where is no pleasure ta'en.
40 In brief, sir, study what you most affect.°

Lucentio. Gramercies,° Tranio, well dost thou advise.
If, Biondello, thou wert come ashore,
We could at once put us in readiness
And take a lodging fit to entertain
45 Such friends as time in Padua shall beget.
But stay awhile, what company is this?

Tranio. Master, some show to welcome us to town.

*Enter Baptista with his two daughters, Kate and
Bianca; Gremio, a pantaloon;° [and] Hortensio,
suitor to Bianca. Lucentio [and]
Tranio stand by.°*

Baptista. Gentlemen, importune me no farther,
For how I firmly am resolved you know,

23 **plash** pool   25 **Mi perdonato** pardon me   26 **affected** inclined
31 **stocks** sticks (with pun on Stoics)   32 **devote** devoted   32 **checks**
restraints   33 **As** so that   33 **Ovid** Roman love poet (cf. 3.1.28–29,
4.2.8)   34 **Balk logic** engage in arguments   36 **quicken** make alive
38 **stomach** taste, preference   40 **affect** like   41 **Gramercies** many
thanks   47s.d. **pantaloon** laughable old man (a stock character with
baggy pants, in Italian Renaissance comedy)   47s.d. **by** nearby

That is, not to bestow my youngest daughter   50
Before I have a husband for the elder.
If either of you both love Katherina,
Because I know you well and love you well,
Leave shall you have to court her at your pleasure.

Gremio. To cart° her rather. She's too rough for me.   55
There, there, Hortensio, will you any wife?

Kate. I pray you, sir, is it your will
To make a stale° of me amongst these mates?°

Hortensio. Mates, maid? How mean you that? No
mates for you
Unless you were of gentler, milder mold.   60

Kate. I' faith, sir, you shall never need to fear:
Iwis° it° is not halfway to her° heart.
But if it were, doubt not her care should be
To comb your noddle with a three-legged stool
And paint° your face and use you like a fool.   65

Hortensio. From all such devils, good Lord deliver us!

Gremio. And me too, good Lord!

Tranio. [*Aside*] Husht, master, here's some good pastime toward.°
That wench is stark mad or wonderful froward.°

Lucentio. [*Aside*] But in the other's silence do I see   70
Maid's mild behavior and sobriety.
Peace, Tranio.

Tranio. [*Aside*] Well said, master. Mum, and gaze
your fill.

Baptista. Gentlemen, that I may soon make good
What I have said: Bianca, get you in,   75
And let it not displease thee, good Bianca,

---

55 **cart** drive around in an open cart (a punishment for prostitutes)
58 **stale** (1) laughingstock (2) prostitute   58 **mates** low fellows (with
pun on *stalemate* and leading to pun on *mate* = husband)   62 **Iwis** certainly   62 **it** i.e., getting a mate   62 **her** Kate's   65 **paint** i.e., red with
blood   68 **toward** coming up   69 **froward** willful

For I will love thee ne'er the less, my girl.

Kate. A pretty peat!° It is best
Put finger in the eye,° and° she knew why.

80   *Bianca.* Sister, content you in my discontent.
Sir, to your pleasure humbly I subscribe.
My books and instruments shall be my company,
On them to look and practice by myself.

Lucentio. [*Aside*] Hark, Tranio, thou mayst hear
Minerva° speak.

85   *Hortensio.* Signior Baptista, will you be so strange?°
Sorry am I that our good will effects
Bianca's grief.

Gremio.   Why will you mew° her up,
Signior Baptista, for this fiend of hell
And make her bear the penance of her tongue?

90   *Baptista.* Gentlemen, content ye. I am resolved.
Go in, Bianca.   [*Exit Bianca.*]
And for° I know she taketh most delight
In music, instruments, and poetry,
Schoolmasters will I keep within my house,
95   Fit to instruct her youth. If you, Hortensio,
Or Signior Gremio, you, know any such,
Prefer° them hither; for to cunning° men
I will be very kind, and liberal
To mine own children in good bringing up.
100 And so, farewell. Katherina, you may stay,
For I have more to commune with° Bianca.   *Exit.*

Kate. Why, and I trust I may go too, may I not?
What, shall I be appointed hours, as though, belike,°
I knew not what to take and what to leave? Ha!

                                                  Exit.

---

78 **peat** pet (cf. "teacher's pet")   79 **Put finger in the eye** cry   79 **and**
if   84 **Minerva** goddess of wisdom   85 **strange** rigid   87 **mew** cage
(falconry term)   92 **for** because   97 **Prefer** recommend   97 **cunning**
talented   101 **commune with** communicate to   103 **belike** it seems
likely

Gremio. You may go to the devil's dam;° your gifts 105
are so good, here's none will hold you. Their love is
not so great,° Hortensio, but we may blow our
nails together° and fast it fairly out. Our cake's
dough on both sides.° Farewell. Yet for the love I
bear my sweet Bianca, if I can by any means light 110
on a fit man to teach her that wherein she delights,
I will wish° him to her father.

Hortensio. So will I, Signior Gremio. But a word, I
pray. Though the nature of our quarrel yet never
brooked parle,° know now, upon advice,° it touch- 115
eth° us both—that we may yet again have access
to our fair mistress and be happy rivals in Bianca's
love—to labor and effect one thing specially.

Gremio. What's that, I pray?

Hortensio. Marry, sir, to get a husband for her sister. 120

Gremio. A husband! A devil.

Hortensio. I say, a husband.

Gremio. I say, a devil. Think'st thou, Hortensio,
though her father be very rich, any man is so very°
a fool to° be married to hell?   125

Hortensio. Tush, Gremio, though it pass your patience and mine to endure her loud alarums,° why,
man, there be good fellows in the world, and° a man
could light on them, would take her with all faults,
and money enough.   130

Gremio. I cannot tell, but I had as lief° take her
dowry with this condition, to be whipped at the
high cross° every morning.

---

105 **dam** mother (used of animals)   107 **great** important   107–08
blow our nails together i.e., wait patiently   108–09 **Our cake's dough
on both sides** we've both failed (proverbial)   112 **wish** commend
115 **brooked parle** allowed negotiation   115 **advice** consideration
115–16 **toucheth** concerns   124 **very** thorough   125 **to** as to   127 **alarums** outcries   128 **and** if   131 **had as lief** would as willingly   133 **high
cross** market cross (prominent spot)

Hortensio. Faith, as you say, there's small choice in
135   rotten apples. But come, since this bar in law°
makes us friends, it shall be so far forth° friendly
maintained, till by helping Baptista's eldest daughter to a husband, we set his youngest free for a husband, and then have to't° afresh. Sweet Bianca!
140   Happy man be his dole!° He that runs fastest gets
the ring. How say you, Signior Gremio?

Gremio. I am agreed, and would I had given him the
best horse in Padua to begin his wooing, that°
would thoroughly woo her, wed her, and bed her
145   and rid the house of her. Come on.

Exeunt ambo.° Manet° Tranio and Lucentio.

Tranio. I pray, sir, tell me, is it possible
That love should of a sudden take such hold?

Lucentio. O Tranio, till I found it to be true
I never thought it possible or likely.
150   But see, while idly I stood looking on,
I found the effect of love-in-idleness°
And now in plainness do confess to thee,
That art to me as secret° and as dear
As Anna° to the Queen of Carthage was,
155   Tranio, I burn, I pine, I perish, Tranio,
If I achieve not this young modest girl.
Counsel me, Tranio, for I know thou canst.
Assist me, Tranio, for I know thou wilt.

Tranio. Master, it is no time to chide you now.
160   Affection is not rated° from the heart.

---

135 **bar in law** legal action of preventive sort   136 **so far forth** so long
139 **have to't** renew our competition   140 **Happy man be his dole** let
being a happy man be his (the winner's) destiny   143 **that** (antecedent
is *his*)   145 s.d. **ambo** both   145 s.d. **Manet** remain (though the Latin
plural is properly *manent*, the singular with a plural subject is common
in Elizabethan texts)   151 **love-in-idleness** popular name for pansy
(believed to have mysterious power in love; cf. *Midsummer Night's
Dream*, 2.1. 165 ff.)   153 **to me as secret** as much in my confidence
154 **Anna** sister and confidante of Queen Dido   160 **rated** scolded

If love have touched you, naught remains but so,°
"Redime te captum, quam queas minimo."°

Lucentio. Gramercies,° lad, go forward. This contents.
 The rest will comfort, for thy counsel's sound.

Tranio. Master, you looked so longly° on the maid, *165*
 Perhaps you marked not what's the pith of all.°

Lucentio. O yes, I saw sweet beauty in her face,
 Such as the daughter of Agenor° had,
 That made great Jove to humble him to her hand
 When with his knees he kissed the Cretan strond.° *170*

Tranio. Saw you no more? Marked you not how her
  sister
 Began to scold and raise up such a storm
 That mortal ears might hardly endure the din?

Lucentio. Tranio, I saw her coral lips to move
 And with her breath she did perfume the air. *175*
 Sacred and sweet was all I saw in her.

Tranio. Nay, then, 'tis time to stir him from his trance.
 I pray, awake, sir. If you love the maid,
 Bend thoughts and wits to achieve her. Thus it
  stands:
 Her elder sister is so curst and shrewd° *180*
 That till the father rid his hands of her,
 Master, your love must live a maid at home;
 And therefore has he closely mewed° her up,
 Because° she will not be annoyed with suitors.

Lucentio. Ah, Tranio, what a cruel father's he! *185*
 But art thou not advised° he took some care
 To get her cunning° schoolmasters to instruct her?

---

161 **so** to act thus 162 **Redime . . . minimo** ransom yourself, a captive, at the smallest possible price (from Terence's play *The Eunuch,* as quoted inaccurately in Lilly's *Latin Grammar*) 163 **Gramercies** many thanks 165 **longly** (1) longingly (2) interminably 166 **pith of all** heart of the matter 168 **daughter of Agenor** Europa, loved by Jupiter, who, in the form of a bull, carried her to Crete 170 **strond** strand, shore 180 **curst and shrewd** sharp-tempered and shrewish 183 **mewed** caged 184 **Because** so that 186 **advised** informed 187 **cunning** knowing

Tranio. Ay, marry, am I, sir—and now 'tis plotted!°

Lucentio. I have it, Tranio!

Tranio.   Master, for° my hand,
190   Both our inventions° meet and jump in one.°

Lucentio. Tell me thine first.

Tranio.   You will be schoolmaster
       And undertake the teaching of the maid.
       That's your device.

Lucentio.   It is. May it be done?

Tranio. Not possible, for who shall bear° your part
195   And be in Padua here Vincentio's son?
       Keep house and ply his book, welcome his friends,
       Visit his countrymen and banquet them?

Lucentio. Basta,° content thee, for I have it full.°
       We have not yet been seen in any house,
200   Nor can we be distinguished by our faces
       For man or master. Then it follows thus:
       Thou shalt be master, Tranio, in my stead,
       Keep house and port° and servants as I should.
       I will some other be—some Florentine,
205   Some Neapolitan, or meaner° man of Pisa.
       'Tis hatched and shall be so. Tranio, at once
       Uncase° thee, take my colored° hat and cloak.
       When Biondello comes he waits on thee,
       But I will charm° him first to keep his tongue.

210 *Tranio.* So had you need.
       In brief, sir, sith° it your pleasure is
       And I am tied° to be obedient—
       For so your father charged me at our parting;

---

188 **'tis plotted** I've a scheme   189 **for** I bet   190 **inventions** schemes
190 **jump in one** are identical   194 **bear** act   198 **Basta** enough
(Italian)   198 **full** fully (worked out)   203 **port** style   205 **meaner** of
lower rank   207 **Uncase** undress   207 **colored** (masters dressed color-
fully; servants wore dark blue)   209 **charm** exercise power over (he
tells him a fanciful tale, lines 225–34)   211 **sith** since   212 **tied** obligated

"Be serviceable to my son," quoth he,
Although I think 'twas in another sense—   *215*
I am content to be Lucentio
Because so well I love Lucentio.

Lucentio. Tranio, be so, because Lucentio loves,
    And let me be a slave, t'achieve that maid
    Whose sudden sight hath thralled° my wounded eye.   *220*

                Enter Biondello.

Here comes the rogue. Sirrah, where have you been?

Biondello. Where have I been? Nay, how now, where
    are you?
    Master, has my fellow Tranio stol'n your clothes,
    Or you stol'n his, or both? Pray, what's the news?

Lucentio. Sirrah, come hither. 'Tis no time to jest,   *225*
    And therefore frame your manners to the time.°
    Your fellow Tranio, here, to save my life,
    Puts my apparel and my count'nance° on,
    And I for my escape have put on his,
    For in a quarrel since I came ashore   *230*
    I killed a man and fear I was descried.°
    Wait you on him, I charge you, as becomes,
    While I make way from hence to save my life.
    You understand me?

Biondello.   I, sir? Ne'er a whit.

Lucentio. And not a jot of Tranio in your mouth.   *235*
    Tranio is changed into Lucentio.

Biondello. The better for him. Would I were so too.

Tranio. So could I, faith, boy, to have the next wish
    after,
    That Lucentio indeed had Baptista's youngest
    daughter.

---

220 **thralled** enslaved   226 **frame your manners to the time** adjust
your conduct to the situation   228 **count'nance** demeanor   231 **descried**
seen, recognized

But, sirrah, not for my sake but your master's, I
240 advise
You use your manners discreetly in all kind of com-
  panies.
When I am alone, why, then I am Tranio,
But in all places else your master, Lucentio.

Lucentio. Tranio, let's go.
245 One thing more rests,° that thyself execute°—
To make one among these wooers. If thou ask me
  why,
Sufficeth my reasons are both good and weighty.
              Exeunt.

   The Presenters° above speaks.

First Servingman. My lord, you nod; you do not mind°
  the play.

Sly. Yes, by Saint Anne, do I. A good matter, surely.
250 Comes there any more of it?

Page. My lord, 'tis but begun.

Sly. 'Tis a very excellent piece of work, madam lady.
  Would 'twere done!   *They sit and mark.°*

   [Scene 2. *Padua. The street in front of*
      Hortensio's house.]

   Enter Petruchio° and his man Grumio.

Petruchio. Verona, for a while I take my leave
  To see my friends in Padua, but of all
  My best belovèd and approvèd friend,

---

245 **rests** remains 245 **execute** are to perform 247s.d. **Presenters**
commentators, actors thought of collectively, hence the singular verb
248 **mind** pay attention to 253s.d. **mark** observe 1.2.s.d. **Petruchio**
(correct form *Petrucio,* with *c* pronounced *tch*)

　　Hortensio, and I trow° this is his house.
　　Here, sirrah Grumio, knock, I say.　　　　　　　　　　5

Grumio. Knock, sir? Whom should I knock? Is there
　　any man has rebused° your worship?

Petruchio. Villain, I say, knock me here° soundly.

Grumio. Knock you here, sir? Why, sir, what am I,
　　sir, that I should knock you here, sir?　　　　　　　10

Petruchio. Villain, I say, knock me at this gate°
　　And rap me well or I'll knock your knave's pate.°

Grumio. My master is grown quarrelsome. I should
　　　　knock you first,
　　And then I know after who comes by the worst.

Petruchio. Will it not be?　　　　　　　　　　　　　15
　　Faith, sirrah, and° you'll not knock, I'll ring° it;
　　I'll try how you can *sol, fa,*° and sing it.
　　　　　　　　　　　　He wrings him by the ears.

Grumio. Help, masters, help! My master is mad.

Petruchio. Now, knock when I bid you, sirrah villain.

　　　　　　　　　　Enter Hortensio.

Hortensio. How now, what's the matter? My old　　20
　　friend Grumio, and my good friend Petruchio! How
　　do you all at Verona?

Petruchio. Signior Hortensio, come you to part the
　　fray?
　　Con tutto il cuore ben trovato,° may I say.

Hortensio. Alla nostra casa ben venuto, molto hono-　　25
　　rato signior mio Petruchio.°

---

4 **trow** think　7 **rebused** (Grumio means *abused*)　8 **knock me here**
knock here for me (Grumio plays game of misunderstanding, taking "me
here" as "my ear")　11 **gate** door　12 **pate** head　16 **and** if　16 **ring**
(pun on *wring*)　17 **sol, fa** go up and down the scales (possibly with
puns on meanings now lost)　24 **Con ... trovato** with all [my] heart
well found (i.e., welcome)　25–26 **Alla ... Petruchio** welcome to our
house, my much honored Signior Petruchio

Rise, Grumio, rise. We will compound° this quarrel.

Grumio. Nay, 'tis no matter, sir, what he 'leges° in
Latin.° If this be not a lawful cause for me to leave
30 his service—look you, sir, he bid me knock him and
rap him soundly, sir. Well, was it fit for a servant to
use his master so, being perhaps, for aught I see,
two-and-thirty, a peep out?°
Whom would to God I had well knocked at first,
35 Then had not Grumio come by the worst.

Petruchio. A senseless villain! Good Hortensio,
I bade the rascal knock upon your gate
And could not get him for my heart° to do it.

Grumio. Knock at the gate? O heavens! Spake you
40 not these words plain, "Sirrah, knock me here, rap
me here, knock me well, and knock me soundly"?
And come you now with "knocking at the gate"?

Petruchio. Sirrah, be gone or talk not, I advise you.

Hortensio. Petruchio, patience, I am Grumio's pledge.
45 Why, this's a heavy chance° 'twixt him and you,
Your ancient, trusty, pleasant servant Grumio.
And tell me now, sweet friend, what happy gale
Blows you to Padua here from old Verona?

Petruchio. Such wind as scatters young men through
   the world
50 To seek their fortunes farther than at home,
Where small experience grows. But in a few,°
Signior Hortensio, thus it stands with me:
Antonio my father is deceased,
And I have thrust myself into this maze,°
55 Happily° to wive and thrive as best I may.

---

27 **compound** settle   28 **'leges** alleges   29 **Latin** (as if he were English,
Grumio does not recognize Italian)   33 **two-and-thirty, a peep out** (1)
an implication that Petruchio is aged (2) a term from cards, slang for
"drunk" (*peep* is an old form of *pip,* a marking on a card)   38 **heart** life
45 **heavy chance** sad happening   51 **few** i.e., words   54 **maze** traveling; uncertain course   55 **Happily** haply, perchance

Crowns in my purse I have and goods at home
And so am come abroad to see the world.

Hortensio. Petruchio, shall I then come roundly° to
    thee
And wish thee to a shrewd ill-favored° wife?
Thou'ldst thank me but a little for my counsel—   60
And yet I'll promise thee she shall be rich,
And very rich—but thou'rt too much my friend,
And I'll not wish thee to her.

Petruchio. Signior Hortensio, 'twixt such friends as we
Few words suffice; and therefore if thou know   65
One rich enough to be Petruchio's wife—
As wealth is burthen° of my wooing dance—
Be she as foul° as was Florentius'° love,
As old as Sibyl,° and as curst and shrewd
As Socrates' Xanthippe° or a worse,   70
She moves me not, or not removes, at least,
Affection's edge in me, were she as rough
As are the swelling Adriatic seas.
I come to wive it wealthily in Padua;
If wealthily, then happily in Padua.   75

Grumio. Nay, look you, sir, he tells you flatly what
his mind is. Why, give him gold enough and marry
him to a puppet or an aglet-baby° or an old trot°
with ne'er a tooth in her head, though she have as
many diseases as two-and-fifty horses. Why, nothing   80
comes amiss so money comes withal.°

Hortensio. Petruchio, since we are stepped thus far in,
I will continue that° I broached in jest.
I can, Petruchio, help thee to a wife
With wealth enough and young and beauteous,   85

58 **come roundly** talk frankly   59 **shrewd ill-favored** shrewish, poorly
qualified   67 **burthen** burden (musical accompaniment)   68 **foul** homely
68 **Florentius** knight in Gower's *Confessio Amantis* (cf. Chaucer's Wife of
Bath's Tale; knight marries hag who turns into beautiful girl)   69 **Sibyl**
prophetess in Greek and Roman myth   70 **Xanthippe** Socrates' wife, leg-
endarily shrewish   78 **aglet-baby** small female figure forming metal tip of
cord or lace (French *aiguillette,* point)   78 **trot** hag   81 **withal** with it
83 **that** what

Brought up as best becomes a gentlewoman.
Her only fault—and that is faults enough—
Is that she is intolerable curst°
And shrewd and froward,° so beyond all measure
90   That were my state° far worser than it is,
I would not wed her for a mine of gold.

Petruchio. Hortensio, peace. Thou know'st not gold's
    effect.
Tell me her father's name, and 'tis enough,
For I will board° her though she chide as loud
95   As thunder when the clouds in autumn crack.°

Hortensio. Her father is Baptista Minola,
An affable and courteous gentleman.
Her name is Katherina Minola,
Renowned in Padua for her scolding tongue.

100 *Petruchio.* I know her father though I know not her,
And he knew my deceasèd father well.
I will not sleep, Hortensio, till I see her,
And therefore let me be thus bold with you,
To give you over° at this first encounter
105 Unless you will accompany me thither.

Grumio. I pray you, sir, let him go while the humor°
lasts. A° my word, and° she knew him as well as I
do, she would think scolding would do little good°
upon him. She may perhaps call him half a score
110 knaves or so—why, that's nothing. And he begin
once, he'll rail in his rope-tricks.° I'll tell you what,
sir, and she stand° him but a little, he will throw a
figure in her face and so disfigure her with it that
she shall have no more eyes to see withal than a
115 cat. You know him not, sir.

---

88 **intolerable curst** intolerably sharp-tempered   89 **froward** willful
90 **state** estate, revenue   94 **board** naval term, with double sense:
(1) accost (2) go on board   95 **crack** make explosive roars   104 **give
you over** leave you   106 **humor** mood   107 **A** on   107 **and** if (also at
lines 110 and 112)   108 **do little good** have little effect   111 **rope-
tricks** (1) Grumio's version of *rhetoric*, going with *figure* just below
(2) rascally conduct, deserving hanging (3) possible sexual innuendo, as
in following lines   112 **stand** withstand

Hortensio. Tarry, Petruchio, I must go with thee,
For in Baptista's keep° my treasure is.
He hath the jewel of my life in hold,°
His youngest daughter, beautiful Bianca,
And her withholds from me and other more,   120
Suitors to her and rivals in my love,
Supposing it a thing impossible,
For° those defects I have before rehearsed,
That ever Katherina will be wooed.
Therefore this order° hath Baptista ta'en,   125
That none shall have access unto Bianca
Till Katherine the curst have got a husband.

Grumio. Katherine the curst!
A title for a maid of all titles the worst.

Hortensio. Now shall my friend Petruchio do me
grace°   130
And offer° me, disguised in sober robes,
To old Baptista as a schoolmaster
Well seen° in music, to instruct Bianca,
That so I may, by this device, at least
Have leave and leisure to make love to her   135
And unsuspected court her by herself.

Enter Gremio, and Lucentio disguised
[as a schoolmaster, Cambio].

Grumio. Here's no knavery! See, to beguile the old
folks, how the young folks lay their heads together!
Master, master, look about you. Who goes there,
ha?   140

Hortensio. Peace, Grumio. It is the rival of my love.
Petruchio, stand by awhile.   *[They eavesdrop.]*

Grumio. A proper stripling,° and an amorous!

Gremio. O, very well, I have perused the note.°

117 **keep** heavily fortified inner tower of castle   118 **hold** stronghold
123 **For** because of   125 **order** step   130 **grace** a favor   131 **offer** present, introduce   133 **seen** trained   143 **proper stripling** handsome youth
(sarcastic comment on Gremio)   144 **note** memorandum (reading list
for Bianca)

145　　Hark you, sir, I'll have them very fairly bound—
　　　All books of love, see that at any hand,°
　　　And see you read no other lectures° to her.
　　　You understand me. Over and beside
　　　Signior Baptista's liberality,
150　　I'll mend it with a largess.° Take your paper° too
　　　And let me have them° very well perfumed,
　　　For she is sweeter than perfume itself
　　　To whom they go to. What will you read to her?

Lucentio. Whate'er I read to her, I'll plead for you
155　　As for my patron, stand you so assured,
　　　As firmly as° yourself were still in place°—
　　　Yea, and perhaps with more successful words
　　　Than you unless you were a scholar, sir.

Gremio. O this learning, what a thing it is!

160　*Grumio.* [*Aside*] O this woodcock,° what an ass it is!

Petruchio. Peace, sirrah!

Hortensio. Grumio, mum! [*Coming forward*] God save
　　　you, Signior Gremio.

Gremio. And you are well met, Signior Hortensio.
　　　Trow° you whither I am going? To Baptista Minola.
165　　I promised to inquire carefully
　　　About a schoolmaster for the fair Bianca,
　　　And, by good fortune, I have lighted well
　　　On this young man—for° learning and behavior
　　　Fit for her turn,° well read in poetry
170　　And other books, good ones I warrant ye.

Hortensio. 'Tis well. And I have met a gentleman
　　　Hath promised me to help me to° another,
　　　A fine musician to instruct our mistress.

---

146 **at any hand** in any case　147 **read no other lectures** assign no
other readings　150 **mend it with a largess** add a gift of money to it
150 **paper** note (line 144)　151 **them** i.e., the books　156 **as** as if you
156 **in place** present　160 **woodcock** bird easily trapped, so considered
silly　164 **Trow** know　168 **for** in　169 **turn** situation (with unconscious bawdy pun on the sense of "copulation")　172 **help me to** (1)
find (2) become (Hortensio's jest)

So shall I no whit be behind in duty
To fair Bianca, so beloved of me.   *175*

Gremio. Beloved of me, and that my deeds shall
  prove.

Grumio. [*Aside*] And that his bags° shall prove.

Hortensio. Gremio, 'tis now no time to vent° our love.
  Listen to me, and if you speak me fair,
  I'll tell you news indifferent° good for either.   *180*
  Here is a gentleman whom by chance I met,
  Upon agreement from us to his liking,°
  Will undertake° to woo curst Katherine,
  Yea, and to marry her if her dowry please.

Gremio. So said, so done, is well.   *185*
  Hortensio, have you told him all her faults?

Petruchio. I know she is an irksome, brawling scold;
  If that be all, masters, I hear no harm.

Gremio. No, say'st me so, friend? What countryman?

Petruchio. Born in Verona, old Antonio's son.   *190*
  My father dead, my fortune lives for me,
  And I do hope good days and long to see.

Gremio. O, sir, such a life with such a wife were
  strange.
  But if you have a stomach,° to't a° God's name;
  You shall have me assisting you in all.   *195*
  But will you woo this wildcat?

Petruchio.   Will I live?

Grumio. [*Aside*] Will he woo her? Ay, or I'll hang her.

Petruchio. Why came I hither but to that intent?
  Think you a little din can daunt mine ears?
  Have I not in my time heard lions roar?   *200*
  Have I not heard the sea, puffed up with winds,
  Rage like an angry boar chafèd with sweat?

177 **bags** i.e., of money   178 **vent** express   180 **indifferent** equally
182 **Upon . . . liking** if we agree to his terms (paying costs)   183 **undertake** promise   194 **stomach** inclination   194 **a** in

Have I not heard great ordnance° in the field
And heaven's artillery thunder in the skies?
205   Have I not in a pitchèd battle heard
Loud 'larums,° neighing steeds, and trumpets'
   clang?
And do you tell me of a woman's tongue,
That gives not half so great a blow to hear
As will a chestnut in a farmer's fire?
Tush, tush, fear° boys with bugs.°

210   *Grumio.* [*Aside*]   For he fears none.

Gremio. Hortensio, hark.
This gentleman is happily arrived,
My mind presumes, for his own good and ours.

Hortensio. I promised we would be contributors
215   And bear his charge of° wooing, whatsoe'er.

Gremio. And so we will, provided that he win her.

Grumio. [*Aside*] I would I were as sure of a good
dinner.

   Enter Tranio brave° [*as Lucentio*] *and Biondello.*

Tranio. Gentlemen, God save you. If I may be bold,
Tell me, I beseech you, which is the readiest way
220   To the house of Signior Baptista Minola?

Biondello. He that has the two fair daughters? Is't
he you mean?

Tranio. Even he, Biondello.

Gremio. Hark you, sir. You mean not her to—

Tranio. Perhaps, him and her, sir. What have you
to do?°

225   *Petruchio.* Not her that chides, sir, at any hand,° I
pray.

---

203 **ordnance** cannon 206 **'larums** calls to arms, sudden attacks
210 **fear** frighten 210 **bugs** bugbears 215 **his charge of** the cost of
his 217s.d. **brave** elegantly attired 224 **to do** i.e., to do with this
225 **at any hand** in any case

Tranio. I love no chiders, sir. Biondello, let's away.

Lucentio. [*Aside*] Well begun, Tranio.

Hortensio.   Sir, a word ere
     you go.
     Are you a suitor to the maid you talk of, yea or no?

Tranio. And if I be, sir, is it any offense?

Gremio. No, if without more words you will get you
     hence.   230

Tranio. Why, sir, I pray, are not the streets as free
     For me as for you?

Gremio.   But so is not she.

Tranio. For what reason, I beseech you?

Gremio. For this reason, if you'll know,
     That she's the choice° love of Signior Gremio.   235

Hortensio. That she's the chosen of Signior Hortensio.

Tranio. Softly, my masters! If you be gentlemen,
     Do me this right: hear me with patience.
     Baptista is a noble gentleman
     To whom my father is not all unknown,   240
     And were his daughter fairer than she is,
     She may more suitors have, and me for one.
     Fair Leda's daughter° had a thousand wooers;
     Then well one more may fair Bianca have.
     And so she shall. Lucentio shall make one,   245
     Though Paris° came° in hope to speed° alone.

Gremio. What, this gentleman will out-talk us all.

Lucentio. Sir, give him head. I know he'll prove a
     jade.°

Petruchio. Hortensio, to what end are all these words?

---

235 **choice** chosen   243 **Leda's daughter** Helen of Troy   246 **Paris**
lover who took Helen to Troy (legendary cause of Trojan War)
246 **came** should come   246 **speed** succeed   248 **prove a jade** soon
tire (cf. "jaded")

250 *Hortensio.* Sir, let me be so bold as ask you,
      Did you yet ever see Baptista's daughter?

Tranio. No, sir, but hear I do that he hath two,
      The one as famous for a scolding tongue
      As is the other for beauteous modesty.

255 *Petruchio.* Sir, sir, the first's for me; let her go by.

Gremio. Yea, leave that labor to great Hercules,
      And let it be more than Alcides'° twelve.

Petruchio. Sir, understand you this of me in sooth:°
      The youngest daughter, whom you hearken° for,
260   Her father keeps from all access of suitors
      And will not promise her to any man
      Until the elder sister first be wed.
      The younger then is free, and not before.

Tranio. If it be so, sir, that you are the man
265   Must stead° us all, and me amongst the rest,
      And if you break the ice and do this feat,
      Achieve° the elder, set the younger free
      For our access, whose hap° shall be to have her
      Will not so graceless be to be ingrate.°

Hortensio. Sir, you say well, and well you do con-
270   ceive,°
      And since you do profess to be a suitor,
      You must, as we do, gratify° this gentleman
      To whom we all rest° generally beholding.°

Tranio. Sir, I shall not be slack, in sign whereof,
275   Please ye we may contrive° this afternoon
      And quaff carouses° to our mistress' health
      And do as adversaries° do in law,
      Strive mightily but eat and drink as friends.

---

257 **Alcides** Hercules (after Alcaeus, a family ancestor) 258 **sooth**
truth 259 **hearken** long 265 **stead** aid 267 **Achieve** succeed with
268 **whose hap** the man whose luck 269 **to be ingrate** as to be ungrateful
270 **conceive** put the case 272 **gratify** compensate 273 **rest** remain
273 **beholding** indebted 275 **contrive** pass 276 **quaff carouses** empty
our cups 277 **adversaries** attorneys

Grumio, Biondello. O excellent motion! Fellows, let's
   be gone.

Hortensio. The motion's good indeed, and be it so.   280
   Petruchio, I shall be your *ben venuto.*°   *Exeunt.*

281 **ben venuto** welcome (i.e., host)

[ACT 2

Scene 1. *In Baptista's house.*]

Enter Kate and Bianca [with her hands tied].

Bianca. Good sister, wrong me not nor wrong your-
    self
    To make a bondmaid and a slave of me.
    That I disdain. But for these other gawds,°
    Unbind my hands, I'll pull them off myself,
5   Yea, all my raiment, to my petticoat,
    Or what you will command me will I do,
    So well I know my duty to my elders.

Kate. Of all thy suitors, here I charge thee, tell
    Whom thou lov'st best. See thou dissemble not.

10 *Bianca.* Believe me, sister, of all the men alive
    I never yet beheld that special face
    Which I could fancy more than any other.

Kate. Minion,° thou liest. Is't not Hortensio?

Bianca. If you affect° him, sister, here I swear
15   I'll plead for you myself but you shall have him.

Kate. O then, belike,° you fancy riches more:
    You will have Gremio to keep you fair.°

Bianca. Is it for him you do envy° me so?
    Nay, then you jest, and now I well perceive
20   You have but jested with me all this while.
    I prithee, sister Kate, untie my hands.

2.1.3 **gawds** adornments   13 **Minion** impudent creature   14 **affect** like
16 **belike** probably   17 **fair** in fine clothes   18 **envy** hate

Kate. If that be jest then all the rest was so.

Strikes her.

Enter Baptista.

Baptista. Why, how now, dame, whence grows this
    insolence?
    Bianca, stand aside. Poor girl, she weeps.
    Go ply thy needle; meddle not with her.   25
    For shame, thou hilding° of a devilish spirit,
    Why dost thou wrong her that did ne'er wrong
        thee?
    When did she cross thee with a bitter word?

Kate. Her silence flouts me and I'll be revenged.

Flies after Bianca.

Baptista. What, in my sight? Bianca, get thee in.   30

Exit [Bianca].

Kate. What, will you not suffer° me? Nay, now I see
    She is your treasure, she must have a husband;
    I must dance barefoot on her wedding day,°
    And, for your love to her, lead apes in hell.°
    Talk not to me; I will go sit and weep   35
    Till I can find occasion of revenge.   [*Exit.*]

Baptista. Was ever gentleman thus grieved as I?
    But who comes here?

Enter Gremio, Lucentio in the habit of a mean° man
    [Cambio], Petruchio, with [Hortensio as a music
    teacher, Litio, and] Tranio [as Lucentio], with his
        boy [Biondello] bearing a lute and books.

Gremio. Good morrow, neighbor Baptista.

Baptista. Good morrow, neighbor Gremio. God save   40
    you, gentlemen.

Petruchio. And you, good sir. Pray, have you not a
    daughter

26 **hilding** base wretch   31 **suffer** permit (i.e., to deal with you)
33 **dance ... day** (expected of older maiden sisters)   34 **lead apes in
hell** (proverbial occupation of old maids; cf. *Much Ado About Nothing*,
2.1.41)   38s.d. **mean** lower class

Called Katherina, fair and virtuous?

Baptista. I have a daughter, sir, called Katherina.

45 *Gremio. [Aside]* You are too blunt; go to it orderly.°

Petruchio. [Aside] You wrong me, Signior Gremio,
   give me leave.
   [*To Baptista*] I am a gentleman of Verona, sir,
   That, hearing of her beauty and her wit,
   Her affability and bashful modesty,
50 Her wondrous qualities and mild behavior,
   Am bold to show myself a forward° guest
   Within your house, to make mine eye the witness
   Of that report which I so oft have heard.
   And, for an entrance to° my entertainment,°
55 I do present you with a man of mine,
                              [*presenting Hortensio*]
   Cunning in music and the mathematics,
   To instruct her fully in those sciences,
   Whereof I know she is not ignorant.
   Accept of him, or else you do me wrong.
60 His name is Litio, born in Mantua.

Baptista. Y'are welcome, sir, and he for your good
   sake.
   But for my daughter Katherine, this I know,
   She is not for your turn,° the more my grief.

Petruchio. I see you do not mean to part with her,
65 Or else you like not of my company.

Baptista. Mistake me not; I speak but as I find.
   Whence are you, sir? What may I call your name?

Petruchio. Petruchio is my name, Antonio's son,
   A man well known throughout all Italy.

Baptista. I know him well. You are welcome for his
70 sake.

Gremio. Saving° your tale, Petruchio, I pray,

45 **orderly** gradually   51 **forward** eager   54 **entrance to** price of admission for   54 **entertainment** reception   63 **turn** purpose (again, with
bawdy pun)   71 **Saving** with all respect for

    Let us, that are poor petitioners, speak too.
    Backare,° you are marvelous° forward.

Petruchio. O pardon me, Signior Gremio, I would
    fain° be doing.°

Gremio. I doubt it not, sir, but you will curse your
    wooing.   75
    Neighbor, this is a gift very grateful,° I am sure of
    it. To express the like kindness myself, that° have
    been more kindly beholding to you than any, freely
    give unto you this young scholar [*presenting Lu-*
    centio] that hath been long studying at Rheims—as   80
    cunning in Greek, Latin, and other languages, as
    the other in music and mathematics. His name is
    Cambio.° Pray accept his service.

Baptista. A thousand thanks, Signior Gremio. Wel-
    come, good Cambio. [*To Tranio*] But, gentle sir,   85
    methinks you walk like° a stranger. May I be so
    bold to know the cause of your coming?

Tranio. Pardon me, sir, the boldness is mine own,
    That,° being a stranger in this city here,
    Do make myself a suitor to your daughter,   90
    Unto Bianca, fair and virtuous.
    Nor is your firm resolve unknown to me
    In the preferment of° the eldest sister.
    This liberty is all that I request,
    That, upon knowledge of my parentage,   95
    I may have welcome 'mongst the rest that woo
    And free access and favor° as the rest.
    And, toward the education of your daughters
    I here bestow a simple instrument,°
    And this small packet of Greek and Latin books.   100
    If you accept them, then their worth is great.

---

73 **Backare** back (proverbial quasi-Latin) 73 **marvelous** very 74
would fain am eager to 74 **doing** (with a sexual jest) 76 **grateful**
worthy of gratitude 77 **myself, that** I myself, who 83 **Cambio**
(Italian for "exchange") 86 **walk like** have the bearing of 89 **That**
who 93 **preferment of** giving priority to 97 **favor** countenance,
acceptance 99 **instrument** i.e., the lute

Baptista. [*Looking at books*] Lucentio is your name.
    Of whence, I pray?

Tranio. Of Pisa, sir, son to Vincentio.

Baptista. A mighty man of Pisa; by report
105   I know him° well. You are very welcome, sir.
    [*To Hortensio*] Take you the lute, [*to Lucentio*]
      and you the set of books;
    You shall go see your pupils presently.°
    Holla, within!

Enter a Servant.

          Sirrah, lead these gentlemen
    To my daughters and tell them both
110   These are their tutors; bid them use them well.
              [*Exit Servant, with Lucentio,*
          Hortensio, and Biondello following.]
    We will go walk a little in the orchard°
    And then to dinner. You are passing° welcome,
    And so I pray you all to think yourselves.

Petruchio. Signior Baptista, my business asketh haste,
115   And every day I cannot come to woo.
    You knew my father well, and in him me,
    Left solely heir to all his lands and goods,
    Which I have bettered rather than decreased.
    Then tell me, if I get your daughter's love
120   What dowry shall I have with her to wife?

Baptista. After my death the one half of my lands,
    And in possession° twenty thousand crowns.

Petruchio. And, for that dowry, I'll assure her of
    Her widowhood,° be it that she survive me,
125   In all my lands and leases whatsoever.
    Let specialties° be therefore drawn between us
    That covenants may be kept on either hand.

---

105 **him** his name   107 **presently** at once   111 **orchard** garden
112 **passing** very   122 **possession** i.e., at the time of marriage   124
widowhood estate settled on a widow (Johnson)   126 **specialties** special contracts

Baptista. Ay, when the special thing is well obtained,
That is, her love, for that is all in all.

Petruchio. Why, that is nothing, for I tell you, father, 130
I am as peremptory° as she proud-minded.
And where two raging fires meet together
They do consume the thing that feeds their fury.
Though little fire grows great with little wind,
Yet extreme gusts will blow out fire and all. 135
So I to her, and so she yields to me,
For I am rough and woo not like a babe.

Baptista. Well mayst thou woo, and happy be thy
speed!°
But be thou armed for some unhappy words.

Petruchio. Ay, to the proof,° as mountains are for
winds 140
That shakes not, though they blow perpetually.

Enter Hortensio with his head broke.

Baptista. How now, my friend, why dost thou look
so pale?

Hortensio. For fear, I promise you, if I look pale.

Baptista. What, will my daughter prove a good musician?

Hortensio. I think she'll sooner prove a soldier. 145
Iron may hold with her,° but never lutes.

Baptista. Why, then thou canst not break° her to
the lute?

Hortensio. Why, no, for she hath broke the lute to me.
I did but tell her she mistook her frets°
And bowed° her hand to teach her fingering, 150
When, with a most impatient devilish spirit,
"Frets, call you these?" quoth she; "I'll fume with
them."

131 **peremptory** resolved   138 **speed** progress   140 **to the proof** in
tested steel armor   146 **hold with her** stand her treatment   147 **break**
train   149 **frets** ridges where strings are pressed   150 **bowed** bent

And with that word she stroke° me on the head,
And through the instrument my pate made way.
155 And there I stood amazèd for a while
As on a pillory,° looking through the lute,
While she did call me rascal, fiddler,
And twangling Jack,° with twenty such vile terms
As° had she studied° to misuse me so.

160 *Petruchio.* Now, by the world, it is a lusty° wench!
I love her ten times more than e'er I did.
O how I long to have some chat with her!

Baptista. [*To Hortensio*] Well, go with me, and be
not so discomfited.
Proceed in practice° with my younger daughter;
165 She's apt° to learn and thankful for good turns.
Signior Petruchio, will you go with us
Or shall I send my daughter Kate to you?
                    Exit [*Baptista, with Gremio, Tranio, and
                    Hortensio*]. *Manet Petruchio.°*

Petruchio. I pray you do. I'll attend° her here
And woo her with some spirit when she comes.
170 Say that she rail,° why then I'll tell her plain
She sings as sweetly as a nightingale.
Say that she frown, I'll say she looks as clear
As morning roses newly washed with dew.
Say she be mute and will not speak a word,
175 Then I'll commend her volubility
And say she uttereth piercing eloquence.
If she do bid me pack,° I'll give her thanks
As though she bid me stay by her a week.
If she deny° to wed, I'll crave the day
180 When I shall ask the banns° and when be marrièd.
But here she comes, and now, Petruchio, speak.

---

153 **stroke** struck   156 **pillory** i.e., with a wooden collar (old structure
for public punishment)   158 **Jack** (term of contempt)   159 **As** as if
159 **studied** prepared   160 **lusty** spirited   164 **practice** instruction
165 **apt** disposed   167s.d. (is in the F position, which need not be
changed; Petruchio speaks to the departing Baptista)   168 **attend**
wait for   170 **rail** scold, scoff   177 **pack** go away   179 **deny** refuse
180 **banns** public announcement in church of intent to marry

Enter Kate.

Good morrow, Kate, for that's your name, I hear.

Kate. Well have you heard,° but something hard of
    hearing.
They call me Katherine that do talk of me.

Petruchio. You lie, in faith, for you are called plain
    Kate,   *185*
And bonny° Kate, and sometimes Kate the curst.
But, Kate, the prettiest Kate in Christendom,
Kate of Kate Hall,° my super-dainty Kate,
For dainties° are all Kates,° and therefore, Kate,
Take this of me, Kate of my consolation.   *190*
Hearing thy mildness praised in every town,
Thy virtues spoke of, and thy beauty sounded°—
Yet not so deeply as to thee belongs—
Myself am moved to woo thee for my wife.

Kate. Moved! In good time,° let him that moved you
    hither   *195*
Remove you hence. I knew you at the first
You were a movable.°

Petruchio.   Why, what's a movable?

Kate. A joint stool.°

Petruchio.   Thou hast hit it; come sit on me.

Kate. Asses are made to bear° and so are you.

Petruchio. Women are made to bear° and so are you.   *200*

Kate. No such jade° as you, if me you mean.

---

183 **heard** (pun: pronounced like *hard*) 186 **bonny** big, fine (perhaps
with pun on *bony,* the F spelling) 188 **Kate Hall** (possible topical reference; several places have been proposed) 189 **dainties** delicacies
189 **Kates** i.e., *cates,* delicacies 192 **sounded** (1) measured (effect of
deeply) (2) spoken of (pun) 195 **In good time** indeed 197 **movable**
article of furniture (with pun) 198 **joint stool** stool made by a joiner
(standard term of disparagement) 199 **bear** carry 200 **bear** i.e., bear
children (with second sexual meaning in Petruchio's "I will not burden
thee") 201 **jade** worn-out horse (Kate has now called him both "ass"
and "sorry horse")

Petruchio. Alas, good Kate, I will not burden thee,
  For, knowing thee to be but young and light—

Kate. Too light for such a swain° as you to catch
205   And yet as heavy as my weight should be.

Petruchio. Should be!° Should—buzz!

Kate.   Well ta'en, and like a buzzard.°

Petruchio. O slow-winged turtle,° shall a buzzard
  take° thee?

Kate. Ay, for a turtle, as he takes a buzzard.°

Petruchio. Come, come, you wasp, i' faith you are
  too angry.

210   *Kate.* If I be waspish, best beware my sting.

Petruchio. My remedy is then to pluck it out.

Kate. Ay, if the fool could find it where it lies.

Petruchio. Who knows not where a wasp does wear
  his sting?
  In his tail.

Kate.   In his tongue.

Petruchio.   Whose tongue?

215   *Kate.* Yours, if you talk of tales,° and so farewell.

Petruchio. What, with my tongue in your tail? Nay,
  come again.
  Good Kate, I am a gentleman—

Kate.   That I'll try.
                          She strikes him.

Petruchio. I swear I'll cuff you if you strike again.

---

204 **swain** country boy   206 **be** (pun on *bee*; hence *buzz*, scandal, i.e.,
about "light" woman)   206 **buzzard** hawk unteachable in falconry
(hence idiot)   207 **turtle** turtledove, noted for affectionateness   207 **take**
capture (with pun, "mistake for," in next line)   208 **buzzard** buzzing
insect (hence "wasp")   215 **of tales** idle tales (leading to bawdy pun on
tail = pudend)

Kate. So may you lose your arms:°
  If you strike me you are no gentleman,   220
  And if no gentleman, why then no arms.

Petruchio. A herald,° Kate? O, put me in thy books.°

Kate. What is your crest?° A coxcomb?°

Petruchio. A combless° cock, so° Kate will be my hen.

Kate. No cock of mine; you crow too like a craven.°   225

Petruchio. Nay, come, Kate, come, you must not look
  so sour.

Kate. It is my fashion when I see a crab.°

Petruchio. Why, here's no crab, and therefore look
  not sour.

Kate. There is, there is.

Petruchio. Then show it me.

Kate.   Had I a glass° I would.   230

Petruchio. What, you mean my face?

Kate.   Well aimed of°
  such a young one.

Petruchio. Now, by Saint George, I am too young
  for you.

Kate. Yet you are withered.

Petruchio.   'Tis with cares.

Kate.   I care not.

Petruchio. Nay, hear you, Kate, in sooth° you scape°
  not so.

 Kate. I chafe° you if I tarry. Let me go.   235

219 **arms** (pun on "coat of arms")   222 **herald** one skilled in heraldry
222 **books** registers of heraldry (with pun on "in your good books")
223 **crest** heraldic device   223 **coxcomb** identifying feature of court
Fool's cap; the cap itself   224 **combless** i.e., unwarlike   224 **so** if
225 **craven** defeated cock   227 **crab** crab apple   230 **glass** mirror
231 **well aimed of** a good shot (in the dark)   234 **sooth** truth   234 **scape**
escape   235 **chafe** (1) annoy (2) warm up

Petruchio. No, not a whit. I find you passing gentle.
 'Twas told me you were rough and coy° and sullen,
 And now I find report a very liar,
 For thou art pleasant, gamesome, passing courteous,
240 But slow in speech, yet sweet as springtime flowers.
 Thou canst not frown, thou canst not look askance,
 Nor bite the lip as angry wenches will,
 Nor hast thou pleasure to be cross in talk,
 But thou with mildness entertain'st thy wooers,
245 With gentle conference,° soft and affable.
 Why does the world report that Kate doth limp?
 O sland'rous world! Kate like the hazel-twig
 Is straight and slender, and as brown in hue
 As hazelnuts and sweeter than the kernels.
250 O, let me see thee walk. Thou dost not halt.°

Kate. Go, fool, and whom thou keep'st° command.

Petruchio. Did ever Dian° so become a grove
 As Kate this chamber with her princely gait?
 O, be thou Dian and let her be Kate,
255 And then let Kate be chaste and Dian sportful!°

Kate. Where did you study all this goodly speech?

Petruchio. It is extempore, from my mother-wit.°

Kate. A witty mother! Witless else° her son.

Petruchio. Am I not wise?

Kate.   Yes,° keep you warm.

Petruchio. Marry, so I mean, sweet Katherine, in thy
260 bed.
 And therefore, setting all this chat aside,
 Thus in plain terms: your father hath consented
 That you shall be my wife, your dowry 'greed on,
 And will you, nill° you, I will marry you.

---

237 **coy** offish   245 **conference** conversation   250 **halt** limp   251 **whom
thou keep'st** i.e., your servants   252 **Dian** Diana, goddess of hunting
and virginity   255 **sportful** (i.e., in the game of love)   257 **mother-wit**
natural intelligence   258 **else** otherwise would be   259 **Yes** yes, just
enough to (refers to a proverbial saying)   264 **nill** won't

Now, Kate, I am a husband for your turn,°   265
For, by this light, whereby I see thy beauty—
Thy beauty that doth make me like thee well—
Thou must be married to no man but me.

Enter Baptista, Gremio, Tranio.

For I am he am born to tame you, Kate,
And bring you from a wild Kate° to a Kate   270
Conformable° as other household Kates.
Here comes your father. Never make denial;
I must and will have Katherine to my wife.

Baptista. Now, Signior Petruchio, how speed° you
with my daughter?

Petruchio. How but well, sir? How but well?   275
It were impossible I should speed amiss.

Baptista. Why, how now, daughter Katherine, in your
dumps?°

Kate. Call you me daughter? Now, I promise° you
You have showed a tender fatherly regard
To wish me wed to one half lunatic,   280
A madcap ruffian and a swearing Jack
That thinks with oaths to face° the matter out.

Petruchio. Father, 'tis thus: yourself and all the world
That talked of her have talked amiss of her.
If she be curst it is for policy,°   285
For she's not froward but modest as the dove.
She is not hot° but temperate as the morn;
For patience she will prove a second Grissel°
And Roman Lucrece° for her chastity.
And to conclude, we have 'greed so well together   290
That upon Sunday is the wedding day.

Kate. I'll see thee hanged on Sunday first.

265 **turn** advantage (with bawdy second meaning)   270 **wild Kate** (pun on "wildcat")   271 **Conformable** submissive   274 **speed** get on   277 **dumps** low spirits   278 **promise** tell   282 **face** brazen   285 **policy** tactics   287 **hot** intemperate   288 **Grissel** Griselda (patient wife in Chaucer's Clerk's Tale)   289 **Lucrece** (killed herself after Tarquin raped her)

Gremio. Hark, Petruchio, she says she'll see thee hanged first.

Tranio. Is this your speeding?° Nay, then good night our part!

Petruchio. Be patient, gentlemen, I choose her for
295   myself.
     If she and I be pleased, what's that to you?
     'Tis bargained 'twixt us twain, being alone,
     That she shall still be curst in company.
     I tell you, 'tis incredible to believe
300   How much she loves me. O, the kindest Kate,
     She hung about my neck, and kiss on kiss
     She vied° so fast, protesting oath on oath,
     That in a twink° she won me to her love.
     O, you are novices. 'Tis a world° to see
305   How tame, when men and women are alone,
     A meacock° wretch can make the curstest shrew.
     Give me thy hand, Kate. I will unto Venice
     To buy apparel 'gainst° the wedding day.
     Provide the feast, father, and bid the guests;
310   I will be sure my Katherine shall be fine.°

Baptista. I know not what to say, but give me your hands.
     God send you joy, Petruchio! 'Tis a match.

Gremio, Tranio. Amen, say we. We will be witnesses.

Petruchio. Father, and wife, and gentlemen, adieu.
315   I will to Venice; Sunday comes apace.
     We will have rings and things and fine array,
     And, kiss me, Kate, "We will be married a Sunday."°

                              Exit Petruchio and Kate.

Gremio. Was ever match clapped° up so suddenly?

---

294 **speeding** success   302 **vied** made higher bids (card-playing terms),
i.e., kissed more frequently   303 **twink** twinkling   304 **world** wonder
306 **meacock** timid   308 **'gainst** in preparation for   310 **fine** well dressed
317 **"We . . . Sunday"** (line from a ballad)   318 **clapped** fixed

Baptista. Faith, gentlemen, now I play a merchant's
    part
  And venture madly on a desperate mart.°   *320*

Tranio. 'Twas a commodity° lay fretting° by you;
  'Twill bring you gain or perish on the seas.

Baptista. The gain I seek is quiet in the match.

Gremio. No doubt but he hath got a quiet catch.
  But now, Baptista, to your younger daughter;   *325*
  Now is the day we long have lookèd for.
  I am your neighbor and was suitor first.

Tranio. And I am one that loves Bianca more
  Than words can witness or your thoughts can guess.

Gremio. Youngling, thou canst not love so dear as I. *330*

Tranio. Graybeard, thy love doth freeze.

Gremio.   But thine doth fry.
  Skipper,° stand back, 'tis age that nourisheth.

Tranio. But youth in ladies' eyes that flourisheth.

Baptista. Content you, gentlemen; I will compound°
    this strife.
  'Tis deeds must win the prize, and he of both°   *335*
  That can assure my daughter greatest dower°
  Shall have my Bianca's love.
  Say, Signior Gremio, what can you assure her?

Gremio. First, as you know, my house within the city
  Is richly furnishèd with plate and gold,   *340*
  Basins and ewers to lave° her dainty hands;
  My hangings all of Tyrian° tapestry;
  In ivory coffers I have stuffed my crowns,
  In cypress chests my arras counterpoints,°

---

320 **mart** "deal"   321 **commodity** (here a coarse term for women; see
Partridge, *Shakespeare's Bawdy*)   321 **fretting** decaying in storage
(with pun)   332 **Skipper** skipping (irresponsible) fellow   334 **compound** settle   335 **he of both** the one of you two   336 **dower** man's
gift to bride   341 **lave** wash   342 **Tyrian** purple   344 **arras counterpoints** counterpanes woven in Arras

345 Costly apparel, tents,° and canopies,
Fine linen, Turkey cushions bossed° with pearl,
Valance° of Venice gold in needlework,
Pewter and brass, and all things that belongs
To house or housekeeping. Then, at my farm
350 I have a hundred milch-kine to the pail,°
Six score fat oxen standing in my stalls
And all things answerable to this portion.°
Myself am struck° in years, I must confess,
And if I die tomorrow, this is hers,
355 If whilst I live she will be only mine.

Tranio. That "only" came well in. Sir, list to me.
I am my father's heir and only son.
If I may have your daughter to my wife,
I'll leave her houses three or four as good,
360 Within rich Pisa walls, as any one
Old Signior Gremio has in Padua,
Besides two thousand ducats° by the year
Of° fruitful land, all which shall be her jointure.°
What, have I pinched° you, Signior Gremio?

Gremio. [*Aside*] Two thousand ducats by the year of
365 land!
My land amounts not to so much in all.
[*To others*] That she shall have besides an argosy°
That now is lying in Marcellus' road.°
What, have I choked you with an argosy?

370 *Tranio.* Gremio, 'tis known my father hath no less
Than three great argosies, besides two galliasses°
And twelve tight° galleys. These I will assure her
And twice as much, whate'er thou off'rest next.

---

345 **tents** bed tester (hanging cover)   346 **bossed** embroidered   347 **Valance** bed fringes and drapes   350 **milch-kine to the pail** cows producing milk for human use   352 **answerable to this portion** corresponding to this settlement (?)   353 **struck** advanced   362 **ducats** Venetian gold coins   363 **Of** from   363 **jointure** settlement   364 **pinched** put the screws on   367 **argosy** largest type of merchant ship   368 **Marcellus' road** Marseilles' harbor   371 **galliasses** large galleys   372 **tight** watertight

Gremio. Nay, I have off'red all. I have no more,
  And she can have no more than all I have.   375
  If you like me, she shall have me and mine.

Tranio. Why, then the maid is mine from all the world
  By your firm promise. Gremio is outvied.°

Baptista. I must confess your offer is the best,
  And let your father make her the assurance,°   380
  She is your own; else you must pardon me.
  If you should die before him, where's her dower?

Tranio. That's but a cavil.° He is old, I young.

Gremio. And may not young men die as well as old?

Baptista. Well, gentlemen,   385
  I am thus resolved. On Sunday next, you know,
  My daughter Katherine is to be married.
  Now on the Sunday following shall Bianca
  Be bride to you if you make this assurance;
  If not, to Signior Gremio.   390
  And so I take my leave and thank you both.   *Exit.*

Gremio. Adieu, good neighbor. Now I fear thee not.
  Sirrah° young gamester,° your father were° a fool
  To give thee all and in his waning age
  Set foot under thy table.° Tut, a toy!°   395
  An old Italian fox is not so kind, my boy.   *Exit.*

Tranio. A vengeance on your crafty withered hide!
  Yet I have faced it with a card of ten.°
  'Tis in my head to do my master good.
  I see no reason but supposed Lucentio   400
  Must get° a father, called "supposed Vincentio,"
  And that's a wonder. Fathers commonly
  Do get their children, but in this case of wooing
  A child shall get a sire if I fail not of my cunning.
                                                    Exit.

---

378 **outvied** outbid   380 **assurance** guarantee   383 **cavil** small point
393 **Sirrah** (used contemptuously)   393 **gamester** gambler   393 **were**
would be   395 **Set foot under thy table** be dependent on you   395 **a
toy** a joke   398 **faced it with a card of ten** bluffed with a ten-spot
401 **get** beget

ACT 3

[Scene 1. *Padua. In Baptista's house.*]

Enter Lucentio [as Cambio], Hortensio [as Litio],
and Bianca.

Lucentio. Fiddler, forbear. You grow too forward, sir.
   Have you so soon forgot the entertainment°
   Her sister Katherine welcomed you withal?

Hortensio. But, wrangling pedant, this is
5   The patroness of heavenly harmony.
   Then give me leave to have prerogative,°
   And when in music we have spent an hour,
   Your lecture° shall have leisure for as much.

Lucentio. Preposterous° ass, that never read so far
10   To know the cause why music was ordained!
   Was it not to refresh the mind of man
   After his studies or his usual pain?°
   Then give me leave to read° philosophy,
   And while I pause, serve in your harmony.

Hortensio. Sirrah, I will not bear these braves° of
15   thine.

Bianca. Why, gentlemen, you do me double wrong
   To strive for that which resteth in my choice.

3.1.2 **entertainment** i.e., "pillorying" him with the lute   6 **prerogative**
priority   8 **lecture** instruction   9 **Preposterous** putting later things
(*post-*) first (*pre-*)   12 **pain** labor   13 **read** give a lesson in   15 **braves**
defiances

I am no breeching° scholar° in the schools.
I'll not be tied to hours nor 'pointed times,
But learn my lessons as I please myself.   20
And, to cut off all strife, here sit we down.
[*To Hortensio*] Take you your instrument, play you
    the whiles;°
His lecture will be done ere you have tuned.

Hortensio. You'll leave his lecture when I am in tune?

Lucentio. That will be never. Tune your instrument.   25

Bianca. Where left we last?

Lucentio. Here, madam:
    Hic ibat Simois, hic est Sigeia tellus,
    Hic steterat Priami regia celsa senis.°

Bianca. Conster° them.   30

Lucentio. Hic ibat, as I told you before, *Simois,* I am
    Lucentio, *hic est,* son unto Vincentio of Pisa, *Sigeia
    tellus,* disguised thus to get your love, *Hic steterat,*
    and that Lucentio that comes a wooing, *Priami,* is
    my man Tranio, *regia,* bearing my port,° *celsa senis,*   35
    that we might beguile the old pantaloon.°

Hortensio. [*Breaks in*] Madam, my instrument's in
    tune.

Bianca. Let's hear. O fie, the treble jars.°

Lucentio. Spit in the hole, man, and tune again.

Bianca. Now let me see if I can conster it. *Hic ibat*   40
    Simois, I know you not, *hic est Sigeia tellus,* I trust
    you not, *Hic steterat Priami,* take heed he hear us
    not, *regia,* presume not, *celsa senis,* despair not.

Hortensio. [*Breaks in again*] Madam, 'tis now in tune.

18 **breeching** (1) in breeches (young) (2) whippable   18 **scholar**
schoolboy   22 **the whiles** meanwhile   28–29 **Hic . . . senis** here flowed
the Simois, here is the Sigeian (Trojan) land, here had stood old Priam's
high palace (Ovid)   30 **Conster** construe   35 **bearing my port** taking
on my style   36 **pantaloon** Gremio (see 1.1.47.s.d. note)   38 **treble
jars** highest tone is off

Lucentio.   All but the bass.

Hortensio. The bass is right; 'tis the base knave that
45   jars.
      [*Aside*] How fiery and forward our pedant is!
      Now, for my life, the knave doth court my love.
      Pedascule,° I'll watch you better yet.

Bianca. In time I may believe, yet I mistrust.

50 Lucentio. Mistrust it not, for sure Aeacides
      Was Ajax,° called so from his grandfather.

Bianca. I must believe my master; else, I promise you,
      I should be arguing still upon that doubt.
      But let it rest. Now, Litio, to you.
55   Good master, take it not unkindly, pray,
      That I have been thus pleasant° with you both.

Hortensio. [*To Lucentio*] You may go walk and give
      me leave° a while.
      My lessons make no music in three parts.°

Lucentio. Are you so formal, sir? [*Aside*] Well, I
      must wait
60   And watch withal,° for but° I be deceived,
      Our fine musician groweth amorous.

Hortensio. Madam, before you touch the instrument,
      To learn the order of my fingering,
      I must begin with rudiments of art
65   To teach you gamut° in a briefer sort,
      More pleasant, pithy, and effectual,
      Than hath been taught by any of my trade;
      And there it is in writing, fairly drawn.

Bianca. Why, I am past my gamut long ago.

70 Hortensio. Yet read the gamut of Hortensio.

---

48 **Pedascule** little pedant (disparaging quasi-Latin)   50–51 **Aeacides/
Was Ajax** Ajax, Greek warrior at Troy, was grandson of Aeacus
(Lucentio comments on next passage in Ovid)   56 **pleasant** merry
57 **give me leave** leave me alone   58 **in three parts** for three voices
60 **withal** besides   60 **but** unless   65 **gamut** the scale

Bianca. [*Reads*]

> *Gamut* I am, the ground° of all accord.°
>   *A re,* to plead Hortensio's passion:
> *B mi,* Bianca, take him for thy lord,
>   *C fa ut,* that loves with all affection;
> *D sol re,* one clef, two notes have I:
>   *E la mi,* show pity or I die.

> Call you this gamut? Tut, I like it not.
> Old fashions please me best; I am not so nice°
> To change true rules for odd inventions.

Enter a Messenger.

Messenger. Mistress, your father prays you leave your
    books
And help to dress your sister's chamber up.
You know tomorrow is the wedding day.

Bianca. Farewell, sweet masters both, I must be gone.
[*Exeunt Bianca and Messenger.*]

Lucentio. Faith, mistress, then I have no cause to stay.
[*Exit.*]

Hortensio. But I have cause to pry into this pedant.
Methinks he looks as though he were in love.
Yet if thy thoughts, Bianca, be so humble
To cast thy wand'ring eyes on every stale,°
Seize thee that list.° If once I find thee ranging,°
Hortensio will be quit with thee by changing.° *Exit.*

75
80
85
90

---

71 **ground** beginning, first note   71 **accord** harmony   78 **nice** whimsical
88 **stale** lure (as in hunting)   89 **Seize thee that list** let him who likes capture you   89 **ranging** going astray   90 **changing** i.e., sweethearts

[Scene 2. *Padua. The street in front of
Baptista's house.*]

*Enter Baptista, Gremio, Tranio [as Lucentio], Kate,
Bianca, [Lucentio as Cambio]
and others, Attendants.*

Baptista. [*To Tranio*] Signior Lucentio, this is the
    'pointed day
That Katherine and Petruchio should be marrièd,
And yet we hear not of our son-in-law.
What will be said? What mockery will it be
5 To want° the bridegroom when the priest attends
To speak the ceremonial rites of marriage!
What says Lucentio to this shame of ours?

Kate. No shame but mine. I must, forsooth, be forced
To give my hand opposed against my heart
10 Unto a mad-brain rudesby,° full of spleen,°
Who wooed in haste and means to wed at leisure.
I told you, I, he was a frantic fool,
Hiding his bitter jests in blunt behavior.
And to be noted for° a merry man,
15 He'll woo a thousand, 'point the day of marriage,
Make friends, invite,° and proclaim the banns,
Yet never means to wed where he hath wooed.
Now must the world point at poor Katherine
And say, "Lo, there is mad Petruchio's wife,
20 If it would please him come and marry her."

Tranio. Patience, good Katherine, and Baptista too.
Upon my life, Petruchio means but well,
Whatever fortune stays° him from his word.

3.2.5 **want** be without   10 **rudesby** uncouth fellow   10 **spleen** caprice
14 **noted for** reputed   16 **Make friends, invite** (some editors emend to
"Make feast, invite friends")   23 **stays** keeps

Though he be blunt, I know him passing° wise;
Though he be merry, yet withal he's honest.   25

Kate. Would Katherine had never seen him though!
        Exit weeping [followed by Bianca and others].

Baptista. Go, girl, I cannot blame thee now to weep.
For such an injury would vex a very saint,
Much more a shrew of thy impatient humor.°

                Enter Biondello.

Biondello. Master, master, news! And such old° news   30
as you never heard of!

Baptista. Is it new and old too? How may that be?

Biondello. Why, is it not news to hear of Petruchio's
coming?

Baptista. Is he come?   35

Biondello. Why, no, sir.

Baptista. What then?

Biondello. He is coming.

Baptista. When will he be here?

Biondello. When he stands where I am and sees you   40
there.

Tranio. But, say, what to thine old news?

Biondello. Why, Petruchio is coming in a new hat and
an old jerkin;° a pair of old breeches thrice turned;°
a pair of boots that have been candle-cases,° one   45
buckled, another laced; an old rusty sword ta'en
out of the town armory, with a broken hilt and
chapeless;° with two broken points;° his horse
hipped° (with an old mothy saddle and stirrups of

---

24 **passing** very   29 **humor** temper   30 **old** strange   44 **jerkin** short
outer coat   44 **turned** i.e., inside out (to conceal wear and tear)
45 **candle-cases** worn-out boots used to keep candle ends in   48 **chapeless** lacking the metal mounting at end of scabbard   48 **points** laces to
fasten hose to garment above   49 **hipped** with dislocated hip

50   no kindred),° besides, possessed with the glanders°
and like to mose in the chine;° troubled with the
lampass,° infected with the fashions,° full of windgalls,° sped with spavins,° rayed° with the yellows,°
past cure of the fives,° stark spoiled with the stag-
55   gers,° begnawn with the bots,° swayed° in the
back, and shoulder-shotten;° near-legged before,°
and with a half-cheeked° bit and a head-stall° of
sheep's leather,° which, being restrained° to keep
him from stumbling, hath been often burst and
60   now repaired with knots; one girth° six times
pieced,° and a woman's crupper° of velure,° which
hath two letters for her name fairly set down in
studs,° and here and there pieced with packthread.°

Baptista. Who comes with him?

65   *Biondello.* O sir, his lackey, for all the world capari-
soned° like the horse: with a linen stock° on one
leg and a kersey boot-hose° on the other, gart'red
with a red and blue list;° an old hat, and the humor
of forty fancies° pricked° in't for a feather—a mon-
70   ster, a very monster in apparel, and not like a Christian footboy° or a gentleman's lackey.

49–50 **of no kindred** not matching   50 **glanders** bacterial disease
affecting mouth and nose   51 **mose in the chine** (1) glanders (2) nasal
discharge   52 **lampass** swollen mouth   52 **fashions** tumors (related
to glanders)   52–53 **windgalls** swellings on lower leg   53 **spavins**
swellings on upper hind leg   53 **rayed** soiled   53 **yellows** jaundice
54 **fives** vives: swelling of submaxillary glands   54–55 **staggers** ner-
vous disorder causing loss of balance   55 **begnawn with the bots**
gnawed by parasitic worms (larvae of the botfly)   55 **swayed** sagging
56 **shoulder-shotten** with dislocated shoulder   56 **near-legged before**
with forefeet knocking together   57 **half-cheeked** wrongly adjusted
to bridle and affording less control   57 **head-stall** part of bridle which
surrounds head   58 **sheep's leather** (weaker than pigskin)   58 **restrained** pulled back   60 **girth** saddle strap under belly   61 **pieced**
patched   61 **crupper** leather loop under horse's tail to help steady
saddle   61 **velure** velvet   63 **studs** large-headed nails of brass or silver
63 **pieced with packthread** tied together with coarse thread   65–66 **ca-
parisoned** outfitted   66 **stock** stocking   67 **kersey boot-hose** coarse
stocking worn with riding boot   68 **list** strip of discarded border-cloth
68–69 **humor of forty fancies** fanciful decoration (in place of feather)
69 **pricked** pinned   71 **footboy** page in livery

Tranio. 'Tis some odd humor° pricks° him to this fashion,
　Yet oftentimes he goes but mean-appareled.

Baptista. I am glad he's come, howsoe'er he comes.

Biondello. Why, sir, he comes not.   75

Baptista. Didst thou not say he comes?

Biondello. Who? That Petruchio came?

Baptista. Ay, that Petruchio came.

Biondello. No, sir, I say his horse comes, with him on his back.   80

Baptista. Why, that's all one.°

Biondello. [*Sings*]

> Nay, by Saint Jamy,
> I hold° you a penny,
> A horse and a man
> Is more than one   85
> And yet not many.

Enter Petruchio and Grumio.

Petruchio. Come, where be these gallants?° Who's at home?

Baptista. You are welcome, sir.

Petruchio.　　　　　　　And yet I come not well.

Baptista. And yet you halt° not.

Tranio.　　　　　　　Not so well appareled
　As I wish you were.   90

Petruchio. Were it better,° I should rush in thus.
　But where is Kate? Where is my lovely bride?
　How does my father? Gentles,° methinks you frown.

---

72 **humor** mood, fancy   72 **pricks** incites   81 **all one** the same thing
83 **hold** bet   87 **gallants** men of fashion   89 **halt** limp (pun on *come*
meaning "walk")   91 **Were it better** even if I were better   93 **Gentles** sirs

And wherefore gaze this goodly company
95 As if they saw some wondrous monument,°
Some comet or unusual prodigy?°

Baptista. Why, sir, you know this is your wedding day.
First were we sad, fearing you would not come,
Now sadder that you come so unprovided.°
100 Fie, doff this habit,° shame to your estate,°
An eyesore to our solemn festival.

Tranio. And tell us what occasion of import°
Hath all so long detained you from your wife
And sent you hither so unlike yourself.

105 *Petruchio.* Tedious it were to tell and harsh to hear.
Sufficeth, I am come to keep my word
Though in some part enforcèd to digress,°
Which, at more leisure, I will so excuse
As you shall well be satisfied with all.
110 But where is Kate? I stay too long from her.
The morning wears, 'tis time we were at church.

Tranio. See not your bride in these unreverent robes.
Go to my chamber; put on clothes of mine.

Petruchio. Not I, believe me; thus I'll visit her.

115 *Baptista.* But thus, I trust, you will not marry her.

Petruchio. Good sooth,° even thus; therefore ha' done
with words.
To me she's married, not unto my clothes.
Could I repair what she will wear° in me
As I can change these poor accoutrements,
120 'Twere well for Kate and better for myself.
But what a fool am I to chat with you
When I should bid good morrow to my bride
And seal the title° with a lovely° kiss.

Exit [with Grumio].

95 **monument** warning sign 96 **prodigy** marvel 99 **unprovided** ill-
outfitted 100 **habit** costume 100 **estate** status 102 **of import** important 107 **enforcèd to digress** forced to depart (perhaps from his plan to
"buy apparel 'gainst the wedding day," 2.1.308) 116 **Good sooth** yes
indeed 118 **wear** wear out 123 **title** i.e., as of ownership 123 **lovely**
loving

Tranio. He hath some meaning in his mad attire.
  We will persuade him, be it possible,   125
  To put on better ere he go to church.

Baptista. I'll after him and see the event° of this.
        Exit [with Gremio and Attendants].

Tranio. But to her love concerneth us to add
  Her father's liking, which to bring to pass,
  As I before imparted to your worship,   130
  I am to get a man—whate'er he be
  It skills° not much, we'll fit him to our turn°—
  And he shall be Vincentio of Pisa,
  And make assurance° here in Padua
  Of greater sums than I have promisèd.   135
  So shall you quietly enjoy your hope
  And marry sweet Bianca with consent.

Lucentio. Were it not that my fellow schóolmaster
  Doth watch Bianca's steps so narrowly,
  'Twere good, methinks, to steal our marriage,°   140
  Which once performed, let all the world say no,
  I'll keep mine own despite of all the world.

Tranio. That by degrees we mean to look into
  And watch our vantage° in this business.
  We'll overreach° the graybeard, Gremio,   145
  The narrow-prying father, Minola,
  The quaint° musician, amorous Litio—
  All for my master's sake, Lucentio.

        Enter Gremio.

Signior Gremio, came you from the church?

Gremio. As willingly as e'er I came from school.   150

Tranio. And is the bride and bridegroom coming
  home?

Gremio. A bridegroom say you? 'Tis a groom° indeed,

127 **event** upshot, outcome   132 **skills** matters   132 **turn** purpose
134 **assurance** guarantee   140 **steal our marriage** elope   144 **vantage** advantage   145 **overreach** get the better of   147 **quaint** artful
152 **groom** menial (i.e., coarse fellow)

A grumbling groom, and that the girl shall find.

Tranio. Curster than she? Why, 'tis impossible.

155 *Gremio.* Why, he's a devil, a devil, a very fiend.

Tranio. Why, she's a devil, a devil, the devil's dam.°

Gremio. Tut, she's a lamb, a dove, a fool to° him.
I'll tell you, Sir Lucentio, when the priest
Should ask, if Katherine should be his wife,
"Ay, by goggs woones!"° quoth he and swore so
160 loud
That, all amazed, the priest let fall the book,
And as he stooped again to take it up,
This mad-brained bridegroom took° him such a cuff
That down fell priest and book and book and priest.
165 "Now, take them up," quoth he, "if any list."°

Tranio. What said the wench when he rose again?

Gremio. Trembled and shook, for why° he stamped
and swore
As if the vicar meant to cozen° him.
But after many ceremonies done
170 He calls for wine. "A health!" quoth he as if
He had been aboard, carousing° to his mates
After a storm; quaffed off the muscadel°
And threw the sops° all in the sexton's face,
Having no other reason
175 But that his beard grew thin and hungerly,°
And seemed to ask him sops as he was drinking.
This done, he took the bride about the neck
And kissed her lips with such a clamorous smack
That at the parting all the church did echo,
180 And I, seeing this, came thence for very shame.

---

156 **dam** mother   157 **fool to** harmless person compared with   160 **goggs woones** by God's wounds (a common oath)   163 **took** gave   165 **list** pleases to   167 **for why** because   168 **cozen** cheat   171 **carousing** calling "Bottoms up"   172 **muscadel** sweet wine, conventionally drunk after marriage service   173 **sops** pieces of cake soaked in wine; dregs   175 **hungerly** as if poorly nourished

And after me, I know, the rout° is coming.
Such a mad marriage never was before.
Hark, hark, I hear the minstrels play.   *Music plays.*

Enter Petruchio, Kate, Bianca, Hortensio [as Litio],
Baptista [with Grumio and others].

Petruchio. Gentlemen and friends, I thank you for
    your pains.
I know you think to dine with me today   185
And have prepared great store of wedding cheer,°
But so it is, my haste doth call me hence
And therefore here I mean to take my leave.

Baptista. Is't possible you will away tonight?

Petruchio. I must away today, before night come.   190
Make it no wonder;° if you knew my business,
You would entreat me rather go than stay.
And, honest company, I thank you all
That have beheld me give away myself
To this most patient, sweet, and virtuous wife.   195
Dine with my father, drink a health to me,
For I must hence, and farewell to you all.

Tranio. Let us entreat you stay till after dinner.

Petruchio. It may not be.

Gremio.   Let me entreat you.

Petruchio. It cannot be.

Kate.   Let me entreat you.   200

Petruchio. I am content.

Kate.   Are you content to stay?

Petruchio. I am content you shall entreat me stay,
But yet not stay, entreat me how you can.

Kate. Now if you love me, stay.

Petruchio.   Grumio, my horse!°

181 **rout** crowd   186 **cheer** food and drink   191 **Make it no wonder**
don't be surprised   204 **horse** horses

205 *Grumio.* Ay, sir, they be ready; the oats have eaten
the horses.°

Kate. Nay then,
Do what thou canst, I will not go today,
No, nor tomorrow, not till I please myself.
210 The door is open, sir, there lies your way.
You may be jogging whiles your boots are green;°
For me, I'll not be gone till I please myself.
'Tis like you'll prove a jolly° surly groom,
That take it on you° at the first so roundly.°

Petruchio. O Kate, content thee; prithee,° be not
215 angry.

Kate. I will be angry. What hast thou to do?°
Father, be quiet; he shall stay my leisure.°

Gremio. Ay, marry, sir, now it begins to work.

Kate. Gentlemen, forward to the bridal dinner.
220 I see a woman may be made a fool
If she had not a spirit to resist.

Petruchio. They shall go forward, Kate, at thy com-
mand.
Obey the bride, you that attend on her.
Go to the feast, revel and domineer,°
225 Carouse full measure to her maidenhead,
Be mad and merry, or go hang yourselves.
But for my bonny Kate, she must with me.
Nay, look not big,° nor stamp, nor stare,° nor fret;
I will be master of what is mine own.
230 She is my goods, my chattels; she is my house,
My household stuff, my field, my barn,
My horse, my ox, my ass, my anything,°

205–06 **oats have eaten the horses** (1) a slip of the tongue or (2) an
ironic jest   211 **You . . . green** (proverbial way of suggesting departure
to a guest, *green* = new, cleaned)   213 **jolly** domineering   214 **take it
on you** do as you please   214 **roundly** roughly   215 **prithee** I pray thee
216 **What hast thou to do** what do you have to do with it   217 **stay my
leisure** await my willingness   224 **domineer** cut up in a lordly fashion
228 **big** challenging   228 **stare** swagger   232 **My horse . . . anything**
(echoing Tenth Commandment)

And here she stands. Touch her whoever dare,
I'll bring mine action° on the proudest he
That stops my way in Padua. Grumio,   235
Draw forth thy weapon, we are beset with thieves.
Rescue thy mistress, if thou be a man.
Fear not, sweet wench; they shall not touch thee,
Kate.
I'll buckler° thee against a million.
          Exeunt Petruchio, Kate [and Grumio].

Baptista. Nay, let them go, a couple of quiet ones.   240

Gremio. Went they not quickly, I should die with
    laughing.

Tranio. Of all mad matches never was the like.

Lucentio. Mistress, what's your opinion of your sister?

Bianca. That being mad herself, she's madly mated.

Gremio. I warrant him, Petruchio is Kated.   245

Baptista. Neighbors and friends, though bride and
    bridegroom wants°
For to supply the places at the table,
You know there wants no junkets° at the feast.
[*To Tranio*] Lucentio, you shall supply the bride-
    groom's place,
And let Bianca take her sister's room.   250

Tranio. Shall sweet Bianca practice how to bride it?

Baptista. She shall, Lucentio. Come, gentlemen, let's
    go.   *Exeunt.*

---

234 **action** lawsuit   239 **buckler** shield   246 **wants** are lacking   248 **junkets** sweetmeats, confections

[ACT 4

Scene 1. *Petruchio's country house.*]

Enter Grumio.

Grumio. Fie, fie, on all tired jades,° on all mad masters, and all foul ways!° Was ever man so beaten? Was ever man so rayed?° Was ever man so weary? I am sent before to make a fire, and they are coming after to warm them. Now were not I a little pot and soon hot,° my very lips might freeze to my teeth, my tongue to the roof of my mouth, my heart in my belly, ere I should come by a fire to thaw me. But I with blowing the fire shall warm myself, for considering the weather, a taller° man than I will take cold. Holla, ho, Curtis!

Enter Curtis [a Servant].

Curtis. Who is that calls so coldly?

Grumio. A piece of ice. If thou doubt it, thou mayst slide from my shoulder to my heel with no greater a run° but my head and my neck. A fire, good Curtis.

Curtis. Is my master and his wife coming, Grumio?

4.1.1 **jades** worthless horses   2 **foul ways** bad roads   3 **rayed** befouled
5–6 **little pot and soon hot** (proverbial for small person of short temper)
10 **taller** sturdier (with allusion to "little pot")   15 **run** running start

66

Grumio. O ay, Curtis, ay, and therefore fire, fire; cast on no water.°

Curtis. Is she so hot a shrew as she's reported?   20

Grumio. She was, good Curtis, before this frost, but thou know'st winter tames man, woman, and beast; for it hath tamed my old master, and my new mistress, and myself, fellow Curtis.

Curtis. Away, you three-inch° fool! I am no beast.   25

Grumio. Am I but three inches? Why, thy horn° is a foot, and so long am I at the least. But wilt thou make a fire, or shall I complain on thee to our mistress, whose hand—she being now at hand—thou shalt soon feel, to thy cold comfort, for being slow   30 in thy hot office?°

Curtis. I prithee, good Grumio, tell me, how goes the world?

Grumio. A cold world, Curtis, in every office but thine, and therefore, fire. Do thy duty and have thy   35 duty,° for my master and mistress are almost frozen to death.

Curtis. There's fire ready, and therefore, good Grumio, the news.

Grumio. Why, "Jack boy, ho boy!"° and as much   40 news as wilt thou.

Curtis. Come, you are so full of cony-catching.°

Grumio. Why therefore fire, for I have caught extreme cold. Where's the cook? Is supper ready, the house trimmed, rushes strewed,° cobwebs swept, the serv-   45

---

19 **cast on no water** (alters "Cast on more water" in a well-known round
25 **three-inch** (1) another allusion to Grumio's small stature (2) a phallic
jest, the first of several   26 **horn** (symbol of cuckold)   31 **hot office**
job of making a fire   35–36 **thy duty** what is due thee   40 **"Jack
boy, ho boy!"** (from another round or catch)   42 **cony-catching**
rabbit-catching (i.e., tricking simpletons; with pun on *catch,* the song)
45 **strewed** i.e., on floor (for special occasion)

ingmen in their new fustian,° the white stockings,
and every officer° his wedding garment on? Be the
jacks° fair within, the jills° fair without, the car-
pets° laid and everything in order?

50 *Curtis.* All ready, and therefore, I pray thee, news.

Grumio. First, know my horse is tired, my master and
mistress fall'n out.

Curtis. How?

Grumio. Out of their saddles into the dirt—and
55 thereby hangs a tale.

Curtis. Let's ha't, good Grumio.

Grumio. Lend thine ear.

Curtis. Here.

Grumio. There.   [*Strikes him.*]

60 *Curtis.* This 'tis to feel a tale, not to hear a tale.

Grumio. And therefore 'tis called a sensible° tale, and
this cuff was but to knock at your ear and beseech
list'ning. Now I begin. *Imprimis,*° we came down
a foul° hill, my master riding behind my mistress—

65 *Curtis.* Both of° one horse?

Grumio. What's that to thee?

Curtis. Why, a horse.

Grumio. Tell thou the tale. But hadst thou not
crossed° me thou shouldst have heard how her
70 horse fell and she under her horse. Thou shouldst
have heard in how miry a place, how she was bemoiled,° how he left her with the horse upon her,
how he beat me because her horse stumbled, how

---

46 **fustian** coarse cloth (cotton and flax)   47 **officer** servant   48 **jacks**
(1) menservants (2) half-pint leather drinking cups   48 **jills** (1) maids
(2) gill-size metal drinking cups   48–49 **carpets** table covers   61 **sensible** (1) rational (2) "feel"-able   63 **Imprimis** first   64 **foul** muddy
65 **of** on   69 **crossed** interrupted   72 **bemoiled** muddied

she waded through the dirt to pluck him off me;
how he swore, how she prayed that never prayed   75
before; how I cried, how the horses ran away, how
her bridle was burst, how I lost my crupper, with
many things of worthy memory which now shall
die in oblivion, and thou return unexperienced° to
thy grave.   80

Curtis. By this reck'ning° he is more shrew than she.

Grumio. Ay, and that thou and the proudest of you
all shall find when he comes home. But what° talk
I of this? Call forth Nathaniel, Joseph, Nicholas,
Philip, Walter, Sugarsop, and the rest. Let their   85
heads be slickly° combed, their blue° coats brushed,
and their garters of an indifferent° knit. Let them
curtsy with their left legs and not presume to touch
a hair of my master's horsetail till they kiss their
hands. Are they all ready?   90

Curtis. They are.

Grumio. Call them forth.

Curtis. Do you hear, ho? You must meet my master
to countenance° my mistress.

Grumio. Why, she hath a face of her own.   95

Curtis. Who knows not that?

Grumio. Thou, it seems, that calls for company to
countenance her.

Curtis. I call them forth to credit° her.

Grumio. Why, she comes to borrow nothing of them. 100

Enter four or five Servingmen.

Nathaniel. Welcome home, Grumio!

---

79 **unexperienced** uninformed   81 **reck'ning** account   83 **what** why
86 **slickly** smoothly   86 **blue** (usual color of servants' clothing)   87 **indifferent** matching (?) appropriate (?)   94 **countenance** show respect to
(with puns following)   99 **credit** honor

Philip. How now, Grumio?

Joseph. What, Grumio!

Nicholas. Fellow Grumio!

105 *Nathaniel.* How now, old lad!

Grumio. Welcome, you; how now, you; what, you; fellow, you; and thus much for greeting. Now, my spruce companions, is all ready and all things neat?

Nathaniel. All things is ready. How near is our 110 master?

Grumio. E'en at hand, alighted by this,° and therefore be not—Cock's° passion, silence! I hear my master.

Enter Petruchio and Kate.

Petruchio. Where be these knaves? What, no man at door
115 To hold my stirrup nor to take my horse?
Where is Nathaniel, Gregory, Philip?

All Servingmen. Here, here, sir, here, sir.

Petruchio. Here, sir, here, sir, here, sir, here, sir!
You loggerheaded° and unpolished grooms!
120 What, no attendance? No regard? No duty?
Where is the foolish knave I sent before?

Grumio. Here, sir, as foolish as I was before.

Petruchio. You peasant swain!° You whoreson° malt-horse drudge!°
Did I not bid thee meet me in the park°
125 And bring along these rascal knaves with thee?

Grumio. Nathaniel's coat, sir, was not fully made
And Gabrel's pumps were all unpinked° i' th' heel.

111 **this** now   112 **Cock's** God's (i.e., Christ's)   119 **loggerheaded** blockheaded   123 **swain** bumpkin   123 **whoreson** bastardly   123 **malt-horse drudge** slow horse on brewery treadmill   124 **park** country-house grounds   127 **unpinked** lacking embellishment made by pinking (making small holes in leather)

There was no link° to color Peter's hat,
And Walter's dagger was not come from sheathing.°
There were none fine but Adam, Rafe, and Gregory;   *130*
The rest were ragged, old, and beggarly.
Yet, as they are, here are they come to meet you.

Petruchio. Go, rascals, go, and fetch my supper in.
                             Exeunt Servants.

[*Sings*] "Where is the life that late I led?"°

Where are those°—Sit down, Kate, and welcome.   *135*
  Soud,° soud, soud, soud!

          Enter Servants with supper.

Why, when,° I say?—Nay, good sweet Kate, be
  merry.—
Off with my boots, you rogues, you villains! When?
[*Sings*] "It was the friar of orders gray,
As he forth walkèd on his way"°—   *140*
Out, you rogue, you pluck my foot awry!
Take that, and mend° the plucking of the other.
                            [Strikes him.]

Be merry, Kate. Some water here! What ho!

          Enter one with water.

Where's my spaniel Troilus? Sirrah, get you hence
And bid my cousin Ferdinand come hither—   *145*
                         [Exit Servant.]
One, Kate, that you must kiss and be acquainted with.
Where are my slippers? Shall I have some water?
Come, Kate, and wash, and welcome heartily.
You whoreson villain, will you let it fall?
                            [Strikes him.]

Kate. Patience, I pray you. 'Twas a fault unwilling.   *150*

Petruchio. A whoreson, beetle-headed,° flap-eared
  knave!

128 **link** torch, providing blacking   129 **sheathing** repairing scabbard
134 **"Where ... led?"** (from an old ballad) 135 **those** servants
136 **Soud** (exclamation variously explained; some editors emend to *Food*)
137 **when** (exclamation of annoyance, as in next line) 139–40 **"It was ...
his way"** (from another old song) 142 **mend** improve 151 **beetle-
headed** mallet-headed

Come, Kate, sit down; I know you have a stomach.°
Will you give thanks,° sweet Kate, or else shall I?
What's this? Mutton?

First Servingman.   Ay.

Petruchio.   Who brought it?

Peter.   I.

155 *Petruchio.* 'Tis burnt, and so is all the meat.
What dogs are these! Where is the rascal cook?
How durst you, villains, bring it from the dresser,°
And serve it thus to me that love it not?
There, take it to you, trenchers,° cups, and all,
                    [*Throws food and dishes at them.*]
160 You heedless joltheads° and unmannered slaves!
What, do you grumble? I'll be with° you straight.°

Kate. I pray you, husband, be not so disquiet.
The meat was well if you were so contented.°

Petruchio. I tell thee, Kate, 'twas burnt and dried away,
165 And I expressly am forbid to touch it,
For it engenders choler,° planteth anger,
And better 'twere that both of us did fast—
Since of ourselves, ourselves are choleric°—
Than feed it° with such overroasted flesh.
170 Be patient. Tomorrow't shall be mended,°
And for this night we'll fast for company.°
Come, I will bring thee to thy bridal chamber.

                                                    Exeunt.

Enter Servants severally.

Nathaniel. Peter, didst ever see the like?

Peter. He kills her in her own humor.°

---

152 **stomach** (1) hunger (2) irascibility   153 **give thanks** say grace
157 **dresser** sideboard   159 **trenchers** wooden platters   160 **joltheads**
boneheads (*jolt* is related to *jaw* or *jowl*)   161 **with** even with   161 **straight**
directly   163 **so contented** willing to see it as it was   166 **choler** bile, the
"humor" (fluid) supposed to produce anger   168 **choleric** bilious, i.e., hot-
tempered   169 **it** i.e., their choler   170 **'t shall be mended** things will be
better   171 **for company** together   174 **kills her in her own humor**
conquers her by using her own disposition

Enter Curtis, a Servant.

Grumio. Where is he?   175

Curtis. In her chamber, making a sermon of continency
    to her,
And rails and swears and rates,° that she, poor soul,
Knows not which way to stand, to look, to speak,
And sits as one new-risen from a dream.   180
Away, away, for he is coming hither.   [*Exeunt.*]

Enter Petruchio.

Petruchio. Thus have I politicly° begun my reign,
And 'tis my hope to end successfully.
My falcon° now is sharp° and passing empty,
And till she stoop° she must not be full gorged,°   185
For then she never looks upon her lure.°
Another way I have to man° my haggard,°
To make her come and know her keeper's call,
That is, to watch° her as we watch these kites°
That bate and beat° and will not be obedient.   190
She eat° no meat today, nor none shall eat.
Last night she slept not, nor tonight she shall not.
As with the meat, some undeservèd fault
I'll find about the making of the bed,
And here I'll fling the pillow, there the bolster,°   195
This way the coverlet, another way the sheets.
Ay, and amid this hurly° I intend°
That all is done in reverent care of her,
And in conclusion she shall watch° all night.
And if she chance to nod I'll rail and brawl   200
And with the clamor keep her still awake.

---

178 **rates** scolds   182 **politicly** with a calculated plan   184 **falcon** hawk
trained for hunting (falconry figures continue for seven lines)   184 **sharp**
pinched with hunger   185 **stoop** (1) obey (2) swoop to the lure   185 **full
gorged** fully fed   186 **lure** device used in training a hawk to return from
flight   187 **man** (1) tame (2) be a man to   187 **haggard** hawk captured
after reaching maturity   189 **watch** keep from sleep   189 **kites** type of
small hawk   190 **bate and beat** flap and flutter (i.e., in jittery resistance
to training)   191 **eat** ate (pronounced *et,* as still in Britain)   195 **bolster** cushion extending width of bed as under-support for pillows
197 **hurly** disturbance   197 **intend** profess   199 **watch** stay awake

This is a way to kill a wife with kindness,°
And thus I'll curb her mad and headstrong humor.
He that knows better how to tame a shrew,°
205 Now let him speak—'tis charity to show.   *Exit.*

[Scene 2. *Padua. The street in front of
Baptista's house.*]

Enter Tranio [as Lucentio] and Hortensio [as Litio].

Tranio. Is't possible, friend Litio, that Mistress Bianca
    Doth fancy° any other but Lucentio?
    I tell you, sir, she bears me fair in hand.°

Hortensio. Sir, to satisfy you in what I have said,
5   Stand by and mark the manner of his teaching.
                                    [*They eavesdrop.*]

        Enter Bianca [and Lucentio as Cambio].

Lucentio. Now mistress, profit you in what you read?

Bianca. What, master, read you? First resolve° me that.

Lucentio. I read that° I profess,° the Art to Love.°

Bianca. And may you prove, sir, master of your art.

Lucentio. While you, sweet dear, prove mistress of my
10   heart.   [*They court.*]

Hortensio. Quick proceeders,° marry!° Now, tell me,
    I pray,
    You that durst swear that your mistress Bianca
    Loved none in the world so well as Lucentio.

---

202 **kill a wife with kindness** (ironic allusion to proverb on ruining a
wife by pampering)   204 **shrew** (rhymes with "show")   4.2.2 **fancy**
like   3 **bears me fair in hand** leads me on   7 **resolve** answer   8 **that**
what   8 **profess** avow, practice   8 **Art to Love** (i.e., Ovid's *Ars
Amandi*)   11 **proceeders** (pun on idiom "proceed Master of Arts"; cf.
line 9)   11 **marry** by Mary (mild exclamation)

Tranio. O despiteful° love! Unconstant womankind!
  I tell thee, Litio, this is wonderful.°   *15*

Hortensio. Mistake no more. I am not Litio,
  Nor a musician, as I seem to be,
  But one that scorn to live in this disguise,
  For such a one as leaves a gentleman
  And makes a god of such a cullion.°   *20*
  Know, sir, that I am called Hortensio.

Tranio. Signior Hortensio, I have often heard
  Of your entire affection to Bianca,
  And since mine eyes are witness of her lightness,°
  I will with you, if you be so contented,   *25*
  Forswear° Bianca and her love forever.

Hortensio. See, how they kiss and court! Signior
    Lucentio,
  Here is my hand and here I firmly vow
  Never to woo her more, but do forswear her,
  As one unworthy all the former favors°   *30*
  That I have fondly° flattered her withal.

Tranio. And here I take the like unfeignèd oath,
  Never to marry with her though she would entreat.
  Fie on her! See how beastly° she doth court him.

Hortensio. Would all the world but he had quite for-
    sworn.°   *35*
  For me, that I may surely keep mine oath,
  I will be married to a wealthy widow
  Ere three days pass, which° hath as long loved me
  As I have loved this proud disdainful haggard.°
  And so farewell, Signior Lucentio.   *40*
  Kindness in women, not their beauteous looks,
  Shall win my love, and so I take my leave
  In resolution as I swore before.   [*Exit.*]

---

14 **despiteful** spiteful   15 **wonderful** causing wonder   20 **cullion** low
fellow (literally, testicle)   24 **lightness** (cf. "light woman")   26 **Forswear** "swear off"   30 **favors** marks of esteem   31 **fondly** foolishly
34 **beastly** unashamedly   35 **Would ... forsworn** i.e., would she had
only one lover   38 **which** who   39 **haggard** (cf. 4.1.187)

Tranio. Mistress Bianca, bless you with such grace
45   As 'longeth to a lover's blessèd case.
      Nay, I have ta'en you napping,° gentle love,
      And have forsworn you with Hortensio.

Bianca. Tranio, you jest. But have you both forsworn
      me?

Tranio. Mistress, we have.

Lucentio.   Then we are rid of Litio.

50   *Tranio.* I' faith, he'll have a lusty° widow now,
      That shall be wooed and wedded in a day.

Bianca. God give him joy!

Tranio. Ay, and he'll tame her.

Bianca.   He says so, Tranio.

Tranio. Faith, he is gone unto the taming school.

Bianca. The taming school! What, is there such a
55   place?

Tranio. Ay, mistress, and Petruchio is the master,
      That teacheth tricks eleven and twenty long°
      To tame a shrew and charm her chattering tongue.

                  Enter Biondello.

Biondello. O master, master, I have watched so long
60   That I am dog-weary, but at last I spied
      An ancient angel° coming down the hill
      Will serve the turn.°

Tranio.   What° is he, Biondello?

Biondello. Master, a mercatante° or a pedant,°
      I know not what, but formal in apparel,

---

46 **ta'en you napping** seen you "kiss and court" (line 27)   50 **lusty**
lively   57 **tricks eleven and twenty long** (1) many tricks (2) possibly
an allusion to card game "thirty-one" (cf.1.2.33)   61 **ancient angel** man
of good old stamp (*angel* = coin; cf. "gentleman of the old school")
62 **Will serve the turn** who will do for our purposes   62 **What** what
kind of man   63 **mercatante** merchant   63 **pedant** schoolmaster

In gait and countenance° surely like a father.   65

Lucentio. And what of him, Tranio?

Tranio. If he be credulous and trust my tale,
I'll make him glad to seem Vincentio,
And give assurance to Baptista Minola
As if he were the right Vincentio.   70
Take in your love and then let me alone.
> [*Exeunt Lucentio and Bianca.*]

Enter a Pedant.

Pedant. God save you, sir.

Tranio.   And you, sir. You are welcome.
Travel you far on, or are you at the farthest?

Pedant. Sir, at the farthest for a week or two,
But then up farther and as far as Rome,   75
And so to Tripoli if God lend me life.

Tranio. What countryman,° I pray?

Pedant.   Of Mantua.

Tranio. Of Mantua, sir? Marry, God forbid!
And come to Padua, careless of your life?

Pedant. My life, sir? How, I pray? For that goes
hard.°   80

Tranio. 'Tis death for anyone in Mantua
To come to Padua. Know you not the cause?
Your ships are stayed° at Venice and the Duke,
For private quarrel 'twixt your duke and him,
Hath published and proclaimed it openly.   85
'Tis marvel, but that you are but newly come,
You might have heard it else proclaimed about.

Pedant. Alas, sir, it is worse for me than so,°
For I have bills for money by exchange
From Florence and must here deliver them.   90

---

65 **gait and countenance** bearing and style   77 **What countryman** a
man of what country   80 **goes hard** (cf. "is rough")   83 **stayed** held
88 **than so** than it appears so far

Tranio. Well, sir, to do you courtesy,
 This will I do and this I will advise° you.
 First tell me, have you ever been at Pisa?

Pedant. Ay, sir, in Pisa have I often been—
95 Pisa, renownèd for grave citizens.

Tranio. Among them, know you one Vincentio?

Pedant. I know him not but I have heard of him—
 A merchant of incomparable wealth.

Tranio. He is my father, sir, and, sooth to say,
100 In count'nance somewhat doth resemble you.

Biondello. [*Aside*] As much as an apple doth an oys-
 ter, and all one.°

Tranio. To save your life in this extremity,
 This favor will I do you for his sake,
105 And think it not the worst of all your fortunes
 That you are like to Sir Vincentio.
 His name and credit° shall you undertake,°
 And in my house you shall be friendly lodged.
 Look that you take upon you° as you should.
110 You understand me, sir? So shall you stay
 Till you have done your business in the city.
 If this be court'sy, sir, accept of it.

Pedant. O sir, I do, and will repute° you ever
 The patron of my life and liberty.

115 *Tranio.* Then go with me to make the matter good.
 This, by the way,° I let you understand:
 My father is here looked for every day
 To pass assurance° of a dower in marriage
 'Twixt me and one Baptista's daughter here.
120 In all these circumstances I'll instruct you.
 Go with me to clothe you as becomes you.   *Exeunt.*

---

92 **advise** explain to   102 **all one** no difference   107 **credit** standing
107 **undertake** adopt   109 **take upon you** assume your role   113 **re-
pute** esteem   116 **by the way** as we walk along   118 **pass assurance**
give a guarantee

[Scene 3. *In Petruchio's house.*]

Enter Kate and Grumio.

Grumio. No, no, forsooth, I dare not for my life.

Kate. The more my wrong,° the more his spite ap-
   pears.
   What, did he marry me to famish me?
   Beggars that come unto my father's door,
   Upon entreaty have a present° alms;   5
   If not, elsewhere they meet with charity.
   But I, who never knew how to entreat
   Nor never needed that I should entreat,
   Am starved for meat,° giddy for lack of sleep,
   With oaths kept waking and with brawling fed.   10
   And that which spites me more than all these wants,
   He does it under name of perfect love,
   As who should say,° if I should sleep or eat
   'Twere deadly sickness or else present death.
   I prithee go and get me some repast,   15
   I care not what, so° it be wholesome food.

Grumio. What say you to a neat's° foot?

Kate. 'Tis passing good; I prithee let me have it.

Grumio. I fear it is too choleric° a meat.
   How say you to a fat tripe finely broiled?   20

Kate. I like it well. Good Grumio, fetch it me.

Grumio. I cannot tell, I fear 'tis choleric.
   What say you to a piece of beef and mustard?

4.3.2 **The more my wrong** the greater the wrong done me   **5 present**
prompt   **9 meat** food   13 **As who should say** as if to say   16 **so** as long
as   17 **neat's** ox's or calf's   19 **choleric** temper-producing

Kate. A dish that I do love to feed upon.

25　*Grumio.* Ay, but the mustard is too hot a little.

Kate. Why then, the beef, and let the mustard rest.

Grumio. Nay then, I will not. You shall have the mustard
　Or else you get no beef of Grumio.

Kate. Then both or one, or anything thou wilt.

30　*Grumio.* Why then, the mustard without the beef.

Kate. Go, get thee gone, thou false deluding slave,
　　　　　　　　　　　　　　　　　Beats him.
　That feed'st me with the very name° of meat.
　Sorrow on thee and all the pack of you
　That triumph thus upon my misery.
35　Go, get thee gone, I say.

　　　　Enter Petruchio and Hortensio with meat.

Petruchio. How fares my Kate? What, sweeting, all
　amort?°

Hortensio. Mistress, what cheer?°

Kate.　　　　　　　　　　Faith, as cold° as can be.

Petruchio. Pluck up thy spirits; look cheerfully upon
　me.
　Here, love, thou seest how diligent I am
40　To dress thy meat° myself and bring it thee.
　I am sure, sweet Kate, this kindness merits thanks.
　What, not a word? Nay then, thou lov'st it not,
　And all my pains is sorted to no proof.°
　Here, take away this dish.

Kate.　　　　　　　　　　I pray you, let it stand.

45　*Petruchio.* The poorest service is repaid with thanks,
　And so shall mine before you touch the meat.

32 **very name** name only　36 **all amort** depressed, lifeless (cf. "morti-
fied")　37 **what cheer** how are things　37 **cold** (cf. "not so hot"; "cold
comfort," 4.1.30)　40 **To dress thy meat** in fixing your food　43 **sorted
to no proof** have come to nothing

Kate. I thank you, sir.

Hortensio. Signior Petruchio, fie, you are to blame.
Come, Mistress Kate, I'll bear you company.

Petruchio. [*Aside*] Eat it up all, Hortensio, if thou   50
    lovest me;
Much good do it unto thy gentle heart.
Kate, eat apace. And now, my honey love,
Will we return unto thy father's house
And revel it as bravely° as the best,   55
With silken coats and caps and golden rings,
With ruffs° and cuffs and fardingales° and things,
With scarfs and fans and double change of brav'ry,°
With amber bracelets, beads, and all this knav'ry.°
What, hast thou dined? The tailor stays thy leisure°   60
To deck thy body with his ruffling° treasure.

Enter Tailor.

Come, tailor, let us see these ornaments.

Enter Haberdasher.

Lay forth the gown. What news with you, sir?

Haberdasher. Here is the cap your Worship did be-
    speak.°

Petruchio. Why, this was molded on a porringer°—
A velvet dish. Fie, fie, 'tis lewd° and filthy.   65
Why, 'tis a cockle° or a walnut shell,
A knack,° a toy, a trick,° a baby's cap.
Away with it! Come, let me have a bigger.

Kate. I'll have no bigger. This doth fit the time,°
And gentlewomen wear such caps as these.   70

---

54 **bravely** handsomely dressed 56 **ruffs** stiffly starched, wheel-
shaped collars 56 **fardingales** farthingales, hooped skirts of petticoats
57 **brav'ry** handsome clothes 58 **knav'ry** girlish things 59 **stays thy
leisure** awaits your permission 60 **ruffling** gaily ruffled 63 **bespeak**
order 64 **porringer** soup bowl 65 **lewd** vile 66 **cockle** shell of a
mollusk 67 **knack** knickknack 67 **trick** plaything 69 **doth fit the
time** is in fashion

Petruchio. When you are gentle you shall have one too,
And not till then.

Hortensio. [*Aside*] That will not be in haste.

Kate. Why, sir, I trust I may have leave to speak,
And speak I will. I am no child, no babe.
75   Your betters have endured me say my mind,
And if you cannot, best you stop your ears.
My tongue will tell the anger of my heart,
Or else my heart, concealing it, will break,
And rather than it shall I will be free
80   Even to the uttermost, as I please, in words.

Petruchio. Why, thou sayst true. It is a paltry cap,
A custard-coffin,° a bauble, a silken pie.°
I love thee well in that thou lik'st it not.

Kate. Love me or love me not, I like the cap,
85   And it I will have or I will have none.

[*Exit Haberdasher.*]

Petruchio. Thy gown? Why, ay. Come, tailor, let us see't.
O mercy, God! What masquing° stuff is here?
What's this? A sleeve? 'Tis like a demi-cannon.°
What, up and down,° carved like an apple tart?
90   Here's snip and nip and cut and slish and slash,
Like to a censer° in a barber's shop.
Why, what, a° devil's name, tailor, call'st thou this?

Hortensio. [*Aside*] I see she's like to have neither cap nor gown.

Tailor. You bid me make it orderly and well,
95   According to the fashion and the time.

Petruchio. Marry, and did, but if you be rememb'red,

---

82 **custard-coffin** custard crust   82 **pie** meat pie   87 **masquing** for masquerades or actors' costumes   88 **demi-cannon** big cannon   89 **up and down** entirely   91 **censer** incense burner with perforated top   92 **a** in the

I did not bid you mar it to the time.°
Go, hop me over every kennel° home,
For you shall hop without my custom, sir.
I'll none of it. Hence, make your best of it.   100

Kate. I never saw a better-fashioned gown,
More quaint,° more pleasing, nor more commend-
     able.
Belike° you mean to make a puppet of me.

Petruchio. Why, true, he means to make a puppet of
     thee.

Tailor. She says your worship means to make a pup-   105
     pet of her.

Petruchio. O monstrous arrogance!
Thou liest, thou thread, thou thimble,
Thou yard, three-quarters, half-yard, quarter, nail!°
Thou flea, thou nit,° thou winter cricket thou!
Braved° in mine own house with° a skein of thread!   110
Away, thou rag, thou quantity,° thou remnant,
Or I shall so bemete° thee with thy yard
As thou shalt think on prating° whilst thou liv'st.
I tell thee, I, that thou hast marred her gown.

Tailor. Your worship is deceived. The gown is made   115
Just as my master had direction.°
Grumio gave order how it should be done.

Grumio. I gave him no order; I gave him the stuff.

Tailor. But how did you desire it should be made?

Grumio. Marry, sir, with needle and thread.   120

Tailor. But did you not request to have it cut?

Grumio. Thou hast faced° many things.

97 **to the time** for all time (cf. line 95, in which "the time" is "the contemporary style") 98 **kennel** gutter (canal) 102 **quaint** skillfully made
103 **Belike** no doubt 108 **nail** 1/16 of a yard 109 **nit** louse's egg
110 **Braved** defied 110 **with** by 111 **quantity** fragment 112 **be-
mete** (1) measure (2) beat 113 **think on prating** remember your silly
talk 116 **had direction** received orders 122 **faced** trimmed

Tailor. I have.

Grumio. Face° not me. Thou hast braved° many men;
125   brave° not me. I will neither be faced nor braved. I
say unto thee, I bid thy master cut out the gown, but
I did not bid him cut it to pieces. *Ergo,*° thou
liest.

Tailor. Why, here is the note° of the fashion to testify.

130 *Petruchio.* Read it.

Grumio. The note lies in's throat° if he° say I said so.

Tailor. "*Imprimis,*° a loose-bodied gown."°

Grumio. Master, if ever I said loose-bodied gown, sew
me in the skirts of it and beat me to death with a
135   bottom° of brown thread. I said, a gown.

Petruchio. Proceed.

Tailor. "With a small compassed° cape."

Grumio. I confess the cape.

Tailor. "With a trunk° sleeve."

140 *Grumio.* I confess two sleeves.

Tailor. "The sleeves curiously° cut."

Petruchio. Ay, there's the villainy.

Grumio. Error i' th' bill,° sir, error i' th' bill. I commanded the sleeves should be cut out and sewed
145   up again, and that I'll prove upon° thee, though thy
little finger be armed in a thimble.

Tailor. This is true that I say. And° I had thee in
place where,° thou shouldst know it.

124 **Face** challenge   124 **braved** equipped with finery   125 **brave**
defy   127 **Ergo** therefore   129 **note** written notation   131 **in's throat**
from the heart, with premeditation   131 **he** it   132 **Imprimis** first
132 **loose-bodied gown** (worn by prostitutes, with *loose* in pun)
135 **bottom** spool   137 **compassed** with circular edge   139 **trunk** full
(cf. line 88)   141 **curiously** painstakingly   143 **bill** i.e., the "note"
145 **prove upon** test by dueling with   147 **And** if   148 **place where**
the right place

Grumio. I am for° thee straight.° Take thou the bill,°
give me thy mete-yard,° and spare not me.   *150*

Hortensio. God-a-mercy, Grumio, then he shall have
no odds.

Petruchio. Well, sir, in brief, the gown is not for me.

Grumio. You are i' th' right, sir; 'tis for my mistress.

Petruchio. Go, take it up unto° thy master's use.°   *155*

Grumio. Villain, not for thy life! Take up my mistress'
gown for thy master's use!

Petruchio. Why sir, what's your conceit° in that?

Grumio. O sir, the conceit is deeper than you think
for.
Take up my mistress' gown to his master's use!   *160*
O, fie, fie, fie!

Petruchio. [*Aside*] Hortensio, say thou wilt see the
tailor paid.
[*To Tailor*] Go take it hence; be gone and say no
more.

Hortensio. Tailor, I'll pay thee for thy gown tomor-
row;   *165*
Take no unkindness of his hasty words.
Away, I say, commend me to thy master.
                                        Exit Tailor.

Petruchio. Well, come, my Kate, we will unto your
father's,
Even in these honest mean habiliments.°
Our purses shall be proud, our garments poor,
For 'tis the mind that makes the body rich,   *170*
And as the sun breaks through the darkest clouds
So honor peereth° in the meanest habit.°

149 **for** ready for   149 **straight** right now   149 **bill** (1) written order
(2) long-handled weapon   150 **mete-yard** yardstick   155 **up unto** away
for   155 **use** i.e., in whatever way he can; Grumio uses these words for
a sex joke   158 **conceit** idea   168 **habiliments** clothes   172 **peereth**
is recognized   172 **habit** clothes

What, is the jay more precious than the lark
Because his feathers are more beautiful?
175   Or is the adder better than the eel
Because his painted skin contents the eye?
O no, good Kate, neither art thou the worse
For this poor furniture° and mean array.
If thou account'st it shame, lay° it on me,
180   And therefore frolic. We will hence forthwith
To feast and sport us at thy father's house.
   [*To Grumio*] Go call my men, and let us straight
   to him;
And bring our horses unto Long-lane end.
There will we mount, and thither walk on foot.
185   Let's see, I think 'tis now some seven o'clock,
And well we may come there by dinnertime.°

Kate. I dare assure you, sir, 'tis almost two,
   And 'twill be suppertime ere you come there.

Petruchio. It shall be seven ere I go to horse.
190   Look what° I speak or do or think to do,
   You are still crossing° it. Sirs, let't alone:
   I will not go today, and ere I do,
   It shall be what o'clock I say it is.

Hortensio. [*Aside*] Why, so this gallant will command
   the sun.   [*Exeunt.*]

---

178 **furniture** outfit   179 **lay** blame   186 **dinnertime** midday   190 **Look
what** whatever   191 **crossing** obstructing, going counter to

[Scene 4. *Padua. The street in front
of Baptista's house.*]

*Enter Tranio [as Lucentio] and the Pedant
dressed like Vincentio.*

Tranio. Sir, this is the house. Please it you that I call?

Pedant. Ay, what else? And but° I be deceived,
Signior Baptista may remember me
Near twenty years ago in Genoa,
Where we were lodgers at the Pegasus.°   5

Tranio. 'Tis well, and hold your own° in any case
With such austerity as 'longeth to a father.

Pedant. I warrant° you. But sir, here comes your boy;
'Twere good he were schooled.°

Enter Biondello.

Tranio. Fear you not him. Sirrah Biondello,   10
Now do your duty throughly,° I advise you.
Imagine 'twere the right Vincentio.

Biondello. Tut, fear not me.

Tranio. But hast thou done thy errand to Baptista?

Biondello. I told him that your father was at Venice   15
And that you looked for him this day in Padua.

Tranio. Th' art a tall° fellow. Hold thee that° to drink.
Here comes Baptista. Set your countenance, sir.

4.4.2 **but** unless 3–5 **Signior Baptista . . . Pegasus** (the Pedant is prac-
ticing as Vincentio) 5 **Pegasus** common English inn name (after mythical winged horse symbolizing poetic inspiration) 6 **hold your own** act
your role 8 **warrant** guarantee 9 **schooled** informed (about his role)
11 **throughly** thoroughly 17 **tall** excellent 17 **Hold thee that** i.e.,
take this tip

Enter Baptista and Lucentio [as Cambio].
Pedant booted and bareheaded.°

Signior Baptista, you are happily met.
[*To the Pedant*] Sir, this is the gentleman I told
20   you of.
I pray you, stand good father to me now,
Give me Bianca for my patrimony.

Pedant. Soft,° son.
Sir, by your leave. Having come to Padua
25   To gather in some debts, my son Lucentio
Made me acquainted with a weighty cause°
Of love between your daughter and himself.
And—for the good report I hear of you,
And for the love he beareth to your daughter,
30   And she to him—to stay° him not too long,
I am content, in a good father's care,
To have him matched. And if you please to like°
No worse than I, upon some agreement
Me shall you find ready and willing
35   With one consent to have her so bestowed,
For curious° I cannot be with you,
Signior Baptista, of whom I hear so well.

Baptista. Sir, pardon me in what I have to say.
Your plainness and your shortness° please me well.
40   Right true it is, your son Lucentio here
Doth love my daughter and she loveth him—
Or both dissemble deeply their affections—
And therefore, if you say no more than this,
That like a father you will deal with him
45   And pass° my daughter a sufficient dower,
The match is made, and all is done.
Your son shall have my daughter with consent.

---

18 s.d. **booted and bareheaded** i.e., arriving from a journey and courte-
ously greeting Baptista   23 **Soft** take it easy   26 **weighty cause** important matter   30 **stay** delay   32 **like** i.e., the match   36 **curious**
overinsistent on fine points   39 **shortness** conciseness   45 **pass** legally
settle upon

Tranio. I thank you, sir. Where, then, do you know°
    best
    We be affied° and such assurance ta'en
    As shall with either part's° agreement stand?   50

Baptista. Not in my house, Lucentio, for you know
    Pitchers have ears, and I have many servants.
    Besides, old Gremio is heark'ning still,°
    And happily° we might be interrupted.

Tranio. Then at my lodging and it like° you.   55
    There doth my father lie,° and there this night
    We'll pass° the business privately and well.
    Send for your daughter by your servant here;
    My boy shall fetch the scrivener° presently.   60
    The worst is this, that at so slender warning°
    You are like to have a thin and slender pittance.°

Baptista. It likes° me well. Cambio, hie you home
    And bid Bianca make her ready straight,
    And, if you will, tell what hath happenèd: 65
    Lucentio's father is arrived in Padua,
    And how she's like to be Lucentio's wife.
                        [Exit Lucentio.]

Biondello. I pray the gods she may with all my heart!
                                 Exit.

Tranio. Dally not with the gods, but get thee gone.
    Signior Baptista, shall I lead the way?
    Welcome, one mess° is like to be your cheer.°   70
    Come, sir, we will better it in Pisa.

Baptista. I follow you.   *Exeunt.*

    Enter Lucentio [as Cambio] and Biondello.

Biondello. Cambio!

Lucentio. What sayst thou, Biondello?

48 **know** think 49 **affied** formally engaged 50 **part's** party's
53 **heark'ning still** listening constantly 54 **happily** perchance 55 **and
it like** if it please 56 **lie** stay 57 **pass** settle 59 **scrivener** notary
60 **slender warning** short notice 61 **pittance** meal 62 **likes** pleases
70 **mess** dish 70 **cheer** entertainment

75 *Biondello.* You saw my master° wink and laugh upon
      you?

    Lucentio. Biondello, what of that?

    Biondello. Faith, nothing, but has° left me here be-
      hind to expound the meaning or moral of his signs
80   and tokens.

    Lucentio. I pray thee, moralize° them.

    Biondello. Then thus. Baptista is safe, talking with
      the deceiving father of a deceitful son.

    Lucentio. And what of him?

85 *Biondello.* His daughter is to be brought by you to
      the supper.

    Lucentio. And then?

    Biondello. The old priest at Saint Luke's church is at
      your command at all hours.

90 *Lucentio.* And what of all this?

    Biondello. I cannot tell, except they are busied about
      a counterfeit assurance.° Take you assurance° of
      her, *"cum previlegio ad impremendum solem."*° To
      th' church! Take the priest, clerk, and some suffi-
95   cient honest witnesses.
      If this be not that you look for, I have no more
        to say,
      But bid Bianca farewell forever and a day.

    Lucentio. Hear'st thou, Biondello?

    Biondello. I cannot tarry. I knew a wench married
100   in an afternoon as she went to the garden for pars-
      ley to stuff a rabbit. And so may you, sir. And so
      adieu, sir. My master hath appointed me to go to

---

75 **my master** i.e., Tranio; cf. line 59   78 **has** he has   81 **moralize**
"expound"   92 **assurance** betrothal document   92 **Take you assurance** make sure   93 **cum ... solem** (Biondello's version of *cum pre-
vilegio ad imprimendum solum,* "with right of sole printing," a licensing
phrase, with sexual pun in *imprimendum,* literally, "pressing upon")

Saint Luke's, to bid the priest be ready to come
　　against you come° with your appendix.°　　　*Exit.*

Lucentio. I may, and will, if she be so contented.　　105
　　She will be pleased; then wherefore should I doubt?
　　Hap what hap may, I'll roundly° go about° her.
　　It shall go hard if Cambio go without her.　　　*Exit.*

[Scene 5. *The road to Padua.*]

Enter Petruchio, Kate, Hortensio
[*with Servants.*]

Petruchio. Come on, a° God's name, once more to-
　　ward our father's.
　　Good Lord, how bright and goodly shines the moon.

Kate. The moon? The sun. It is not moonlight now.

Petruchio. I say it is the moon that shines so bright.

Kate. I know it is the sun that shines so bright.　　5

Petruchio. Now, by my mother's son, and that's my-
　　self,
　　It shall be moon or star or what I list,°
　　Or ere° I journey to your father's house.
　　[*To Servants*] Go on and fetch our horses back
　　again.
　　Evermore crossed and crossed, nothing but crossed!°　　10

Hortensio. [*To Kate*] Say as he says or we shall never
　　go.

Kate. Forward, I pray, since we have come so far,
　　And be it moon or sun or what you please.

104 **against you come** in preparing for your coming　104 **appendix**
(1) servant (2) wife (another metaphor from printing)　107 **roundly**
directly　107 **about** after　4.5.1 **a** in　7 **list** please　8 **Or ere** before
10 **crossed** opposed, challenged

And if you please to call it a rush-candle,°
15 Henceforth I vow it shall be so for me.

Petruchio. I say it is the moon.

Kate.   I know it is the moon.

Petruchio. Nay, then you lie. It is the blessèd sun.

Kate. Then God be blessed, it is the blessèd sun.
    But sun it is not when you say it is not,
20 And the moon changes even as your mind.
    What you will have it named, even that it is,
    And so it shall be so for Katherine.

Hortensio. [*Aside*] Petruchio, go thy ways. The field
    is won.

Petruchio. Well, forward, forward! Thus the bowl°
    should run
25 And not unluckily against the bias.°
    But soft,° company° is coming here.

Enter Vincentio.

[*To Vincentio*] Good morrow, gentle mistress;
    where away?
Tell me, sweet Kate, and tell me truly too,
Hast thou beheld a fresher° gentlewoman?
30 Such war of white and red within her cheeks!
What stars do spangle heaven with such beauty
As those two eyes become that heavenly face?
Fair lovely maid, once more good day to thee.
Sweet Kate, embrace her for her beauty's sake.

35 *Hortensio.* [*Aside*] 'A° will make the man mad, to
    make a woman of him.

Kate. Young budding virgin, fair and fresh and sweet,
    Whither away, or where is thy abode?

---

14 **rush-candle** rush dipped in grease and used as candle   24 **bowl**
bowling ball   25 **against the bias** not in the planned curving route, made
possible by a lead insertion (bias) weighting one side of the ball   26 **soft**
hush   26 **company** someone   29 **fresher** more radiant   35 **'A** he

Happy the parents of so fair a child!
Happier the man whom favorable stars   40
Allots thee for his lovely bedfellow!

Petruchio. Why, how now, Kate, I hope thou are not
  mad.
  This is a man, old, wrinkled, faded, withered,
  And not a maiden, as thou sayst he is.

Kate. Pardon, old father, my mistaking eyes   45
  That have been so bedazzled with the sun
  That everything I look on seemeth green.°
  Now I perceive thou art a reverend father;
  Pardon, I pray thee, for my mad mistaking.

Petruchio. Do, good old grandsire, and withal make
  known   50
  Which way thou travelest. If along with us,
  We shall be joyful of thy company.

Vincentio. Fair sir, and you my merry mistress,
  That with your strange encounter° much amazed
  me,
  My name is called Vincentio, my dwelling Pisa,   55
  And bound I am to Padua, there to visit
  A son of mine which long I have not seen.

Petruchio. What is his name?

Vincentio.   Lucentio, gentle sir.

Petruchio. Happily met, the happier for thy son.
  And now by law as well as reverend age,   60
  I may entitle thee my loving father.
  The sister to my wife, this gentlewoman,
  Thy son by this° hath married. Wonder not
  Nor be not grieved. She is of good esteem,
  Her dowry wealthy, and of worthy birth;   65
  Beside, so qualified° as may beseem°
  The spouse of any noble gentleman.
  Let me embrace with old Vincentio

47 **green** young   54 **encounter** mode of address   63 **this** now   66 **so
qualified** having qualities   66 **beseem** befit

And wander we to see thy honest son,
70 Who will of thy arrival be full joyous.

Vincentio. But is this true, or is it else your pleasure,
  Like pleasant° travelers, to break a jest
  Upon the company you overtake?

Hortensio. I do assure thee, father, so it is.

75 *Petruchio.* Come, go along, and see the truth hereof,
  For our first merriment hath made thee jealous.°
                    Exeunt [all but Hortensio].

Hortensio. Well, Petruchio, this has put me in heart.
  Have to° my widow, and if she be froward,°
  Then hast thou taught Hortensio to be untoward.°
                                Exit.

---

72 **pleasant** addicted to pleasantries   76 **jealous** suspicious   78 **Have to** on to   78 **froward** fractious   79 **untoward** difficult

[ACT 5

Scene 1. *Padua. The street in front of
Lucentio's house.*]

*Enter Biondello, Lucentio [as Cambio], and
Bianca; Gremio is out before.*°

Biondello. Softly and swiftly, sir, for the priest is
ready.

Lucentio. I fly, Biondello. But they may chance to
need thee at home; therefore leave us.
                              Exit [with Bianca].

Biondello. Nay, faith, I'll see the church a your back,°   5
and then come back to my master's as soon as I
can.   [*Exit.*]

Gremio. I marvel Cambio comes not all this while.

*Enter Petruchio, Kate, Vincentio, [and] Grumio,
with Attendants.*

Petruchio. Sir, here's the door, this is Lucentio's
house.
My father's bears° more toward the marketplace;   10
Thither must I, and here I leave you, sir.

Vincentio. You shall not choose but drink before you
go.
I think I shall command your welcome here,
And by all likelihood some cheer is toward.° *Knock.*

5.1.s.d. **out before** precedes, and does not see, the others   5 **a your
back** on your back (see you enter the church? or, married?)   10 **bears**
lies   14 **toward** at hand

95

15 *Gremio.* They're busy within. You were best knock
      louder.

> *Pedant [as Vincentio] looks out of*
> *the window [above].*

Pedant. What's° he that knocks as he would beat
      down the gate?

Vincentio. Is Signior Lucentio within, sir?

20 *Pedant.* He's within, sir, but not to be spoken withal.°

Vincentio. What if a man bring him a hundred pound
      or two, to make merry withal?

Pedant. Keep your hundred pounds to yourself; he
      shall need none so long as I live.

25 *Petruchio.* Nay, I told you your son was well beloved
      in Padua. Do you hear, sir? To leave frivolous cir-
      cumstances,° I pray you tell Signior Lucentio that
      his father is come from Pisa and is here at the door
      to speak with him.

30 *Pedant.* Thou liest. His father is come from Padua°
      and here looking out at the window.

Vincentio. Art thou his father?

Pedant. Ay sir, so his mother says, if I may believe
      her.

35 *Petruchio.* [*To Vincentio*] Why how now, gentleman?
      Why this is flat° knavery, to take upon you another
      man's name.

Pedant. Lay hands on the villain. I believe 'a° means
      to cozen° somebody in this city under my counte-
40   nance.°

> *Enter Biondello.*

---

17 **What's** who is   20 **withal** with   26–27 **frivolous circumstances**
trivial matters   30 **Padua** (perhaps Shakespeare's slip of the pen for
Pisa, home of the real Vincentio, or *Mantua*, where the Pedant comes
from; cf. 4.2.77)   36 **flat** unvarnished   38 **'a** he   39 **cozen** defraud
39–40 **countenance** identity

Biondello. I have seen them in the church together;
    God send 'em good shipping!° But who is here?
    Mine old master, Vincentio! Now we are undone°
    and brought to nothing.°

Vincentio. Come hither, crack-hemp.°   *45*

Biondello. I hope I may choose,° sir.

Vincentio. Come hither, you rogue. What, have you
    forgot me?

Biondello. Forgot you? No, sir. I could not forget you,
    for I never saw you before in all my life.   *50*

Vincentio. What, you notorious° villain, didst thou
    never see thy master's father, Vincentio?

Biondello. What, my old worshipful old master? Yes,
    marry, sir, see where he looks out of the window.

Vincentio. Is't so, indeed?   *He beats Biondello.*   *55*

Biondello. Help, help, help! Here's a madman will
    murder me.   *[Exit.]*

Pedant. Help, son! Help, Signior Baptista!
                           [Exit from above.]

Petruchio. Prithee, Kate, let's stand aside and see the
    end of this controversy.   *60*
                           [They stand aside.]

    Enter Pedant [below] with Servants, Baptista,
         [and] Tranio [as Lucentio].

Tranio. Sir, what are you that offer° to beat my
    servant?

Vincentio. What am I, sir? Nay, what are you, sir? O
    immortal gods! O fine° villain! A silken doublet,

---

42 **shipping** journey   43 **undone** defeated   44 **brought to nothing** (cf.
"annihilated")   45 **crack-hemp** rope-stretcher (i.e., subject for hanging)
46 **choose** have some choice (in the matter)   51 **notorious** extraordinary   61 **offer** attempt   64 **fine** well dressed

65 a velvet hose, a scarlet cloak, and a copatain° hat!
O, I am undone, I am undone! While I play the
good husband° at home, my son and my servant
spend all at the university.

Tranio. How now, what's the matter?

70 *Baptista.* What, is the man lunatic?

Tranio. Sir, you seem a sober ancient gentleman by
your habit,° but your words show you a madman.
Why sir, what 'cerns° it you if I wear pearl and
gold? I thank my good father, I am able to main-
75 tain it.

Vincentio. Thy father! O villain, he is a sailmaker in
Bergamo.

Baptista. You mistake, sir, you mistake, sir. Pray,
what do you think is his name?

80 *Vincentio.* His name! As if I knew not his name! I
have brought him up ever since he was three years
old, and his name is Tranio.

Pedant. Away, away, mad ass! His name is Lucentio,
and he is mine only son and heir to the lands of me,
85 Signior Vincentio.

Vincentio. Lucentio! O he hath murd'red his master.
Lay hold on him, I charge you in the Duke's name.
O my son, my son! Tell me, thou villain, where is
my son Lucentio?

90 *Tranio.* Call forth an officer.

[*Enter an Officer.*]

Carry this mad knave to the jail. Father Baptista,
I charge you see that he be forthcoming.°

Vincentio. Carry me to the jail!

Gremio. Stay, officer. He shall not go to prison.

---

65 **copatain** high conical 67 **husband** manager 72 **habit** manner
73 **'cerns** concerns 92 **forthcoming** available (for trial)

Baptista. Talk not, Signior Gremio. I say he shall go   95
to prison.

Gremio. Take heed, Signior Baptista, lest you be cony-
catched° in this business. I dare swear this is the
right Vincentio.

Pedant. Swear, if thou dar'st.   100

Gremio. Nay, I dare not swear it.

Tranio. Then thou wert best° say that I am not
Lucentio.

Gremio. Yes, I know thee to be Signior Lucentio.

Baptista. Away with the dotard,° to the jail with him!   105

Vincentio. Thus strangers may be haled° and abused.
O monstrous villain!

Enter Biondello, Lucentio, and Bianca.

Biondello. O we are spoiled°—and yonder he is. Deny
him, forswear him, or else we are all undone.
*Exit Biondello, Tranio, and Pedant as fast
as may be.*

Lucentio. Pardon, sweet father.   *Kneel.*

Vincentio.   Lives my sweet son?   110

Bianca. Pardon, dear father.

Baptista.   How hast thou offended?
Where is Lucentio?

Lucentio.   Here's Lucentio,
Right son to the right Vincentio,
That have by marriage made thy daughter mine
While counterfeit supposes° bleared thine eyne.°   115

97–98 **cony-catched** fooled   102 **thou wert best** maybe you'll dare
105 **dotard** old fool   106 **haled** pulled about   108 **spoiled** ruined
115 **supposes** pretendings (evidently an allusion to Gascoigne's play
Supposes, one of Shakespeare's sources)   115 **eyne** eyes

Gremio. Here's packing,° with a witness,° to deceive us all!

Vincentio. Where is that damnèd villain Tranio
That faced and braved° me in this matter so?

120 *Baptista.* Why, tell me, is not this my Cambio?

Bianca. Cambio is changed into Lucentio.

Lucentio. Love wrought these miracles. Bianca's love
Made me exchange my state with Tranio
While he did bear my countenance° in the town,
125 And happily I have arrived at the last
Unto the wishèd haven of my bliss.
What Tranio did, myself enforced him to.
Then pardon him, sweet father, for my sake.

Vincentio. I'll slit the villain's nose that would have
130 sent me to the jail.

Baptista. [*To Lucentio*] But do you hear, sir? Have
you married my daughter without asking my good
will?

Vincentio. Fear not, Baptista; we will content you, go
135 to.° But I will in, to be revenged for this villainy.
                                                  Exit.

Baptista. And I, to sound the depth° of this knavery.
                                                  Exit.

Lucentio. Look not pale, Bianca. Thy father will not
frown.   *Exeunt [Lucentio and Bianca].*

Gremio. My cake is dough,° but I'll in among the rest
140 Out of hope of all but my share of the feast.   [*Exit.*]

Kate. Husband, let's follow, to see the end of this ado.

Petruchio. First kiss me, Kate, and we will.

116 **packing** plotting   116 **with a witness** outright, unabashed   119 **faced and braved** impudently challenged and defied   124 **bear my countenance** take on my identity   134–35 **go to** (mild remonstrance; cf. "go on," "come, come," "don't worry")   136 **sound the depth** get to the bottom of   139 **cake is dough** project hasn't worked out (proverbial; cf. 1.1.108–09)

Kate. What, in the midst of the street?

Petruchio. What, art thou ashamed of me?

Kate. No sir, God forbid, but ashamed to kiss.   *145*

Petruchio. Why, then let's home again. [*To Grumio*]
 Come sirrah, let's away.

Kate. Nay, I will give thee a kiss. Now pray thee, love,
 stay.

Petruchio. Is not this well? Come, my sweet Kate.
 Better once° than never, for never too late.° *Exeunt.*

[Scene 2. *Padua. In Lucentio's house.*]

*Enter Baptista, Vincentio, Gremio, the Pedant,
Lucentio, and Bianca, [Petruchio, Kate, Hortensio,]
Tranio, Biondello, Grumio, and Widow; the
Servingmen with Tranio bringing in a banquet.°*

Lucentio. At last, though long,° our jarring notes agree,
 And time it is, when raging war is done,
 To smile at 'scapes and perils overblown.°
 My fair Bianca, bid my father welcome
 While I with self-same kindness welcome thine.   *5*
 Brother Petruchio, sister Katherina,
 And thou, Hortensio, with thy loving widow,
 Feast with the best and welcome to my house.
 My banquet is to close our stomachs° up
 After our great good cheer.° Pray you, sit down,   *10*
 For now we sit to chat as well as eat.

Petruchio. Nothing but sit and sit, and eat and eat.

---

149 **once** at some time   149 **Better ... late** better late than never
5.2.s.d. **banquet** dessert   1 **At last, though long** at long last   3 **overblown** that have blown over   9 **stomachs** (with pun on "irascibility";
cf.4.1.152)   10 **cheer** (reception at Baptista's)

Baptista. Padua affords this kindness, son Petruchio.

Petruchio. Padua affords nothing but what is kind.

15 *Hortensio.* For both our sakes I would that word were true.

Petruchio. Now, for my life, Hortensio fears° his widow.

Widow. Then never trust me if I be afeard.°

Petruchio. You are very sensible and yet you miss my sense:
  I mean Hortensio is afeard of you.

20 *Widow.* He that is giddy thinks the world turns round.

Petruchio. Roundly° replied.

Kate.   Mistress, how mean you that?

Widow. Thus I conceive by° him.

Petruchio. Conceives by° me! How likes Hortensio that?

Hortensio. My widow says, thus she conceives her tale.°

Petruchio. Very well mended. Kiss him for that, good
25   widow.

Kate. "He that is giddy thinks the world turns round."
  I pray you, tell me what you meant by that.

Widow. Your husband, being troubled with a shrew,
  Measures° my husband's sorrow by his° woe,
30   And now you know my meaning.

Kate. A very mean° meaning.

---

16 **fears** is afraid of (the Widow puns on the meaning "frightens")
17 **afeard** (1) frightened (2) suspected   21 **Roundly** outspokenly
22 **conceive by** understand   23 **Conceives by** is made pregnant by
24 **conceives her tale** understands her statement (with another pun)
29 **Measures** estimates   29 **his** his own   31 **mean** paltry

Widow.   Right, I mean you.

Kate. And I am mean° indeed, respecting you.

Petruchio. To her, Kate!

Hortensio. To her, widow!

Petruchio. A hundred marks, my Kate does put her   35
  down.°

Hortensio. That's my office.°

Petruchio. Spoke like an officer. Ha'° to thee, lad.
                            Drinks to Hortensio.

Baptista. How likes Gremio these quick-witted folks?

Gremio. Believe me, sir, they butt° together well.

Bianca. Head and butt!° An hasty-witted body   40
  Would say your head and butt were head and horn.°

Vincentio. Ay, mistress bride, hath that awakened
  you?

Bianca. Ay, but not frighted me; therefore I'll sleep
  again.

Petruchio. Nay, that you shall not. Since you have
  begun,
  Have at you° for a bitter° jest or two.   45

Bianca. Am I your bird?° I mean to shift my bush,
  And then pursue me as you draw your bow.
  You are welcome all.
             Exit Bianca [with Kate and Widow].

Petruchio. She hath prevented me.° Here, Signior
  Tranio,

---

32 **am mean** (1) am moderate (2) have a low opinion   35 **put her down**
defeat her (with sexual pun by Hortensio)   36 **office** job   37 **Ha'**
here's, hail   39 **butt** (perhaps also "but," i.e., argue or differ)   40 **butt**
(with pun on "bottom")   41 **horn** (1) butting instrument (2) symbol of
cuckoldry (3) phallus   45 **Have at you** let's have   45 **bitter** biting (but
good-natured)   46 **bird** prey   49 **prevented me** beaten me to it

50   This bird you aimed at, though you hit her not;
         Therefore a health to all that shot and missed.

Tranio. O sir, Lucentio slipped° me, like his grey-
     hound,
     Which runs himself and catches for his master.

Petruchio. A good swift° simile but something currish.

55   *Tranio.* 'Tis well, sir, that you hunted for yourself;
         'Tis thought your deer° does hold you at a bay.°

Baptista. O, O, Petruchio, Tranio hits you now.

Lucentio. I thank thee for that gird,° good Tranio.

Hortensio. Confess, confess, hath he not hit you here?

60   *Petruchio.* 'A has a little galled° me, I confess,
         And as the jest did glance away from me,
         'Tis ten to one it maimed you two outright.

Baptista. Now, in good sadness,° son Petruchio,
     I think thou hast the veriest° shrew of all.

65   *Petruchio.* Well, I say no. And therefore, for assur-
     ance,°
         Let's each one send unto his wife,
         And he whose wife is most obedient
         To come at first when he doth send for her
         Shall win the wager which we will propose.

Hortensio. Content. What's the wager?

70   *Lucentio.*
                                     Twenty crowns.

Petruchio. Twenty crowns!
     I'll venture so much of° my hawk or hound,
     But twenty times so much upon my wife.

Lucentio. A hundred then.

Hortensio.   Content.°

---

52 **slipped** unleashed   54 **swift** quick-witted   56 **deer** (1) doe (2) dear
56 **at a bay** at bay (i.e., backed up at a safe distance)   58 **gird** gibe
60 **galled** chafed   63 **sadness** seriousness   64 **veriest** most genuine
65 **assurance** proof   72 **of** on   74 **Content** agreed

Petruchio.   A match,° 'tis done.

Hortensio. Who shall begin?

Lucentio.   That will I.   *75*
  Go Biondello, bid your mistress come to me.

Biondello. I go.   *Exit.*

Baptista. Son, I'll be your half,° Bianca comes.

Lucentio. I'll have no halves; I'll bear it all myself.

                    Enter Biondello.

  How now,° what news?

Biondello.   Sir, my mistress sends you
    word   *80*
  That she is busy and she cannot come.

Petruchio. How?° She's busy and she cannot come?
  Is that an answer?

Gremio.   Ay, and a kind one too.
  Pray God, sir, your wife send you not a worse.

Petruchio. I hope, better.   *85*

Hortensio. Sirrah Biondello, go and entreat my wife
  To come to me forthwith.°   *Exit Biondello.*

Petruchio.   O ho, entreat her!
  Nay, then she must needs come.

Hortensio.   I am afraid, sir,
  Do what you can, yours will not be entreated.

                    Enter Biondello.

  Now where's my wife?   *90*

Biondello. She says you have some goodly jest in hand.
  She will not come. She bids you come to her.

---

74 **A match** (it's) a bet   78 **be your half** assume half your bet
80 **How now** (mild exclamation; cf. "well")   82 **How** what   87 **forthwith** right away

Petruchio. Worse and worse. She will not come. O vile,
Intolerable, not to be endured!
95 Sirrah Grumio, go to your mistress; say
I command her come to me.   *Exit [Grumio].*

Hortensio. I know her answer.

Petruchio.   What?

Hortensio.   She will not.

Petruchio. The fouler fortune mine, and there an end.

Enter Kate.

Baptista. Now, by my holidame,° here comes Katherina.

100 *Kate.* What is your will, sir, that you send for me?

Petruchio. Where is your sister and Hortensio's wife?

Kate. They sit conferring° by the parlor fire.

Petruchio. Go fetch them hither. If they deny° to come,
Swinge° me them soundly° forth unto their husbands.
105 Away, I say, and bring them hither straight.

[Exit Kate.]

Lucentio. Here is a wonder, if you talk of a wonder.

Hortensio. And so it is. I wonder what it bodes.

Petruchio. Marry, peace it bodes, and love, and quiet life,
An awful° rule and right supremacy;
110 And, to be short, what not° that's sweet and happy.

Baptista. Now fair befall° thee, good Petruchio.

---

99 **holidame** holy dame (some editors emend to *halidom,* sacred place or relic)   102 **conferring** conversing   103 **deny** refuse   104 **Swinge** thrash   104 **soundly** thoroughly (cf. "sound beating")   109 **awful** inspiring respect   110 **what not** i.e., everything   111 **fair befall** good luck to

The wager thou hast won, and I will add
Unto their losses twenty thousand crowns,
Another dowry to another daughter,
For she is changed as she had never been.   *115*

Petruchio. Nay, I will win my wager better yet
And show more sign of her obedience,
Her new-built virtue and obedience.

> *Enter Kate, Bianca, and Widow.*

See where she comes and brings your froward°
     wives
As prisoners to her womanly persuasion.   *120*
Katherine, that cap of yours becomes you not.
Off with that bauble, throw it under foot.
                              [*She throws it.*]

Widow. Lord, let me never have a cause to sigh
Till I be brought to such a silly pass.°

Bianca. Fie, what a foolish—duty call you this?   *125*

Lucentio. I would your duty were as foolish too.
The wisdom of your duty, fair Bianca,
Hath cost me five hundred° crowns since supper-
     time.

Bianca. The more fool you for laying° on my duty.

Petruchio. Katherine, I charge thee, tell these head-
     strong women   *130*
What duty they do owe their lords and husbands.

Widow. Come, come, you're mocking. We will have
     no telling.

Petruchio. Come on, I say, and first begin with her.

Widow. She shall not.

---

119 **froward** uncooperative   124 **pass** situation   128 **five hundred**
(1) Lucentio makes it look worse than it is, or (2) he made several bets,
or (3) the text errs (some editors emend to "a hundred," assuming that the
manuscript's "a" was misread as the Roman numeral v)   129 **laying**
betting

135 *Petruchio.* I say she shall—and first begin with her.

Kate. Fie, fie, unknit that threatening unkind° brow
And dart not scornful glances from those eyes
To wound thy lord, thy king, thy governor.
It blots thy beauty as frosts do bite the meads,
Confounds thy fame° as whirlwinds shake° fair
140   buds,
And in no sense is meet or amiable.
A woman moved° is like a fountain troubled,
Muddy, ill-seeming, thick, bereft of beauty,
And while it is so, none so dry or thirsty
145 Will deign to sip or touch one drop of it.
Thy husband is thy lord, thy life, thy keeper,
Thy head, thy sovereign—one that cares for thee,
And for thy maintenance commits his body
To painful labor both by sea and land,
150 To watch° the night in storms, the day in cold,
Whilst thou li'st warm at home, secure and safe;
And craves no other tribute at thy hands
But love, fair looks, and true obedience:
Too little payment for so great a debt.
155 Such duty as the subject owes the prince,
Even such a woman oweth to her husband,
And when she is froward, peevish, sullen, sour,
And not obedient to his honest° will,
What is she but a foul contending rebel
160 And graceless traitor to her loving lord?
I am ashamed that women are so simple°
To offer war where they should kneel for peace,
Or seek for rule, supremacy, and sway,
When they are bound to serve, love, and obey.
165 Why are our bodies soft and weak and smooth,
Unapt to° toil and trouble in the world,
But that our soft conditions° and our hearts

---

136 **unkind** hostile   140 **Confounds thy fame** spoils people's opinion of
you   140 **shake** shake off   142 **moved** i.e., by ill temper   150 **watch**
stay awake, be alert during   158 **honest** honorable   161 **simple** silly
166 **Unapt to** unfitted for   167 **conditions** qualities

Should well agree with our external parts?
Come, come, you froward and unable worms,°
My mind hath been as big° as one of yours,   *170*
My heart as great, my reason haply more,
To bandy word for word and frown for frown.
But now I see our lances are but straws,
Our strength as weak, our weakness past compare,
That seeming to be most which we indeed least are.   *175*
Then vail your stomachs,° for it is no boot,°
And place your hands below your husband's foot,
In token of which duty, if he please,
My hand is ready, may it° do him ease.

Petruchio. Why, there's a wench! Come on and kiss
    me, Kate.   *180*

Lucentio. Well, go thy ways, old lad, for thou shalt
    ha't.

Vincentio. 'Tis a good hearing° when children are
    toward.°

Lucentio. But a harsh hearing when women are fro-
    ward.

Petruchio. Come, Kate, we'll to bed.
    We three are married, but you two are sped.°   *185*
    'Twas I won the wager, [*to Lucentio*] though you
        hit the white,°
    And, being a winner, God give you good night.
                        Exit Petruchio [*with Kate*].

Hortensio. Now, go thy ways; thou hast tamed a curst
    shrow.

Lucentio. 'Tis a wonder, by your leave, she will be
    tamèd so.   [*Exeunt.*]

FINIS

169 **unable worms** weak, lowly creatures   170 **big** inflated (cf. "think
big")   176 **vail your stomachs** fell your pride   176 **no boot** useless,
profitless   179 **may it** (1) I hope it may (2) if it may   182 **hearing** thing
to hear; report   182 **toward** tractable   185 **sped** done for   186 **white**
(1) bull's eye (2) *Bianca* means white

Textual Note

The authority for the present text is the Folio of 1623 (F). Based on it were the Quarto of 1631 and three later folios. These introduce a number of errors of their own but also make some corrections and some changes accepted by most subsequent editors. The present text adheres as closely as possible to F, accepting standard emendations only when F seems clearly erroneous. These emendations come mainly from such early editors as Rowe, Theobald, and Capell.

F's incomplete division into acts is almost universally altered by modern editors, and the present text conforms to standard practice. F has "*Actus primus. Scoena [sic] Prima*" at the beginning, whereas in modern practice approximately the first 275 lines are placed in an "Induction" with two scenes. F lacks a designation for Act 2. F's "*Actus Tertia [sic],*" beginning with Lucentio's "Fiddler, forbear, etc.," is universally accepted. F's "*Actus Quartus. Scena Prima*" generally becomes modern 4.3, and F's "*Actus Quintus,*" modern 5.2.

F makes a number of erroneous or unclear speech assignments (at one time naming an actor, Sincklo, instead of the character). These are at Ind.1.88; 3.1.46ff.; 4.2.4ff. They are specifically listed below. Names of speakers, nearly always abbreviated in F, are regularly spelled out in the present edition. Speakers in F designated *Beggar*, *Lady*, and *Man* are given as *Sly*, *Page*, and *Servingman*, respectively.

F is not consistent in the spelling of some proper names. In the stage directions, the shrew, for instance, appears as *Katerina*, *Katherina*, *Katherine* (sometimes with *a* in the second syllable), and *Kate*; she is spoken to and of as

Katherine and *Kate*; her speeches are headed *Ka*, *Kat*, and *Kate*. Since *Kate* is the most frequent form, this edition uses it throughout and does not include the change in the following list. In F, the name adopted by Hortensio when he pretends to be a music teacher appears three times as *Litio*, which we use here, and four times as *Lisio*. Many editors follow F2 and Rowe in emending to *Licio*.

Editors vary in the treatment of F's short lines, sometimes letting a short line stand independently, and sometimes joining several short lines into a quasi-pentameter. The latter practice is generally followed in the present edition. Modern editors are quite consistent in identifying as verse a few passages set as prose in F, and vice versa.

Errors in foreign languages in F are allowed to stand if they are conceivably errors made by the speaker, e.g., errors in Latin and Spanish. Spellings of English words are corrected and modernized. The punctuation is modern. Obvious typographical errors, of which there are a great many, are corrected silently. The following materials, lacking in F, are given in square brackets in this edition: cast of characters, missing act and scene designations, indications of place of action, certain stage directions (F has an unusually copious supply of stage directions, some of which make interesting references to properties).

The following list includes all significant variations from F. The reading in the present text is in italics, followed by the F reading in roman.

Ind.1.s.d. *Hostess and Beggar* Begger and Hostes   12 *thirdborough* Head-borough   17 *Broach* Brach   82 *A Player* 2. Player   88 *2. Player* Sincklo

Ind.2.2 *lordship* Lord   18 *Sly's* Sies   137 *play it. Is* play, it is

1.1.13 *Vincentio* Vincentio's   25 *Mi perdonato* Me Pardonato 47s.d. *suitor* sister   73 *master* Mr   162 *captum* captam   207 *colored* Conlord   243 *your* you

1.2.13 *master* Mr   17s.d. *wrings* rings   18 *masters* mistris   24 *Con . . . trovato* Contutti le core bene trobatto   25 *ben* bene   25 *molto* multo   45 *this's* this   69, 89 *shrewd* shrow'd   70 *Xanthippe* Zentippe   72 *she* she is   120 *me and other* me. Other   172 *help me* helpe one   190 *Antonio's* Butonios   213 *ours* yours   266 *feat* seeke

2.1.3 *gawds* goods   8 *charge thee* charge   73 *Backare* Bacare   75–76 *wooing. Neighbor,* wooing neighbors: 79 *unto you this*

vnto this   104 *Pisa; by report* Pisa by report   158 *vile* vilde   186
bonny bony   241 *askance* a sconce   323 *in* me

3.1.28 *Sigeia* Sigeria (also in 32, 41)   46 *[Aside]* Luc.   49 *Bianca*
[F omits]   50 *Lucentio* Bian.   52 *Bianca* Hort.   73 *B mi* Beeme
79 *change* charge   79 *odd* old   80 *Messenger* Nicke

3.2.29 *of thy* of   30 *such old* such   33 *hear* heard   55 *swayed*
Waid   57 *half-cheeked* halfe-chekt   128 *to her love* sir, Loue
130 *As I* As

4.1.25 *Curtis* Grumio   100s.d. *Enter ... Servingmen* [F places
after 99]   174s.d. [in F, after 175]   198 *reverent* reuerend

4.2.4 *Hortensio* Luc.   6 *Lucentio* Hor.   8 *Lucentio* Hor.   13 *none*
me   31 *her* them   63 *mercatante* Marcantant   71 *Take in* Par. Take me.

4.3.63 *Haberdasher* Fel.   81 *is a* is   88 *like a* like   179 *account'st*
accountedst

4.4.1 *Sir* Sirs   5 [in F, Tranio's speech begins here]   9s.d. [F
places after 7]   19 *Signior* Tra. Signior   68 [F adds s.d., Enter
Peter]   91 *except* expect

4.5.18 *is* in   36 *make a* make the   38 *Whither* Whether   38 *where*
whether   41 *Allots* A lots   48 *reverend* reuerent (also in 60)   78 *she
be* she

5.1.6 *master's* mistris   52 *master's* Mistris   107s.d. [F places after
105]   145 *No* Mo

5.2.2 *done* come   37 *thee, lad* the lad   45 *bitter* better   65 *for* sir

A Note on the Sources of
The Taming of the Shrew

Some time ago it was a rather generally held opinion that *The Taming of the Shrew* was Shakespeare's reworking of an anonymous play, *The Taming of a Shrew* (the conventional shorter form of a much longer title), published in 1594. There were at least two variations of the basic theory—one, that *A Shrew* itself was based on an earlier play; the other (and more widely held), that there was an intermediate play between *A Shrew* and Shakespeare's *The Shrew*. Such speculations were ways of explaining the similarities and dissimilarities between the two plays, and to some extent, also, the apparent inconsistencies within the plays. The latter led likewise, it may be added, to much theorizing about authorship: *A Shrew* was attributed to various contemporary dramatists whose styles were supposedly recognizable in it, and *The Shrew* was believed to reveal the hand, not only of Shakespeare, but of a less gifted collaborator.

Another theory of the relationship between *The Shrew* and *A Shrew* was that they were siblings—different offspring of a single parent play (either by Shakespeare or by someone else). Another theory of authorship was that Shakespeare himself had helped write *A Shrew*. Long before the putting forward of these hypotheses, Alexander Pope (1725) attributed *A Shrew* entirely to Shakespeare, and in his *History of English Poetry* (1895–1910), W. J. Courthope expressed the same conviction, though it ran counter to orthodox views at the time. The justification for mentioning these points of view here is that, in different ways and in different measure, they anticipate what is apparently the prevailing view at the present time—namely, that Shakespeare's *The Shrew* is the prior play and that *A Shrew* in some way derives from it. One theory is that *A Shrew* is a "memorial reconstruction" of *The Shrew*, that is, an acting company's effort to put together from memory a script perhaps sold to another company. This explains parts of *A Shrew* that sound like badly remembered parts of *The Shrew*, but it hardly explains the larger extent of the Christopher Sly framework plot in *A Shrew*, the addition of a third daughter for Baptista, or the changing of the names of all the characters. To deal with these problems there is the hypothesis that though *A Shrew* is based on *The Shrew*, it is a conscious revision, for whatever reasons, rather than a reassembling from memory. Obviously, much is still left unexplained. But that is true of all these theories, most of which are based on assumptions and likelihoods rather than on very hard evidence. In the end, we do not really know what the relation between the two plays is.

Scholars who believed that *The Shrew* was the later play tended to date it after 1595. Those who accept it as the prior play date it 1592 or 1593.

If *The Shrew* is the prior play, the problem of sources is simplified, for we need not consider the differences between the two plays. *The Shrew* is usually admired for its ingenious merging of three different bodies of material—the Christopher Sly business in the Induction, the taming plot, and the straight love story involving rival lovers (Bianca, Lucentio, etc.)—that are all, so to speak, old stories.

The story of the trick played upon the sleeper when he awakes is at least as old as the *Arabian Nights* (collected c. 1450), in which Harun al-Rashid victimizes Abu Hassan. One scholar theorizes that ambassadors from the East may have told this story to Philip the Good (1396–1467), Duke of Burgundy, who is said to have played the trick upon a drunken man in Brussels. An officer of the Duke told it to the theologian and educator Juan Luis Vives (1492–1540), who reported it in a letter (*Epistolarum* . . .

Farrago, Antwerp, 1556). From him it passed to Heuterus, whose version in *De rebus burgundicis* (1584) is the most probable immediate source for Shakespeare (from Heuterus the story went via France into other English works later than *The Shrew*). Shakespeare may also have known the story in Richard Edwards' 1570 version, one of a collection of prose tales now lost.

In the taming plot Shakespeare utilized another old story of which there were versions in many countries. A possible immediate source is a long ballad (over 1100 lines) published in the mid-sixteenth century, *A Merry Jest of a Shrewd and Curst Wife Lapped in Morel's Skin for Her Good Behavior,* but this is a cruder story of a rough and unsubtle husband ("Morel's Skin" is the salt hide of an old horse that the husband kills). Shakespeare, as Professor Hosley has shown, follows the humanist tradition embodied in, and perhaps derived some details from, Erasmus's colloquy, *A Merry Dialogue Declaring the Properties of Shrewd Shrews and Honest Wives* (1557). Several features of the Shakespeare story had appeared in Don Juan Manuel's *El Conde Lucanor,* a fourteenth-century collection of tales, of which there was a sixteenth-century edition. Sisters somewhat like Baptista's daughters are contrasted in a tale in Giovanni Straparola's *Piacevoli notti* (1553).

Of the three main elements in *The Shrew,* the Bianca story is the only one whose source may be securely identified. That source is George Gascoigne's *Supposes* (acted 1566, published 1573; alluded to in *The Shrew,* 5.1.115). Gascoigne's play, in turn, is a translation of an Italian play, Ariosto's *I Suppositi* (first acted at Ferrara in 1509). Ariosto, in turn, makes use of comic conventions that derive from the Romans Plautus and Terence and the Athenian Menander. The names *Tranio* and *Grumio* both come from Plautus. The Latin lesson may derive from a scene in R. W.'s *Three Lords and Three Ladies of London* (c. 1590).

The farcical elements in *The Shrew* seem to have inspired revisers to outdo the farce of the original; Shakespeare's play is high comedy in contrast with versions of it that held the stage from the mid-seventeenth to mid-nineteenth centuries. In 1667 Pepys saw an adaptation by John Lacy called *Sauny the Scot*: this magnifies Grumio's part (in *A Shrew*, the Grumio character was named Sander) and gives Grumio (i.e., Sauny) a Scots accent. Garrick's *Catherine and Petruchio* (1756), which cut out the Sly and Bianca parts, was popular for over a century; indeed, toward the end of the nineteenth century Shaw was attacking Garrick for this commercialistic version that was still competing with Shakespeare's play. In the 1920s Fritz Leiber mounted a production in which Grumio was a Negro comic in a bellhop's uniform, and Grumio and Petruchio rode motorcycles. In 1948 Cole Porter wrote the musical *Kiss Me, Kate*, which is only nominally related to the original. However, modern productions tend, with variations, to produce *The Taming of the Shrew* in the 1623 version; the return to this began in 1844, with J. R. Planché's production at the Haymarket in London (under the sponsorship of Ben Webster, an ancestor of Margaret Webster, the modern director of Shakespeare).

Commentaries

RICHARD HOSLEY

Sources and Analogues of
The Taming of the Shrew

I

The problem of establishing the sources and analogues of Shakespeare's *Taming of the Shrew* is greatly complicated by the undecided question of the relationship of that play to the anonymous *Taming of a Shrew*.[1] The older theory that *A Shrew* is a source of *The Shrew*, though it dies hard,[2] is now generally rejected in favor of the theory that *A Shrew* is a "bad quarto"—that is to say, a memorial reconstruction. There is a sharp disagreement, however, about the play from which *A Shrew* is supposed to derive. Some scholars hold the theory that *A Shrew* is simply a bad quarto of *The Shrew*, albeit of an unusual type,[3] whereas others hold the theory that *A Shrew* is a bad quarto of a "lost Shrew play" which itself served as a source of *The Shrew*.[4] The issue has not been resolved,

From *The Huntington Library Quarterly* 27 (1963–64): 289–308. Reprinted by permission of the Huntington Library and the author.

[1] For *The Shrew* I have used the Folio text (1623) in the Yale facsimile edition (1954); for *A Shrew*, the quarto text (1594) in the Praetorius facsimile edition (1886).

[2] Artificial respiration is applied by John W. Schroeder, "The Taming of a Shrew and The Taming of the Shrew: A Case Reopened," *JEGP* 57 (1958): 424–43.

[3] E.g., Peter Alexander, "The Taming of a Shrew," *TLS*, September 16, 1926, p. 614; J. Dover Wilson, ed. *The Taming of the Shrew* (Cambridge, Eng., 1928), pp. 104 ff.; E. A. J. Honigmann, "Shakespeare's 'Lost Source Plays,'" *MLR* 49 (1954): 302–04.

[4] E.g., R. A. Houk, "The Evolution of The Taming of the Shrew," *PMLA* 57 (1942): 1009–39; G. I. Duthie, "The Taming of a Shrew and The Taming of the Shrew," *RES* 19 (1943): 337–56; W. W. Greg, *The Shakespeare First Folio* (Oxford, 1955), pp. 211–12.

yet the particular theory which we accept makes a big difference in our understanding of the sources. For example, if we accept the first bad-quarto theory, *A Shrew*, being derivative from *The Shrew*, does not enter the picture at all. On the other hand, if we accept the second bad-quarto theory, *A Shrew* is very much in the picture—not, to be sure, as a source of *The Shrew*, but as a reflection of the lost play which textual scholars have postulated as a source of *The Shrew*. Faced with this difficult situation, Kenneth Muir, in his general study of Shakespeare's sources, in effect threw up his hands: "The state of our knowledge is such that it would be unprofitable to discuss the question of sources."[5]

Muir's caution was in part motivated, one suspects, by an understandable reluctance to decide what eminent textual scholars have been unable to agree upon. But it may well have been motivated also by his tentative acceptance of the theory that *A Shrew* is a bad quarto of a lost Shrew play which served as a source of *The Shrew*. For how can we know the changes which Shakespeare assuredly would have made in the materials he took from X? And how can we know the changes which the author or authors of *A Shrew* would assuredly have made in the materials they also took from X? There is so much room for lost motion here that one can only agree with Muir that if the textual situation is indeed as he tentatively supposes, discussion of the question of sources would be unprofitable. The situation has been rather less troublesome in what might be the parallel case of *Hamlet*, precisely for the reason that we do not have a bad quarto of the *Ur-Hamlet*.[6]

---

[5]*Shakespeare's Sources* (London, 1957), p. 259. Compare A. L. Attwater, "Shakespeare's Sources," in *A Companion to Shakespeare Studies* (Cambridge, 1941), p. 226n: "*The Taming of the Shrew* is excluded from this discussion as a source play or a 'bad' quarto." Compare also J. Payne Collier's failure to include sources of *The Taming of the Shrew* in his *Shakespeare's Library* (London, 1843).

[6]Although *The Taming of the Shrew* did not escape the attention of the disintegrators, it is now generally assumed that the entire play is Shakespeare's uncollaborated work. Compare Ernest P. Kuhl, "The Authorship of *The Taming of the Shrew*," *PMLA* 40 (1925): 551–618; and K. Wentersdorf, "The Authenticity of *The Taming of the Shrew*," *SQ* 5 (1954): 311–32.

When we turn to Geoffrey Bullough's treatment of the sources of *The Taming of the Shrew*, in his anthology of Shakespearean sources, we find a certain amount of confusion but not many sources or analogues.[7] Rejecting the generally accepted modern view that *A Shrew* is a bad quarto, Bullough returns to the older theory that *A Shrew* is a source of *The Shrew*, even suggesting that *A Shrew* may represent Shakespeare's early draft! His position on the text does not require comment, but it does need to be made clear in order that we may understand why he prints (and discusses) *A Shrew* as a source of *The Shrew*. Bullough prints also two other sources or analogues: Simon Goulart's version of "The Sleeper Awakened" in Edward Grimeston's translation, as representing a source or analogue (Heuterus) of the Sly-Lord action not in *The Shrew* but in *A Shrew*; and George Gascoigne's *Supposes*, as a source of the Bianca-Lucentio action in *The Shrew*, the assumption being that Shakespeare, though he used *A Shrew* as a source of the Sly-Lord action and of the Kate-Petruchio action, here abandoned *A Shrew* in favor of the *Supposes*. Thus Bullough prints only one generally acknowledged source (the *Supposes*), one representative version (Grimeston) of an acknowledged source or analogue (Heuterus), and one "source" (*A Shrew*) which practically all modern scholars would consider to be neither a source nor an analogue; and he fails to print or discuss a number of other possible sources or analogues, most prominent among them the ballad *A Shrewde and Curste Wyfe*, which he seems to regard as merely an interesting example of the wife-beating tradition from which Shakespeare obviously departed.

II

Clearly the source problem in *The Taming of the Shrew* is intimately connected with the textual problem of the relationship between *The Shrew* and *A Shrew*. Can the textual problem be solved? Probably not, I suspect, at least not by the usual method of detailed comparison of texts—witness the impasse arrived at by the scholars of footnote 3 and those of footnote 4. One reason for the impasse is that any variation between *The Shrew* and *A Shrew* can be explained equally well by the one theory as by the other; and another is that while the theory that *A Shrew* is a bad quarto of *The Shrew* lies open to the kinds of attack to which such theories are liable, the theory that *A Shrew* is a bad quarto of a lost Shrew play cannot be attacked at all since there is nothing there!

But if the problem will not yield to scholarly logic, it may yet yield to scholarly prejudice. We are offered two hypotheses; may we not opt for the one we prefer? Naturally we may, though most nonspecialist scholars hesitate to make a choice (in print) lest it later transpire that they have backed the wrong horse. I began my own study of the question by accepting the theory of a lost Shrew play. Gradually, however, I grew dissatisfied with the theory and in time came to believe that *A Shrew* is simply a bad quarto of *The Shrew*. My purpose is not to argue with the specialists who hold with the theory of an *Ur-Shrew*. It is, rather, to emphasize to nonspecialist readers that since neither theory can be disproved conclusively, we may reasonably prefer one or the other theory without entering the wandering mazes of detailed textual comparison; and to point out, to them and to the specialists, three considerations which led me to my present opinion and which might conceivably lead them to a similar one.

The first is economy of hypothesis. *(Entia non sunt multiplicanda praeter necessitatem.)** There is no external evidence for the existence of a lost Shrew play. (Thus the situation is not to be compared, except conjecturally, with that of *Hamlet* and the *Ur-Hamlet,* for the existence of the latter play is attested to by several witnesses.) The theory of a lost Shrew play is merely a postulate by textual scholars designed to explain the unusual variations between

---

*Things should not unnecessarily be multiplied.

Shakespeare's *Taming of the Shrew* and the bad-quarto text *The Taming of a Shrew*.

The second consideration is that the difficulties which have seemed to stand in the way of accepting the theory that *A Shrew* is simply a bad quarto of *The Shrew* are by no means insuperable. There are, in general, two such difficulties. The first is that there are, within a framework of basic similarities indicating a connection of some sort between the two texts, variations between them in language, structure, and characters greater than are usually to be observed in the comparison of corresponding "good" and "bad" texts. For example, the basic situation of *A Shrew* involves three sisters, whereas that of *The Shrew* involves only two; *A Shrew* lacks characters corresponding to Tranio and Gremio in *The Shrew* and provides the character of a page for Polidor (Hortensio in *The Shrew*); the induction to *A Shrew* is balanced by a "dramatic epilogue" in which we return to the story of Christopher Sly, whereas there is no dramatic epilogue to *The Shrew*—and so on. But such wide variations are not without distant analogues in other bad quartos. For example, the bad quarto of *Romeo and Juliet* contains a scene which, in language at least, varies widely from the corresponding scene of Shakespeare's text (2.6). The bad quarto of *Henry V* omits one of Shakespeare's scenes (3.1) and reverses the order of two others (4.4 and 5). The bad quarto of *The Merry Wives of Windsor* has nothing to correspond to the first four scenes of Act 5 in Shakespeare's text, and the last scene of the play varies widely from Shakespeare's corresponding scene (5.5). The bad quarto of *Hamlet* shifts the nunnery scene from a point in 3.1 in Shakespeare's text to a point several hundred lines earlier, in a scene corresponding to 2.2; and it converts Shakespeare's scene in which Horatio receives Hamlet's letter about the England voyage (4.6) into a quite different scene in which Horatio gives Gertrude the information contained in that letter. These variations are not, to be sure, exactly analogous to the variations we are concerned with between *The Shrew* and *A Shrew*, but they do suggest that the authors of bad-quarto texts could, upon occasion, depart considerably from their sources in corresponding good texts. *The Taming of a Shrew* may well involve, upon a grander scale, comparable departures from its supposed source in *The Shrew*, many of them undoubtedly originating in memorial error, but some of them conceivably originating in conscious design. The other difficulty is posed by variant nomenclature. The names of characters in *A Shrew*, with the exception of Sly and Kate, vary in substance from those of *The Shrew*—for example, Grumio is called Sander in *A Shrew*, Petruchio Ferando, Bianca Philema, and so on; and the scene of *A Shrew* is Athens instead of Padua. Certainly the reporters could not have "forgotten" that the shrew-tamer's name was Petruchio or that the play was laid in Italy. But they might—for reasons that for the moment remain obscure— intentionally have altered the scene and most of the names in their reconstruction; and presumably such alterations would not have been out of keeping with the larger variations in language, structure, and characters which are observable between the two texts. To sum up: the theory of a lost Shrew play is of great convenience in explaining the two kinds of "difficulty" noted. Wherever the "gap" between *The Shrew* and *A Shrew* seems too large for a "normal" good- and bad-text relationship, we can explain the variation by postulating the influence of X. But the postulate is not strictly necessary. We may suppose *A Shrew* to be simply a bad quarto of *The Shrew* if we concede that it is of rather a different type from the bad quartos of other Shakespearean plays—an "abnormal" type, that is to say, which involves a good deal more conscious originality on the part of its author or authors than is usually to be observed in bad-quarto texts.

The third consideration follows from recognition of the artistic excellence of *The Taming of the Shrew*. Shakespeare's play (as preserved in the Folio text) had little appreciation during the two centuries from the Restoration to the Victorian period, as witness the long series of adaptations and "improvements" of which Garrick's *Catherine and Petruchio* (which dispenses with both induction and subplot) is perhaps the best known. Early critics occasionally express an appreciation of the play's excellence. Dr.

Johnson, for example, admired the unity of the play proper: "Of this play the two plots are so well united, that they can hardly be called two without injury to the art with which they are interwoven. The attention is entertained with all the variety of a double plot, yet is not distracted by unconnected incidents."[8] Nor does it seem an exaggeration to suggest that the structural unity of main plot and subplot is comparable in excellence to that of such plays as *The Merchant of Venice* and *Twelfth Night*. But it has remained for quite recent critics—notably Donald A. Stauffer,[9] Maynard Mack,[10] and especially Cecil C. Seronsy[11]—to give proper emphasis to the brilliant threefold structure of induction, main plot, and subplot, unified as these elements are by the "Supposes" theme.[12] This thematic unity of a three-action play is perhaps all the more remarkable for being without parallel in Elizabethan drama. Now—to return to the relationship between *The Shrew* and *A Shrew*—if we concede the brilliance of the threefold structure of Shakespeare's *Shrew*, and if we postulate that *The Shrew* had a source in a lost Shrew play of which *A Shrew* is a bad quarto, we are assuming that Shakespeare was not responsible for the basic tripartite conception, for the essential threefold structure would have been present in the supposed *Ur-Shrew*, whence of course *A Shrew* would have derived its own essentially threefold structure. In this case we should be assuming, around 1593, the existence of a dramatist other than Shakespeare who was capable of devising a three-part structure more impressive than the structure of any extant play by Lyly, Peele, Greene, Marlowe, or Kyd. The assumption seems an unlikely one. Furthermore, in this case we should also be denying Shakespeare the powers of synthesis and invention which are so evident in plays like *The*

[8] *Johnson on Shakespeare,* ed. Walter Raleigh (London, 1925), p. 96.

[9] *Shakespeare's World of Images* (New York, 1949), p. 46.

[10] "Engagement and Detachment in Shakespeare's Plays," in *Essays on Shakespeare and Elizabethan Drama in Honor of Hardin Craig* (Columbia, 1962), pp. 279–80.

[11] "'Supposes' as the Unifying Theme in *The Taming of the Shrew*," *SQ* 14 (1963): 15–30.

[12] Interpretation along the same lines is proposed in my edition for the Pelican Shakespeare (Baltimore, 1964), pp. 24–25.

Merchant of Venice and *King Lear*, especially when these are compared with their sources. Such a denial seems both unnecessary and undesirable. As M. C. Bradbrook puts it, "It is unnecessary to postulate a lost source play unless Shakespeare is held to be constitutionally incapable of inventing a plot; for there is no sound external evidence for it."[13]

The reader, then, is invited to accept the following line of argument. (1) *The Taming of the Shrew* has a structural and thematic unity which is peculiarly characteristic of Shakespeare. Hence (2) we may reject the theory that Shakespeare's play had a source in a lost Shrew play of which *A Shrew* is a bad quarto. And hence (3) we may accept the theory that *A Shrew* is simply a bad quarto of *The Shrew*. Adopting this approach to *The Taming of a Shrew,* we may approach the problem of establishing Shakespeare's sources and analogues without the necessity of considering either *A Shrew* or a supposed *Ur-Shrew*. A small but important point will illustrate the advantages of the position. Accepting it, we need not search for a source or analogue necessarily involving three sisters (as in *A Shrew*), [14] and we should be inclined to recognize the special relevance, potentially, of a source or analogue involving two sisters (as in *The Shrew*).

III

As it happens, such a source has been under our noses all along, in an anonymous verse tale printed by Hugh Jackson about 1550 under the title *Here Begynneth a Merry Jest of a Shrewde and Curste Wyfe, Lapped in Morrelles Skin, for Her Good Behavyour.*[15] This is generally considered not to be a source of Shakespeare's play. Bullough, for instance, who does not anthologize it, mentions

---

[13]"Dramatic Role as Social Image: A Study of *The Taming of the Shrew*," *SJ* 94 (1958): 138. This article contains an excellent discussion of the shrew-taming theme in Elizabethan drama.

[14]E.g., the Jutland tale of the Three Shrewish Sisters; see Reinhold Köhler, "Zu Shakespeare's *The Taming of the Shrew*," *SJ* 3 (1868): 397–401. Nor need we search for a source of *A Shrew*, as John W. Shroeder does in "A New Analogue and Possible Source for *The Taming of a Shrew*," *SQ* 10 (1959): 251–55.

[15]*STC* 14521. I have used the copy in the Huntington Library. The poem was edited by Thomas Amyot for the Shakespeare Society (London, 1844); and by W. C. Hazlitt, in *Shakespeare's Library* (London, 1875), IV, 415–48.

it only in passing as an example of "the Shrew theme common in fabliaux from classical times." "*The Ballad of the Curst Wife Wrapt* [sic] *in a* [sic] *Morell's Skin* (*c.* 1550) given in *ShLib* iv.415ff., also shows the interest taken in unusual methods of taming" (p. 63). And Hazlitt, who did anthologize it, denied a relationship between the *Shrewde and Curste Wyfe* and Shakespeare's play. "The following humorous tale in verse has no special relation in its incidents to Shakespeare's 'Taming of the Shrew,' and consequently none to the older comedy [*A Shrew*] reprinted in the present work; but it is of a similar character, and has always been mentioned in connection with both: it is therefore appended, in order that the ancient materials existing in the time of our great dramatist, and most likely well known to him, may be at one view before the reader."[16] Since both writers regard *A Shrew* as a source of *The Shrew*, it is perhaps not surprising that they fail to see any particular relevance in the *Shrewde and Curste Wyfe*: a lion stands in the path. (As also in the path of believers in an *Ur-Shrew*.) Another reason (I would conjecture) for the position of these and other scholars who have seen no special relevance in the *Shrewde and Curste Wyfe* is an understandable distaste for the sadistic relish with which the husband of the ballad "tames" his truly "shrewde and curste" wife—a virago in the best tradition of medieval farce and *fabliau* (but not unchaste). He takes her down into the cellar and locks the door, tears off her clothes, beats her with birch rods till the blood runs on the floor and she faints, and then wraps her in the skin of an old lame plough-horse, Morel, killed and flayed especially for the occasion. Morel's salted skin quickly "revives" the wife, and the husband threatens to keep her in it all her life unless she yields him the mastership. At this threat the wife's "mood begins to sink": she calls for "grace," promises obedience, and becomes an exemplary wife. This Tudor Grand Guignol is so far removed from Petruchio's "taming" of Kate (even if we accept the deplorable modern stage traditions of having

[16]Hazlitt, IV, 415. Compare Israel Gollancz, ed. *The Shrew* (1896): "The nearest analogue in Elizabethan literature to *The Taming of the Shrew* is to be found in a popular poem . . . [the *Shrewde and Curste Wyfe*], but this poem cannot be considered the direct source of the play."

him enter cracking a whip and later administer a spanking to Kate) that it is difficult to see, at first glance, how the *Shrewde and Curste Wyfe* can have any connection with *The Taming of the Shrew*.

Yet when we look closer we find parallels in the basic situation, the characterization, the development of the action, and the language. A man with a shrewish wife has two daughters. (Baptista. Shakespeare omits the mother, as in many of his other plays.) The younger daughter is the father's favorite, "*meek,* and gentle" (sig. Aii[r]), sought after by many suitors. (Bianca. Compare Lucentio: "Maid's *mild* behavior"—1.1.71.) Because she pleases him so, the father is reluctant to give the younger daughter in marriage. (Similarly Baptista, with a difference that tightly links main plot and subplot at their very beginning, refuses to permit the marriage of Bianca before that of Kate.) The older daughter is the mother's favorite and, like her, a shrew; she is "Sometime franticke and sometime *mad*" (sig. Aii[r]); and she has no suitors. (Kate. Compare Tranio: "That wench is stark *mad*"—1.1.69. Bianca: "—being *mad* herself, she's *madly* mated"—3.2.244. Petruchio: "And thus I'll curb her *mad* and headstrong humor"— 4.2.203.) Finally, however, a suitor appears who wishes to marry the older daughter. (Petruchio.) There is also a suitor for the younger daughter, but this couple drops out of the action and is not mentioned again. (Lucentio.) The father is willing to pay generously to get rid of his older daughter, but, "loth any man to beguile" (sig. Aii[r]), he attempts to dissuade the suitor from marrying her: "Golde and sylver I would thee give: / If thou her marry by sweete Saynt John, / But thou shouldest repent it all thy live" (sig. Aiii[r]). (Similarly Baptista attempts to dissuade Petruchio from marrying Kate but offers a good dowry: "She is not for your turn, the more my grief. . . . After my death the one half of my Lands / And in possession twenty thousand crowns"—2.1.63, 121–22.) Moreover, in warning the suitor against his shrewish daughter, the father likens her to a devil: "She is conditioned I tell thee playne, / Moste like a *Fiend,* this no nay: / . . . It were great pity, thou werte forlore, / With such a *devillishe Fende of Hell*" (sig. Aiii^v). (Compare Baptista: "thou hilding of a *devilish spirit*"—2.1.26. Hortensio: "From all such *devils,* good Lord deliver us"—1.1.66. Gremio: "*this fiend of hell*"—88. Tranio: "Why she's *a devil, a devil, the devil's dam*"—3.2.156.) The suitor is unperturbed by the father's warning: "Me thinketh she is *withouten evell*" (sig. [Aiv]^r). (Compare Petruchio: "I know she is an irksome, brawling scold; / If that be all, masters, I heare *no harm*" 1.2.187–88.) Accordingly the wedding goes forward: the bride and groom go to church, "And *after them* followed a full great *rout*" (sig. Biii^v). (Compare Gremio's report upon returning from the church: "and *after me* I know, the *rout* is coming"—3.2.181.) At the wedding feast the father sadly reflects that his daught is "as *angry* y wis as ever was *waspe*" (sig. [Biv]^v). (Compare Petruchio: "Come, come, you *wasp,* i' faith you are too *angry*"—2.1.209.) Removed to the husband's house in the country, the wife behaves very badly indeed, openly challenging the husband for the mastery, tyrannizing over the servants, reducing the household to a state of disorder, at one point refusing to provide dinner for the husband, and finally striking him: "And sodaynly with her fyst she did him hit" (sig. [Eiv]^v). (Similarly Kate, in the "wooing" scene, strikes Petruchio, for he says, "I sweare I'll cuff you if you strike again"—2.1.215.) At this the husband proceeds to "tame" the wife, by dint of birch rods and Morel's skin. At the end of the story the father, mother, and neighbors, entertained at a dinner, marvel at the wife's "good behavyour." (Similarly the guests at Lucentio's banquet marvel at the demonstration of Kate's obedience.) And in a jingling postscript the author or narrator makes a handsome offer to his readers or auditors: "*He that can charme a shrewde wyfe, / Better then thus: / Let him come to me, and fetch ten pound, / And a golden purse*" (sig. [Fiv]^v). (Compare Petruchio's challenge, in soliloquy, to the theater audience: "*He that knows better how to tame a shrew, / Now let him speak—*'tis charity to show"—4.2.205.) All of these details but the shrewish mother, the termagant behavior of a wife in the *fabliau* tradition (as opposed to the ill-tempered behavior of a spoiled young woman), and the brutal "taming" crop up, transmuted, in Shakespeare's play.

Petruchio "tames" Kate not by beating her but by bringing her to an awareness of her shrewishness and thus inducing her to mend her ways. Or, to put it differently, he "cures" her of chronic bad temper. And he effects the cure, as the more perceptive critics have noted, by behaving every bit as capriciously and exasperatingly as she does. More shrew than she, he kills her in her own humor; in fact, he out-Kates Kate. The business of driving out poison with poison, of fighting fire with fire, of driving out one nail with another, is typically Elizabethan—though Petruchio's particular use of the technique appears to be Shakespeare's original contribution to the literature of shrew-taming. And the business of "training" a wife to accept a viable social relationship to her husband, as one would teach a colt to go through its paces or a hawk to fly to the lure, is a commonplace of humanist discussions of marriage. One example seems especially relevant to *The Taming of the Shrew*.

This, which may be regarded as either a source or an analogue, is a colloquy of Erasmus anonymously translated into English as *A Mery Dialogue, Declaringe the Propertyes of Shrowde Shrewes, and Honest Wyves* (1557).[17] The persons of the dialogue are Xantippa, a young wife grown shrewish in response to her husband's habitual drunkenness and general bad behavior, and her friend Eulalia, a more experienced wife who counsels Xantippa to be patient and gently lead her husband to amendment.

> *Xantippa.* He his beyonde goddes forbode, he will never amende[.]
> *Eulalia.* Eye saye not so, there is no beest so wild but by fayre handling be tamed, . . . yet recken what paines ye toke or ye colde teache your paret to speake. (sigs. B5ᵛ, C1ᵛ)

(Earlier [sig. A6], Eulalia had compared the managing of her own husband to the taming of "Elephantes and Lyons

[17]*STC* 10455. I have used the copy in the British Museum. The analogue was noted by R. A. Houk, "Shakespeare's Heroic Shrew," *SAB* 18 (1943): 181–82.

or suche beastes that can not be wonne by strength.") Xantippa's situation has two aspects, both significant in the present context. She is a shrew who must cope with a male shrew. (Similarly Kate must cope with Petruchio.) But, being only shrewish in response to her husband's shrewishness, Xantippa is also a potentially "reasonable" wife who is advised to alter her customary behavior in order to induce her husband to mend his ways. (Similarly, the sexes being reversed, the "reasonable" Petruchio—in behaving like a shrew—alters *his* customary behavior in order to induce Kate to mend *her* ways.) These resemblances of situation are admittedly general, but their relevance is strengthened, I believe, by two specific verbal links with Shakespeare's play. In relating how her husband went to attack her after she had remonstrated with him for coming home drunk in the middle of the night, Xantippa says: "I gat me *a thre foted stole* in hand, and he had but ones layd his littell finger on me, he shulde not have found me lame" (sig. A3ᵛ). (Compare Kate's words to Hortensio: "But if it were, doubt not her care should be / To comb your noddle with a *three-legged stoole*"—1.1.63–64.) The other verbal link (which crops up in Shakespeare only a few lines after the first) is found in an *exemplum,* narrated by Eulalia, which is itself an analogue to *The Taming of the Shrew,* containing several details which have general parallels in the play. It is the story of a young wife who had been brought up in the country by her mother and father to hunt and to hawk. Her husband "would have one that were unbroken, because he might the soner breake her after hys owne mind" (sig. A8ᵛ). He attempts to instruct his wife in learning, singing, playing, repetition of what she had heard at sermons, and "other things that myght have doone her more good in time to come."

This gere, because it was strange unto this young woman which at home was brought up in all ydelnesse, and with the light communication of her Fathers servauntes, and other pastimes, began to waxe grevouse and paynfull, unto her. She withdrew her good mynde and dylygence and when her husband called upon her she *put the finger in the eye,* and wepte and many times she would fal downe on the grounde, beatynge her head ageynst the floure, as one that woulde be out of thys worlde.

(Compare Kate's sarcasm at Bianca's expense: "A pretty peat, it is best *Put finger in the eye,* and she knew why"— 1.1.78–79.) At a loss, the husband takes the wife home to her father's house, where he asks the father "to lay to hys hande in amendinge his doughters fautes."

her father answered that he had ones given him his doughter, and yf that she woulde not be rewled by wordes (a goddes name take Stafforde lawe) she was his owne. Then the gentylman sayd agayne, I know that I may do but I had lever have her amended eyther by youre good counsell or commaundement, then to come unto that extreme waies, her father promised that he woulde fynde a remedye. (sigs. B1ᵛ–2ʳ)

The father scolds his daughter, frightens her, and prevails upon her to repent; and she proceeds to mend her ways. The parallels with Shakespeare are the bad behavior of a spoiled young woman (not a virago in the *fabliau* tradition), the return of husband and wife to her father's house, and the husband's bringing about an amendment of his wife's bad behavior without resort to beating her.

Two other contemporary discussions of marriage, both by Princess Mary's tutor, Juan Vives, are neither sources nor analogues to *The Taming of the Shrew* but do help to define the humanist tradition of inducing a shrewish wife to mend her ways, which Shakespeare evidently preferred to the *fabliau* tradition of wife-beating. The first is *The Office and Duetie of an Husband*, translated by Thomas Paynell.[18] In this, Vives advises the husband never to proceed to the extreme of violence—so long as his wife is chaste (sig. 2A5ʳ). "The bow must not be broken with to muche bendynge therof" (sig. 2A5ᵛ). Rather, the husband should seek to "purge" his wife of a vice (sig. 2B2ᵛ). And Vives, like Erasmus, uses the image of training an animal:

---

[18]London, ca. 1553, *STC* 24855 (copy in the Huntington Library).

The Breaker of horsses that doeth use to ride and to pace theym, doeth handle the rough and sturdy colte with all crafte and fearcenes that maye be, but with it that is more tractable, he taketh not so great payne. A sharpe wyfe must be pleased and mitigated with love, and ruled wyth Majestye. (sig. N7ᵛ)

(Similarly Petruchio compares, at some length, his "taming" of Kate to the training of a hawk.) The other discussion of marriage by Vives is in *A Very Fruteful and Pleasant Boke Callyd the Instruction of a Christen Woman*, translated by Richard Hyrde in about 1529.[19] A significant passage deals with the relation of the wife to the husband:

The woman is nat rekened the more worshipfull amonge men, that presumeth to have maystrye above hir housbande: but the more folysshe, and the more woorthy to be mocked: yea and more over than that, cursed and unhappy: the whiche turneth backewarde the lawes of nature, lyke as though a souldiour wolde rule his capi- tayne, or the mone wolde stande above the sonne, or the arme above the head. For in wedlocke the man resembleth the reason, and the woman the body. Nowe reason ought to rule, and the body to obey, if a man wyll lyve. Also saynte Paule sayth: The head of the woman is the man. (foll. 71ᵛ–72ʳ)

(Compare Kate's long speech on the proper subordination of wife to husband: "Such duty as the subject owes the prince, / Even such a woman oweth to her husband"— 5.2.155–56.) And another significant passage suggests the paradox (sometimes emphasized in modern productions by an ironic delivery of Kate's speech on subordination of the wife) that she who is ruled can also rule:

But on the other partie, if thou by vertuous lyvyng and buxumnes, geve hym cause to love the, thou shalte be maistres in a mery house, thou shalte rejoyse, thou shalt be gladde, thou shalt blesse the daie that thou were maryed unto hym, and all them that were helping there unto. The wyse sentence saieth: *A good woman by lowely obeysaunce ruleth hir husbande.* (fol. 64)

[19]I have used the edition of 1541, *STC* 24858 (copy in the Huntington Library).

At least three elements of the main plot of *The Taming of the Shrew* have identifiable sources or analogues. The first is the episode of Petruchio's rating the tailor for cutting Kate's gown in fantastical fashion (4.3). A source or analogue of this episode appears in Gerard Legh's *Accedens of Armory* (1562), a discursive dialogue on the science of armorial bearings.[20] Legh relates the following anecdote about Sir Philip Caulthrop, a knight of Norwich in the time of Henry VII. Sir Philip brought some fine French tawny and commissioned his tailor to make it into a gown. John Drakes, a shoemaker, happened to see the cloth at the tailor's, was pleased by it, and asked the tailor to make him a gown of the same material and in the same fashion as the knight's. During a fitting the knight noticed the second gown and, when apprised of the situation, commanded that his own gown be "made as full of cuts as thy sheres can make it." Both gowns, of course, were so treated, and Drakes was furious when he discovered the state of his. "I have don nothing quoth the Tailor, but that you bade mee, for as sir Philip Caltrops is, even so have I made yours. By my latchet quoth John Drake, I will never were gentlemans fashion againe" (fol. 112).

The second is the episode of Kate's agreeing with Petruchio in his assertion of what is palpably untrue, to the consternation of Vincentio whom they have met on the road (4.5). An analogue of this episode occurs in *El Conde Lucanor*, a collection of stories made by Don Juan Manuel, Infante of Castile, in 1335–47.[21] Vascuñana, the wife of Don Alvar Fañez, is a paragon, and accordingly he treats her very well. His nephew criticizes him as uxorious. Shortly thereafter Don Alvar and the nephew go on a journey together, and Don Alvar sends for his wife. While they are waiting they see a herd of cows which Don Alvar calls mares. The nephew protests. When Vascuñana

---

[20]I have used the edition of 1568, *STC* 15389 (copy in the Huntington Library).

[21]*Count Lucanor*, trans. James York (London, 1898), Ch. 5. The analogue was noted by J. O. Halliwell, ed., *The Shrew* (1856). A direct connection with Shakespeare has been (rightly) denied by M. Alcalá, "Don Juan Manuel y Shakespeare: Una Influencia Imposible," *Filosofía y Letras*, 10 (1945), 55–67.

arrives she supports her husband, maintaining that the animals are indeed mares, even though she knows perfectly well that they are cows. She behaves similarly in the case of a herd of mares which Don Alvar calls cows, and in that of a river which he insists is flowing toward its source. The nephew is confounded, and Don Alvar lectures him on the satisfactions of having an agreeable wife.

And the third is the wager which Petruchio, Lucentio, and Hortensio make on their waives' obedience (5.2). An analogue of this episode occurs in *The Book of the Knight of La Tour-Landry,* a collection of stories made by the Angevin knight Geoffrey de la Tour-Landry in 1372–73 and translated into English by Caxton (who printed his own translation in 1484).[22] Here three merchants wager a jewel, to be won by him whose wife obeys best. Each will order his wife to jump into a basin set before her. The first and second wives in turn refuse to obey, and each is in turn beaten by her husband. The merchants then pass to the house of the third merchant, where he entertains them at a dinner. Before being put to the test, the third wife misunderstands her husband to say jump on the table ("Sayle sur table") when he is only calling for salt ("Sail" or "Sel sur table"). She obeys his supposed command, making a frightful mess of the food, wine, and tableware, and this so amuses the others that they judge her husband to have won the wager and do not require the test of the basin. Points of contact with *The Taming of the Shrew* are the wager and the obedience test won by the third wife, the merchant's closing dinner-table comment on the impropriety of beating a wife of gentle station (compare Petruchio's forbearance in this regard).

The source of the subplot of *The Taming of the Shrew* is generally acknowledged to be Ariosto's *Suppositi,* or rather Gascoigne's English translation of Ariosto, the *Supposes* (1573; printed by Bullough). Shakespeare's

---

[22]*STC* 15296. I have used the edition by G. B. Rawlings, *The Booke of Thenseygnementes and Techynge that the Knyght of the Towre Made to His Doughters* (London, 1902). A variant translation in manuscript has been edited by Thomas Wright for the EETS (Oxford, 1868). The analogue was noted by Albert H. Tolman, "Shakespeare's Part in *The Taming of the Shrew,*" *PMLA* 5 (1890): 238–39.

debt to the tradition of Renaissance romantic comedy
(whether English or Italian) is generally recognized in his
suppression of Polynesta's promiscuity and pregnancy,[23]
as also in his giving Bianca a much larger share in the
action than Polynesta (who comes on stage only twice, and
then to speak in only one scene). Other significant aspects
of Shakespeare's handling of the story are perhaps less
widely recognized. Chief among these are the shift of the
story from the retrospective to the progressive mode of
drama (and Ariosto's skillful conformance to the unities,
incidentally, is itself deserving of praise); the provision in
Hortensio of a second undercover wooer for Bianca, with
the result that the girl exercises choice between competi-
tive suitors who have secret access to her; and the addition
of a "stolen marriage"—not strictly necessary for the
conduct of the plot (since the arrival of the true Vincentio would itself untie all knots) but expressive of the
romantic-comedy principle (as in *The Merry Wives of
Windsor*) that true lovers should proceed to marry whom
they like, without regard for their parents' wishes. The
character type of the sympathetic rival suitor (Hortensio,
as opposed to the aged suitor, Gremio, or the fake suitor,
Tranio) and the device of the stolen marriage, since these
occur neither in Roman comedy nor in the *Supposes,* evidently came to Shakespeare from the tradition of Renaissance romantic comedy—perhaps specifically from the
commedia erudita. Hortensio serves also to link main plot
and subplot, and since his character as suitor is essentially
sympathetic (though gently mocked) he is matched with
the Widow—a sort of *madonna ex machina*—at the end of
the play.

Shakespeare took the names *Petruchio* and *Litio* (Hortensio's alias) from the names of servants in the *Supposes.*
The former is of course a phonetic spelling (with vocalic
"i") of *Petrucio* or *Petruccio* (with nonvocalic "i") and
should never be given the vulgar pronunciation *Petrukio.*
A short textual note may be advanced about the latter. In

---

[23]Compare H. B. Charlton, *Shakespearian Comedy* (London, 1938), Ch. 4.
This essay is especially useful in relating *The Taming of the Shrew* to traditions of the *commedia erudita.*

the Folio text (1623) the name is spelled *Litio* at 2.1.60, 3.1.54, and 3.2.147, *Lisio* at 4.2.1, 15, 16 and 49. The Second Folio (1632) reads *Licio* at 2.1.60, and Rowe (1709) and subsequent editors read *Licio* throughout (whence occasionally the mispronunciation *Leechi-io* or *Leech-o*). But *Litio*, the form in the *Supposes*, is a spelling variant of *Lizio*, the form in Ariosto's verse version of the *Suppositi* (*Lico* in the prose). The name is apparently a joke in the New Comedy tradition of significant names, for *lizio* is an old Italian word for garlic (Hoare's *Italian Dictionary*; the word does not appear in Florio's *World of Words*). Since *Lisio* appears to be a phonetic spelling of *Litio*, an editor may justifiably read Litio throughout a normalized old-spelling text. One other, rather puzzling, aspect of Shakespeare's text may be mentioned. In Gascoigne (and Ariosto) the fake father is a merchant. The corresponding character in Shakespeare is also a merchant, though this does not seem to have been generally noticed: "For I have bills for money by exchange / From Florence, and must here deliver them" (4.2.89–90). Yet he is invariably called a Pedant in the stage directions and speech-headings! Apparently Shakespeare chose the wrong profession from the alternatives which, in the dialogue (64–65), he himself put into Biondello's mouth: "Master, a Marcantant [i.e., *mercatante*], or a pedant, / I know not what."

Shakespeare's names *Tranio* (connoting "revealer, clarifier") and *Grumio* (connoting "clodhopper") have sources in the *Mostellaria* of Plautus, as do also the contrasting characters of clever servant and thickheaded one.[24] (But the two types of slave are generally characteristic of Roman comedy.) Grumio's beating at Petruchio's hands is paralleled in the *Mostellaria*, and the Tranio of that play (like Shakespeare's Tranio and Ariosto's Dulipo) deceives the father of his young master. Two devices of the plot which came to Shakespeare from the *Supposes* have ultimate origins in Roman comedy: the exchange of identity between servant and master, in *The Captives* of Plautus

---

[24]*Mostellaria*, ed. Edwin W. Fay (New York, 1902), pp. 63–64.

(where, however, the context of the device is not amatory);
and (as Bullough points out) the "lock-out," in the
Amphitruo of Plautus (where the context of the device is
amatory), already used by Shakespeare in *The Comedy of
Errors*. Ariosto followed Plautus (*The Captives*) in providing an end-of-the-play "recognition" of Dulipo as Cleander's long-lost son. By this token Shakespeare's Tranio
should turn out to be Gremio's son—but perhaps Shakespeare (who in any case did not give Gremio Cleander's
strong motivation to get a son and heir) wished to avoid an
additional complication of his last scene, even at the
expense of seeming to leave both Tranio and Gremio out
in the cold. For that matter, the curious treatment (in the
last scene) of Tranio as Lucentio's equal in rank may well
be a fossil of Dulipo's "recognition" in the *Supposes*.

At least one element of the subplot of *The Taming of the
Shrew* has an identifiable analogue. This is the device of
Lucentio's wooing of Bianca under the guise of construing
a Latin text (3.1). The analogue occurs in R.W.'s play *The
Three Lords and Three Ladies of London* (1590).[25] In Simplicity's directions for the punishment of Fraud we are
again in the classroom—though in a lower form from that
to which Bianca, in reading Ovid's *Epistolae heroidum*,
has attained:

> O Singulariter *Nominativo,* wise Lord *pleasure: Genetivo* bind him
> to that poste, *Dativo.* give me my torch, *Accusat.* For I say he's a
> cosoner. *Vocat.* O give me roome to run at him. *Ablat.* take and
> blind me. *Pluraliter, per omnes casus.* Laugh all you to see mee in
> my choller adust to burne and to broile that false *Fraud* to dust.
> (sig. 13ᵛ)

But the general conception of Shakespeare's scene may
have a source or analogue in some example of the *commedia erudita* in which an *innamorato* disguises himself
as a *pedante* in order to gain access to a *donzella*.

Finally, the induction to *The Taming of the Shrew* has a
generally acknowledged source in the story of "The

[25] *STC* 25783 (copy in the Huntington Library). The analogue was noted by
Gollancz, ed., *The Shrew* (1896).

Sleeper Awakened" (ultimately from *The Arabian Nights*), either in the version contained in a letter from Vives to Francis Duke of Béjar,[26] in a lost collection of stories compiled by Richard Edwards and printed in 1570,[27] or in the *De rebus burgundicis* of Heuterus (1584). The story in Heuterus was translated into French by Goulart, in his *Thrésor d'histoires admirables et mémorables de nostre temps* (1600); and Goulart's version was translated into English by Grimeston (1607). (Bullough prints Grimeston.) The version in Heuterus (as represented by Grimeston) is suggestive since the viewing of "a pleasant Comedie" is included in the entertainment of the deluded artisan who corresponds to Shakespeare's Sly. In all narrative versions of the story we are told of the return of the artisan to his original condition before elevation to high rank. But in Shakespeare's dramatic version (the first in which the story is used as introduction to an actual play) Sly drops out of the action after the first scene of the play proper and is (apparently) forgotten. This fact and the appearance of a "dramatic epilogue" in *The Taming of a Shrew* have led some scholars to suppose that the Folio text of *The Shrew* is defective in omitting a dramatic epilogue by Shakespeare. However, as I have suggested elsewhere,[28] there would have been a number of reasons for Shakespeare's apparent failure to provide a dramatic epilogue: a desire to avoid the anticlimax which would result from a return, at the end of the play proper, to the different fictional situation of the induction; a desire to present, not (as in *A Shrew*) Sly's learning of a lesson in shrew-taming (Shakespeare's Sly seems not to have a wife), but Sly's being persuaded by the Lord to accept a new personality (for exactly so will Petruchio persuade Kate); and a desire to facilitate the Elizabethan theatrical practice of doubling parts of the induction with parts of the play proper—for an awkward pause would have been

[26]See Foster Watson, "Shakespeare and Two Stories of Luis Vives," *Nineteenth Century* 85 (1919): 297–306.

[27]Thomas Warton records having seen the book in his *History of English Poetry* (London, 1775), Sec. 52.

[28]"Was There a 'Dramatic Epilogue' to *The Taming of the Shrew*?" *SEL* 1 (1961): 17–34; ed. *The Shrew* (1964), p. 24.

necessary to enable actors on stage at the end of the play to return to the costumes of their roles in the induction.

From the present study there emerges an understanding of Shakespeare's *Taming of the Shrew* as a synthesis of many sources and traditions.[29] The induction derives from the story of "The Sleeper Awakened," perhaps as told by Heuterus in *De rebus burgundicis.* The basic situation of the play proper is taken from the anonymous ballad of *A Shrewde and Curste Wyfe.* The main plot is animated, however, not by the *fabliau* tradition of beating a virago into submission, but by the humanist tradition of inducing a spoiled young wife to mend her ways—perhaps specifically by the *Shrewd Shrews and Honest Wives* of Erasmus. The basic situation of the play proper is filled out with a subplot derived from Gascoigne's *Supposes,* and both actions are embellished with episodes taken from traditions represented by analogues in Gerard Legh's *Accedens of Armory,* Don Juan Manuel's *Conde Lucanor, The Book of the Knight of La Tour-Landry,* and R.W.'s *Three Lords and Three Ladies of London.* Two names come from the *Mostellaria* of Plautus, and much of the spirit and technique of the play comes from Roman comedy in general, much also from romantic comedy of the Renaissance— perhaps specifically from the *commedia erudita.* Further search should turn up additional sources and analogues, certainly of details, possibly of major elements in the three actions of the play.[30]

[29]A story (viii.2) in Straparola's *Piacevoli notti* (1560), though suggested as an analogue by Halliwell, ed. *The Shrew* (1856), and subsequent editors, seems to have no particular connection with *The Taming of the Shrew.*

[30]It is a pleasure to record my indebtedness to the Director and Trustees of the Henry E. Huntington Library for a fellowship grant which made possible the research on which this article is based.

MAYNARD MACK

From Engagement and Detachment in
Shakespeare's Plays

Finally, toward the beginning of Shakespeare's career, we have Sly in *The Taming of the Shrew*. Even in the anonymous play *A Shrew*, but much more in Shakespeare's version, we confront in Sly's experience after being thrown out of the alehouse what appears to be an abstract and brief chronicle of how stage illusion takes effect. Sly, having fallen briefly into one of those mysterious sleeps that Shakespeare elsewhere attributes to those who are undergoing the power of a dramatist, wakes to find the identity of a rich lord thrust upon him, rejects it at first, knowing perfectly well who he is ("Christopher Sly, old Sly's son, of Burton-heath. . . . Ask Marian Hacket, the fat ale-wife of Wincot, if she know me not"— Induction, 2.17–22), then is engulfed by it, accepts the dream as reality, accepts also a dressed-up players' boy to share the new reality with him as his supposed lady, and at last sits down with her beside him to watch the strolling players put on *The Taming of the Shrew*. Since Sly's newly assumed identity has no result whatever except to bring him face to face with a play, it is tempting to imagine him a witty paradigm of all of us as theatergoers, when we awake out of our ordinary reality of the alehouse, or whatever other reality ordinarily encompasses us, to the super-

From *Essays on Shakespeare and Elizabethan Drama in Honor of Hardin Craig,* edited by Richard Hosley (Columbia, Missouri: University of Missouri Press, 1962), pp. 279–80. Reprinted by permission of the University of Missouri Press. Copyright © 1962 by the Curators of the University of Missouri.

imposed reality of the playhouse, and find that there (at any rate, so long as a comedy is playing) wishes are horses and beggars do ride. Sly, to be sure, soon disengages himself from the strollers' play and falls asleep; but in Shakespeare's version—the situation differs somewhat in *A Shrew*[1]—his engagement to his identity as a lord, though presumably broken when the play ends, stretches into infinity for anything we are ever told.

This way of considering Sly is the more tempting in that the play as a whole manipulates the theme of displaced identity in a way that can hardly be ignored. For what the Lord and his Servants do in thrusting a temporary identity on Sly is echoed in what Petruchio does for Kate at a deeper level of psychic change. His gambits in taming her are equally displacements of identity: first, in thrusting on himself the rude self-will which actually belongs to her, so that she beholds what she now is in his mirror, and he (to quote his man Peter) "kills her in her own humor" (4.1.174); and second, in thrusting on her the semblance of a modest, well-conducted young woman—

> 'Twas told me you were coy and rough and sullen,
> And now I find report a very liar,
> For thou art pleasant, gamesome, passing courteous—
>
> (2.1.237–39)

so that she beholds in another mirror what she may become if she tries, in the manner of Hamlet's advice to his mother:

> Assume a virtue, if you have it not.
> That monster, custom, who all sense doth eat
> Of habits evil, is angel yet in this,
> That to the use of actions fair and good
> He likewise gives a frock or livery
> That aptly is put on.
>
> (3.4.161–66)

---

[1] In *A Shrew*, Sly wakes up resolved to try out what he has gleaned of the play's purport before falling asleep, and tame his own shrew at home.

Petruchio's stratagem is thus more than an entertaining stage device. It parodies the idolatrousness of romantic love which, as Theseus says, is always seeing Helen in a brow of Egypt; but it also reflects love's genuine creative power, which can on occasion make the loved one grow to match the dream. Lucentio, possibly because identity for him is only skin-deep, as the nature of his disguises seems to show, takes the surface for what it appears to be (like Aragon and Morocco in *The Merchant of Venice*), and though he wins the girl discovers he has not won the obedient wife he thought. In Geoffrey Bullough's words, he falls victim to "the last (and richest) 'Suppose' of all."[2]

---

[2] *Narrative and Dramatic Sources of Shakespeare* (1957), p. 68.

GERMAINE GREER

From The Female Eunuch

The opposition between women who are people and women who are something less does not only rest in the vague contrast between the women of the comedies and the women of tragedies. There are more explicit examples of women who may earn love, like Helena who pursued her husband through military brothels to marriage and honor in *All's Well*, the women who must lose it through inertia and gormlessness, like Cressida. In *The Taming of the Shrew* Shakespeare contrasted two types in order to present a theory of marriage which is demonstrated by the explicit valuation of both kinds of wooing in the last scene. Kate is a woman striving for her own existence in a world where she is a *stale*, a decoy to be bid for against her sister's higher market value, so she opts out by becoming unmanageable, a scold. Bianca has found the women's way of guile and feigned gentleness to pay better dividends: she woos for herself under false colors, manipulating her father and her suitors in a perilous game which could end in her ruin. Kate courts ruin in a different way, but she has the uncommon good fortune to find Petruchio, who is man enough to know what he wants and how to get it. He wants her spirit and her energy because he wants a wife worth keeping. He tames her as he might a hawk or a high-mettled horse, and she rewards him with strong

From *The Female Eunuch* by Germaine Greer. (New York: McGraw-Hill, 1971), pp. 205–06. Reprinted with the permission of McGraw-Hill Book Company and International Creative Management, Inc.

sexual love and fierce loyalty. Lucentio finds himself saddled with a cold, disloyal woman, who has no objection to humiliating him in public. The submission of a woman like Kate is genuine and exciting because she has something to lay down, her virgin pride and individuality: Bianca is the soul of duplicity, married without earnestness or good will. Kate's speech at the close of the play is the greatest defense of Christian monogamy ever written. It rests upon the role of a husband as protector and friend, and it is valid because Kate has a man who is capable of being both, for Petruchio is both gentle and strong (it is a vile distortion of the play to have him strike her ever). The message is probably twofold: only Kates make good wives, and then only to Petruchios; for the rest, their cake is dough.

ALEXANDER LEGGATT

From Shakespeare's Comedy of Love

As in *The Comedy of Errors*, a world of romance and a world of money collide. But the ultimate outcome is rather different. In the end, the marriage of Bianca and Lucentio is shown as satisfying both the conventions of romance and the conventions of society: the young man is both a successful lover and a good catch. But this satisfaction does not outlast the final scene. An extra factor is introduced, which plays havoc with both conventions—the character of Bianca herself. The heroine of *Supposes*, though technically the center of the action, appeared only briefly; but Bianca is given a character, and a will, of her own. Her sweet disposition is part of a deeper strategy, as Katherina recognizes: "Her silence flouts me and I'll be revenged" (2.1.29). When we see her with her rival tutors, her essential nature is revealed:

> I am no breeching scholar in the schools.
> I'll not be tied to hours nor 'pointed times,
> But learn my lessons as I please myself.

(3.1.18–20)

And throughout the scene she keeps a subtle but firm control over the men. Her conduct at the end will be more surprising for Lucentio than for the audience. Both socially and artistically, he has won a conventional sweetheart in a

From *Shakespeare's Comedy of Love* by Alexander Leggatt (London: Methuen, 1974), pp. 48–62.

conventional way; and when the prize turns out to have been a baited trap, not merely the character but the conventions he has operated under are mocked.

The inadequacy of both conventions is that they take too little account of personality. Bianca can play her role in a courtship, and her role in a business transaction, without revealing her true face. But the play, unlike so many romantic comedies, goes on for one scene after marriage, and Lucentio learns to his dismay what lay behind that romantic sweetness. On the other hand, Petruchio has been concerned with personality all along. The taming plot presents in a deeper, more psychological way ideas that are handled superficially and externally in the romantic plot. Education is one such idea: Bianca is surrounded by instructors, none of whose credentials would bear examination; they have really come to win her, not to teach her (the one real pedant in the play is disguised as someone else). But Petruchio, in his "taming school" (4.2.54), really does teach Kate, and teaches her that inner order of which the music and the mathematics offered to Bianca are only a reflection. Disguise is also treated differently in the two plots: Petruchio disguises himself as a ruffian and a bully (I will argue later that this *is* only a disguise); and he achieves more with this psychological transformation than do the suitors of the other plot, no matter how many hats, robes, and false noses they may don. This repeats a process I have mentioned before: one world builds on features of another world, but develops them in its own way. The Bianca plot is introduced first, and the taming plot may be said to be (in part) a reflection of it at a deeper level; but in the bulk of the play the two plots run along side by side, and we are led to compare them. The most striking effect, perhaps, is in 5.1, when the false Vincentio confronts the real one. Here the external, farcical confusion of the Bianca plot reaches its climax; and this frantic scene is watched by Katherina and Petruchio, who are above the battle, having achieved their own peace already in a scene with the same Vincentio, playing a game of confusion with ideas rather than names and faces.

Petruchio, like Lucentio, has a literary tradition behind

him; but it is the older, more elusive tradition of folktale.[1] Lucentio is irrational, but in a familiar way; he lives in a daylight world, and we have no difficulty understanding anything he does. Petruchio's behavior can in the end be rationalized, but it strikes us at first as strange and eccentric, a series of private jokes he does not always share with us: Motive and action are connected in an oblique, sometimes puzzling way. He has a tinge of the exotic, bringing with him suggestions of a world of adventure quite different from the closeted worlds of money and learning inhabited by the other characters:

> Have I not in my time heard lions roar?
> Have I not heard the sea, puffed up with winds,
> Rage like an angry boar chafèd with sweat?
> Have I not heard great ordnance in the field,
> And heaven's artillery thunder in the skies?
> Have I not in a pitchèd battle heard
> Loud 'larums, neighing steeds, and trumpets' clang?

                                              (1.2.200–6)

He invades the ordered propriety of Padua like a natural force, and the feelings of the inhabitants are considerably ruffled in the process. (His behavior at his wedding is much more piquant for being seen through the outraged eyes of Gremio than it would be if we saw it straight.) No small part of the disruption is that he professes the conventional social motives, but more blatantly than is socially acceptable:

> I come to wive it wealthily in Padua;
> If wealthily, then happily in Padua.

                                              (74–75)

> She is my goods, my chattels; she is my house,
> My household stuff, my field, my barn,
> My horse, my ox, my ass, my anything,
> And here she stands. Touch her whoever dare.

                                              (3.2.230–33)

---

[1]Folktale analogies with the taming plot are discussed by Jan Harold Brunvald, "The folktale origin of *The Taming of the Shrew*," *Shakespeare Quarterly* XVII (Autumn 1966): 345-59.

The citizens of Padua would probably agree with both attitudes; but it is part of their decorum not to insist on them so brazenly (though Baptista comes quite close). And Petruchio at times is simply rude: "If she and I be pleased, what's that to you?" (2.1.296). He woos roughly, dresses like a madman and brawls at his own wedding; and the native population responds with a mixture of chuckling appreciation and shock. But the occasional attempts by other characters to insist on proper behavior are undermined by irony. Gremio says of his wooing, "You are too blunt; go to it orderly" (45), but since Petruchio's entrance has been accompanied by no fewer than three other characters in disguise (one of them introduced by Gremio himself), the old man's insistence on the proprieties seems comically out of place. Similarly, the character who rebukes him most roundly for his appearance at the wedding—"See not your bride in these unreverent robes. / Go to my chamber; put on clothes of mine" (3.2.112–13)—is Tranio, who has much less right to the clothes he is wearing than Petruchio does.

Katherina is a match for him in that she too is unorthodox. Instead of playing, as Bianca does, the dutiful, submissive daughter, she asserts her own will quite overtly. She objects to being treated simply as part of Bianca's wedding arrangements: "I pray you, sir, is it your will / To make a stale of me amongst these mates?" (1.1.57–58). It should be noted that she has wrung one important concession from her father by her behavior: he insists that whoever marries her must do so "when the special thing is well obtained, / That is, her love, for that is all in all" (2.1.128–29). There is obviously no point in trying to match her against her will. But he makes no such conditions with Bianca, whose will he assumes he can control, whose love he thinks he can give to the highest bidder:

'Tis deeds must win the prize, and he of both
That can assure my daughter greatest dower
Shall have my Bianca's love.

                                                    (335–37)

The shrew's unorthodox behavior has its value, forcing attention to her personality and her wishes, keeping her from being simply a counter in a social game.

It is in this sense, however, that Petruchio "kills her in her own humor" (4.1.174), for he attacks her through a disruption of orthodox behavior far more drastic than her own. It is more drastic, paradoxically, because it operates at a seemingly more trivial level: he disrupts the ordinary social amenities that she has taken for granted all her life—food, sleep, clothing. The devastating effect on Katherina demonstrates the truth of the Abbess's lecture to Adriana in *The Comedy of Errors*: "In food, in sport, and life-preserving rest / To be disturbed, would mad or man or beast" (5.1.83–84). Our comfort and our sense of well-being depend on the smooth operation of the normal domestic round. Yet in denying her this Petruchio claims, paradoxically, that he is acting the loving husband:

> As with the meat, some undeservèd fault
> I'll find about the making of the bed,
> And here I'll fling the pillow, there the bolster,
> This way the coverlet, another way the sheets.
> Ay, and amid this hurly I intend
> That all is done in reverent care of her.

> (4.1.193–98)

He concludes, "This is a way to kill a wife with kindness" (202). Throughout his behavior runs this constant sense of paradox, of a crazy inversion of motive and action: with a fine display of choler, he throws the meat away—because it engenders choler (155–69); in their bedchamber, on their wedding night, he preaches "a sermon of continency to her, / And rails and swears and rates" (176–77). Simple bullying would, one feels, produce an equally simple reaction, enraged resistance or blind submission. But Petruchio's paradoxical behavior teases Katherina's mind into action. She picks up the incongruity in his "kindness":

And that which spites me more than all these wants,
He does it under name of perfect love,
As who should say, if I should sleep or eat
'Twere deadly sickness or else present death.

(4.3.11–14)

She offers no explicit explanation; but clearly her mind is running on the nature of "perfect love," and her worries over food and sleep are a stimulus to reflection on this deeper issue.

In place of the clear motives and two-dimensional action of the Bianca plot, we have a more oblique dramatic method. There is no explicit statement from Katherina or Petruchio as to why this bizarre, inverted image of love should have the effect it does. We, like Katherina, are teased into working it out for ourselves. In rejecting clothing that is merely "fashionable" (4.3.69–70, 94–97), or in overcoming Katherina's scruples about kissing in the street (5.1.142–49), Petruchio appears at first glance to be insisting on the unimportance of the more superficial social conventions. As he puts it, " 'tis the mind that makes the body rich" (4.3.170). And he had flouted conventional taste at his wedding, with an equally solemn assurance that "To me she's married, not unto my clothes" (3.2.117). The usual clichés about appearance and reality come to mind at once. But I wonder. In taking such elaborate care to dress absurdly at his wedding, and in criticizing the tailor's efforts so severely and in such detail, Petruchio actually demonstrates a concern for the importance of clothing, and a considerable fascination with it. And his behavior over Katherina's dress is of a piece with his other attacks on her domestic comfort. He seems to be demonstrating to her the *importance* of small social amenities, by denying them to her and forcing her to realize how much she depends on them. Over and over again, her dismay and indignation—at having her groom show up late for the wedding, at not being allowed her own marriage feast, at being denied food and sleep, at not being allowed to dress in the fashion, like other gentlewomen—push her, unwittingly, into being a spokesman for unconventional decent behavior. I say "unwittingly," for her responses at this point do seem to be instinctive and automatic; one imagines that if she realized too clearly what Petruchio was doing, her stubborn nature would find some means of resisting; his attack has to be oblique and paradoxical if he is to penetrate her defences—as he does.

What Petruchio is doing, as G. R. Hibbard has pointed out, is forcing Katherina "to see the value of that order and decency for which she previously had no use."[2] And, expert teacher that he is, he does this not by telling her about it himself, but by maneuvering her into telling him. She also learns sympathy for the victims of bullying, as she finds herself begging forgiveness for Petruchio's servants (4.1.150).[3] Petruchio's ironic claim to be tormenting her out of love may also be a way of demonstrating how much love—love within marriage, as distinct from the romantic love of Lucentio—expresses itself through the provision of ordinary decent comfort. All these may seem like curious lessons for Petruchio to be teaching, since he impresses us at first as a breezy disrupter of convention; but here we touch on the essential paradox of the character. After all the brawling and shouting, the end and aim of his campaign is summed up:

> Marry, peace it bodes, and love, and quiet life,
> An awful rule, and right supremacy,
> And, to be short, what not that's sweet and happy.

> (5.2.108–10)

His program is a comic exorcism of noise and violence, to achieve peace and order in the end. When we hear him assuring Vincentio that his son is well married—and this is *after* his own marriage is comfortably settled—he speaks in what, for him, is a new, surprising manner:

---

[2]Penguin introduction, p. 21.
[3]See Hibbard, Penguin introduction, and Derek Traversi, *Will'am Shakespeare: The Early Comedies* (London, 1964), p. 20.

Wonder not

Nor be not grieved. She is of good esteem,
Her dowry wealthy, and of worthy birth;
Beside, so qualified as may beseem
The spouse of any noble gentleman.

(4.5.63–67)

The madcap seems as much concerned with the respectable, nonromantic side of marriage as any citizen of
Padua.

But while analysing Petruchio's methods and abstract-
ing a philosophical pattern from them may be a necessary
critical exercise, it is not finally an adequate account of
the play. Something more intangible has to be reckoned
with: the spirit in which Petruchio goes to work. It is here
that the modern sensibility is on dangerous ground with
The Taming of the Shrew. We feel a little uncomfortable
with the harshness of Petruchio's method, with the very
real suffering he inflicts; we try to reassure ourselves
that he and Katherina are really in love all the time—
romantically in love, in the manner we are used to in
comedy—and toying affectionately with each other.[4] We
think hopefully of Beatrice and Benedick. In the theater,
performers are at great pains to assure us that since the
couple love each other, no real harm is being done; and
since the dialogue is uncooperative, they frequently resort
to mime to make the point clear.[5] It is true enough that
Petruchio is not just a sadist who beats his wife into dumb

---

[4]Modern attempts to soften the play have been surveyed—and amusingly
dissected—by Robert B. Heilman, "The 'Taming' Untamed, or the Return of
the Shrew," *Modern Language Quarterly* XXVII (June 1966): 147–51.

[5]In the Royal Shakespeare Company's 1962 production (redirected by
Maurice Daniels from John Barton's 1960 production) Katherina was re-
warded for her submission by being given back the hat Petruchio had refused
her; in Trevor Nunn's 1967 production for the same company, their first
meeting began with a long pantomime in which Petruchio pretended to have
only one arm. Katherina approached him with an expression of sympathy; her
reaction when the "missing" arm suddenly appeared combined indignation
with wry amusement. She and Petruchio were thus established as characters
who enjoyed playing games with each other. In both cases the effect was to
soften the characters' relationship, to assure us that no real wounds were being
inflicted.

submission; but to react against this view by importing too much romantic softness into the play would be to falsify it in the other direction.

One cannot deny that the taming is a rough, brutal business, and for all its effect on Katherina's mind the initial impact is physical. She journeys, dirty, wet, and starving, to an ice-cold house, where she is denied food and sleep. And yet the effect is different from the earlier, cruder shrew plays (such as *Tom Tyler and his Wife*) where if the shrew submits at all it is, in M. C. Bradbrook's words, "either to high theological argument or to a taste of the stick."[6] The taming of Katherina is more interesting, more fun to watch; otherwise the play would not be so consistently successful in the theater. It is not just that we sense the philosophical purpose behind the knockabout; there is something attractive in the knockabout itself. A clue is provided, I think, in one of the key images Petruchio uses to describe his method:

> My falcon now is sharp and passing empty,
> And till she stoop she must not be full gorged,
> For then she never looks upon her lure.
> Another way I have to man my haggard,
> To teach her come and know her keeper's call,
> That is, to watch her as we watch these kites
> That bate and beat and will not be obedient.

> (4.1.184–90)

The style of the speech reflects the tough, alert mind of the seasoned sportsman. Katherina is trained, quite literally, as one would train a hawk. (In contrast, Bianca is described in the following scene as a "proud disdainful haggard" (4.2.39) who will not be tamed.) Petruchio greets her submission with another image drawn from sport: "Thus the bowl should run / And not unluckily against the bias" (4.5.24–25). The taming of Katherina is not just a lesson but a game—a test of skill and a source of pleasure. The

[6]"Dramatic Rôle as Social Image: A Study of *The Taming of the Shrew*," *Shakespeare Jahrbuch* XCIV (1958): 134.

roughness is, at bottom, part of the fun: such is the peculiar psychology of sport that one is willing to endure aching muscles and risk the occasional broken limb for the sake of the challenge and the pleasure it provides. And the sports most often recalled throughout the play are blood sports, hunting and hawking—thus invoking in the audience the state of mind in which cruelty and violence are acceptable, even exciting, because their scope is limited by tacit agreement and they are made the occasion for a display of skill.

Similarly, the cruelty is made limited and acceptable by reminders that Petruchio is putting on an act. The memory of Sly may create some detachment in any case; but even in terms of the shrew play Petruchio is seen as a performer. In their first interview, Katherina says of his bombast, "Where did you study all this goodly speech?" (2.1.256). And a slight but visible gap opens between the character and his performance when, after his flamboyant abuse of the tailor, he asks Hortensio, aside, to assure his victim that he will be paid (4.3.162). When, by the end of the play, we realize the value Petruchio places on settled domesticity, the suggestion that his brawling was a performance becomes a virtual certainty. (It might also be noted, by the way, that Petruchio uses the sense of detachment given by a performance as the basis of one of his most ingenious taming devices: he assures the other characters that Katherina's shrewishness is only a pretence, since "'Tis bargained 'twixt us twain, being alone, / That she shall still be curst in company" (2.1.297–98). This robs Katherina of the chief means of exerting her will, since the others can no longer be sure if her displays of temper are serious. This device, however, is not developed, since, from this point on, the real issue is not her relation to the other characters but her relation to Petruchio.)

We can enjoy Petruchio's brutality, then, because it is limited and conventionalized; and this, rather than any notion of romantic love, is the real source of our pleasure in the taming. This is, when viewed dispassionately, a peculiar frame of mind, but it is common enough in spectators of sport and drama. However, it is not automatically

created by drama (as it is by some sports), and one of the
functions of the Induction is to invoke this state of mind in
preparation for Petruchio. The Lord is in many ways analogous to Petruchio. When he first appears we hear him
speaking of his hounds, with appreciation, enjoyment and
concern:

> Huntsman, I charge thee, tender well my hounds.
> Brach Merriman—the poor cur, is embossed—
> And couple Clowder with the deep-mouth'd brach.
> Saw'st thou not, boy, how Silver made it good
> At the hedge-corner in the coldest fault?
> I would not lose the dog for twenty pound.
>
> (Induction, 1.16–21)

(We may recall this passage later when Petruchio, returning
home, demands "where's my spaniel Troilus?"—4.1.134.)
The Lord is also a connoisseur of acting:

> This fellow I remember
> Since once he played a farmer's eldest son;
> 'Twas where you wooed the gentlewoman so well.
> I have forgot your name, but sure that part
> Was aptly fitted and naturally perform'd.
>
> (Induction, 1.83–87)

He later tries a hand at acting himself, impersonating one
of his own servants. Quickly but firmly, Shakespeare
establishes the Lord as a cultivated lover of pleasure. And,
like Petruchio, he has a sense of propriety beneath his
sense of fun. The first sight of Sly offends him: "O monstrous beast, how like a swine he lies! / Grim death, how
foul and loathsome is thine image!" (Induction, 1.34–35).
His joke on Sly is one more sport, a pleasant relaxation
after the day's hunting; but he sees that if it is to remain
sport, it must remain under control: "It will be pastime
passing excellent / If it be husbanded with modesty"
(Induction, 1.67–68). He looks forward to the page's performance, and the servants' reactions, but adds,

I'll in to counsel them; haply my presence
May well abate the over-merry spleen
Which otherwise would grow into extremes.

(Induction, 1.136–38)

To a compassionate eye, the Lord's treatment of Sly, like Petruchio's of Katherina, is cruel fun; but we are not allowed to be so compassionate. Sport and acting are both invoked to give us the detachment necessary to take pleasure in the trick, and the Lord's essential restraint ensures that the balance is maintained.

The appeal to our sense of sport also has important implications for the development of Katherina herself: We watch her progress, not just as a wife, but as a player in Petruchio's game. Their first interview is revealing. He begins by laying out his plan of attack quite simply: he will turn everything she does upside down, and throw her into a state of confusion (2.1.170–81). But when she appears, his early attempt to dominate the conversation breaks down as she engages him in tight, fast repartee, demonstrating that she is a keen fighter, worthy of his best efforts; and the result, as we have seen, is that his simple device of contradiction is replaced by a more subtle and intricate strategy. This increases the pleasure of the game, since there is no sport in playing too weak an opponent. And in her final transformation her sporting nature is not crushed but redirected. The location of the scene is unusual: often enough, in Shakespeare's comedies, we see the beginning or end of a journey; but here, as the dialogue emphasizes, we are on the open road, in transit between Petruchio's house and Baptista's—as it were, on neutral ground, in a free area where anything can happen. And here Katherina finally displays the fruits of Petruchio's teaching. Her obedience is signaled by submission to her husband on the most basic of matters—perception itself. She sees literally with his eyes, her mind becomes a reflection of his:

Then, God be blessed, it is the blessèd sun.
But sun it is not when you say it is not,

And the moon changes even as your mind.

(4.5.18–20)

But there is a sly rebuke in that last line, and with it an awareness that they are really playing a game. Through this awareness something like the initial balance between them is restored. Attacking her on the physical and social levels, he could break her down; but in a battle of pure wit they are well matched, and it is to this level that their relationship now returns. We see this more clearly—and we see how it squares with her new obedience—when she not only accepts her husband's description of Vincentio as a young maid, but matches the relish with which he pursues the jest, and adds a few touches of her own:

> Young budding virgin, fair and fresh and sweet,
> Whither away, or where is thy abode?
> Happy the parents of so fair a child!
> Happier the man whom favorable stars
> Allots thee for his lovely bed fellow.

(37–41)

As a wife she submits, but as a player in the game she is now a full and skillful partner. Most important, she is helping to create her own role as an obedient spouse, and the process of creation gives her pleasure. Her obedience is not meekly accepted, but embraced and enjoyed.[7]

It is this sense of pleasure that one misses most in the other shrew play, *The Taming of a Shrew*. In external action the taming scenes are much the same, but their development is too bare and economical; the fullness

---

[7]I have drawn the analogy between the Lord and Petruchio: at this point, John Russell Brown draws the analogy between Katherina and Sly, both of whom "show the gusto of actors who have been given congenial roles." See *Shakespeare and his Comedies* (2nd edition, revised: London, 1968), p. 98. Nevill Coghill also points to the "sense of fun" Katherina displays in this scene, though he comes to a conclusion about their relationship rather different from mine: "Like most of those wives that are the natural superiors of their husbands, she allows Petruchio the mastery in public." See "The Basis of Shakespearian Comedy," *Essays and Studies* III (1950): 12.

of detail is missing, and with it the zest displayed by Katherina at the beginning and end, and by Petruchio throughout. But this sense of the importance of pleasure is not just a palliative to make the taming acceptable: it is close to the heart—arguably it *is* the heart—of the play's vision of social life. It is presented as the *raison d'être* of the play performed for Sly, and for us:

> Your Honor's players, hearing your amendment,
> Are come to play a pleasant comedy.
> For so your doctors hold it very meet,
> Seeing too much sadness hath congealed your blood,
> And melancholy is the nurse of frenzy.
> Therefore they thought it good you hear a play
> And frame your mind to mirth and merriment,
> Which bars a thousand harms and lengthens life.

> (Induction, 2.129–36)

This genial theory of the function of art is matched shortly afterwards by Tranio's view of education: while acknowledging the importance of "This virtue and this moral discipline" he insists, "No profit grows where is no pleasure ta'en" (1.1.30,39). The same may be said of Petruchio's education of his wife. The final image of social pleasure is the wedding feast—which, for the only time in Shakespeare, is held on stage. Throughout we have been reminded of the civilizing influence of food and drink. It softens the rivalry of Bianca's suitors: Tranio proposes they should "do as adversaries do in law, / Strive mightily, but eat and drink as friends" (1.2.277–78). It consoles Gremio in his defeat: "My cake is dough, but I'll in among the rest / Out of hope of all but my share of the feast" (5.1.139–40). And it provides the setting for Katherina's display of obedience, placing it in a context of social pleasure and pastime.

In the wager the men lay on their wives, the analogy with sport is invoked once more, and more explicitly than ever. When Katherina spars with the Widow, their husbands cheer them on:

Petruchio.   To her, Kate!
Hortensio.   To her, Widow!
Petruchio.   A hundred marks, my Kate does put her down.

(5.2.33–35)

And when Petruchio objects to the stake—

Twenty crowns!
I'll venture so much of my hawk or hound,
But twenty times so much upon my wife—

(71–73)

the difference in the wagers seems to be one of degree, not kind. He displays a confident player's zest for the game; and he displays also a complete trust in his partner, a confidence in her ability to play her own hand. If he enjoys making the wager, Katherina enjoys winning it: The sheer length of her speech, the care she lavishes on its rhetoric, tell us that. Here, as with the taming itself, we must not be too quick to adjust the play to our own assumptions about love and marriage. The fact that Katherina relishes her speech as a performance does not necessarily mean she is ironic or insincere.[8] She is simply enjoying herself. Her submission to her husband is not something to be admitted with shame, or rationalized, but celebrated—particularly in the presence of women who have just failed the test she has so triumphantly passed.

Sport, playacting, education—the taming of Katherina is not finally any of these things, but something *sui generis*, the working out of a personal relationship. But these other activities are analogous, and are placed in the play as points of reference. The achievement of "peace . . . and love, and quiet life" (108) in Petruchio's marriage is seen as part of a whole range of activities whereby men

---

[8]Critics have varied widely in their reactions to the speech. Coghill, ibid., clearly sees it as ironic. For George Ian Duthie, in *Shakespeare* (London, 1951), Katherina speaks "with fervent conviction" (p. 58). Charles Brooks concludes "she plays her part so well that only she and Petruchio know how much is serious and how much put on." See "Shakespeare's Romantic Shrews," *Shakespeare Quarterly* XI (Summer 1970): 354.

try to bring order and pleasure into their lives. In showing this, the play also shows us as creatures of convention: our most pleasurable activities are organized, limited, bounded by rules; and Petruchio's ultimate lesson may be that order and pleasure are inseparable. We also load ourselves with superficial conventions: The play identifies romantic love and a stuffy sense of propriety as two of these, and comically explodes them. But sport and playacting—both highly conventionalized activities—are seen as genuine sources of strength and enjoyment, and Petruchio's application of these activities to his marriage, while it may seem bizarre to the citizens of Padua, is triumphantly justified.

The characters of *The Comedy of Errors* and *The Two Gentlemen of Verona* are comically trapped by limited orders of understanding; they find it difficult, if not impossible, to rise out of their private worlds and see them in relation to other worlds (though Julia is to some degree an exception). But in *The Taming of the Shrew* Petruchio, Katherina, and the Lord have a special vision, an awareness of life as a play or a game, that gives them a power to control not only their own lives but other people's. They have a sense of convention, and therefore a power to manipulate convention, to create experiences rather than have experiences forced upon them. The Lord in creating a new identity for Sly, Petruchio in creating a new life for Katherina, and she herself when she finally joins in this act of creation—all of them convey some of what we imagine to be their own creator's zest in the act of making a new world come to life.

LINDA BAMBER

Sexism and the Battle of Sexes in *The Taming of the Shrew*

In *The Taming of the Shrew* a feminist argument is not explicit, but as we watch the battle between Kate and Petruchio, sexual politics must be on our minds. Kate's resistance to Petruchio is at least in part the resistance of the feminine to male dominance; as in *The Comedy of Errors*, the feminist possibilities of his story provoke the author's partiality for the status quo. Whenever Shakespeare's comedies challenge the limits to sexual equality, they end by strenuously reaffirming those limits. Shakespeare's later comedies, however, seem to avoid both the feminist challenge and the heavy-handed defense against it. In *Twelfth Night* and *As You Like It*, Viola and Rosalind do not confront the political order; they simply preside in its absence. In *The Taming of the Shrew*, we are triumphant over the feminine, but in *Twelfth Night* and *As You Like It*, the happy ending does not depend on masculine control of women. When we leave the domain of the comic heroine (as opposed to the world of the shrew), we do so without triumph and without finality. Illyria and the Forest of Arden are not, like Kate's resistance, shown up as errors; they are states of mind that we visit and leave, revisit and leave again. The later comedies do not share social and political power with the women; but they do emphasize areas of experience to which other kinds of power—emotional, imaginative, personal—are more relevant.

The Taming of the Shrew deserves extended consideration as the play in which the theme of the battle of the sexes is fully and finally elaborated. Here the rebellion of the feminine is sullen and pointless. It is not analogous, like Hermia's rebellion in *A Midsummer Night's Dream*, to the periodic rebellion of all citizens against the restraints of their society; it does not send us off into an alternative world in which we experience the terror and delight of life beyond the social order. Kate's challenge is entirely negative: she resists the arrangements of society but does not call to mind what is beyond society itself. If Kate were in love with another man, or even merely found Petruchio antipathic, she would call to mind the irrationalities of sexual attraction, something beyond the power of society to control. But Kate is no Juliet. Her antagonism to her father's choice is not based on her own sexual preference or on sexual antipathy to her father's choice. It does not resonate with anything larger than itself. Petruchio, on the other hand, represents not only his own desires but the arrangements of society itself. He does so by his cheerful insistence on society's archetypal institution, married cohabitation, which Kate resists. The dialectic between the two is unequal because Kate represents the alternative possibilities very feebly while Petruchio is splendid and triumphant as a representative of the status quo.

Petruchio dominates Kate physically, socially, and economically; he is also the central consciousness of the play and the one character whose will prevails. Insofar as the play dramatizes the battle of the sexes, it ends in complete humiliation for the feminine; insofar as it is a power struggle, Kate loses. By the end of the play Kate herself speaks for wifely obedience. "Thy husband," she instructs her sister,

is thy lord, thy life, thy keeper,
Thy head, thy sovereign—one that cares for thee

. . . .

Such duty as the subject owes the prince,
Even such a woman oweth to her husband,
And when she is froward, peevish, sullen, sour,
And not obedient to his honest will,
What is she but a foul contending rebel
And graceless traitor to her loving lord?
I am ashamed that women are so simple
To offer war where they should kneel for peace,
Or seek for rule, supremacy, and sway,
When they are bound to serve, love, and obey.

> (5.2.146–47, 155–64)

In *The Taming of the Shrew*, the difference of the feminine from the masculine implies only its inferiority. Kate is less powerful, less wealthy, less cheerful, less in the playwright's confidence—less everything than Petruchio. When the conflict with women is stressed but unequal, as it is here, we are surely justified in leveling the charge of sexism.

Many critics, however, have argued against doing so. One of the most interesting articles to take up the issue is Coppelia Kahn's "*The Taming of the Shrew*: Shakespeare's Mirror of Marriage." Kahn's article illuminates both the play's intentions and its limitations when judged from a feminist point of view. Kahn's major argument is that Petruchio "has gained Kate's outward compliance in the form of a public display while her spirit remains mischievously free."[1] Surely the play *invites* us to accept just such a distinction between Kate's public and private selves and to agree that Kate's taming has not crushed her spirit. If we do accept this distinction, we may go so far as to read the final speech as though it were ironic. Though the speech "pleads subordination," says Kahn, "as a speech—

[1]Coppelia Kahn, "*The Taming of the Shrew*: Shakespeare's Mirror of Marriage," *Modern Language Studies* 5 (1975): 98.

a lengthy, ambitious verbal performance before an audience—it allows the speaker to dominate that audience."[2] But the distinction between Kate's public and private selves seems to me a false one. The public forms of equality are important (as Kahn, elsewhere in her article, agrees) because they affect the life of the spirit itself. It is true, of course, that the limits to Kate's equality as a wife are only public. As long as Kate publicly defers to her husband, comes when he calls and says what he wants her to say, their private relationship may be quite playful, equal, and happy. Male dominance is merely a social form, irrelevant to the private relationship—or so the play implies. But this is Shakespeare at his most self-flattering: he imagines the feminine offering explicit social subservience without sacrificing its delightful equality as a sexual partner. Kahn sometimes seems to accept the bargain Shakespeare offers in *The Taming of the Shrew*: If women will go along with male dominance as a mere formality, we may all agree that it is as silly a formality as you like. But the price is to go along with it.

Elsewhere in her article Kahn refuses this easygoing bargain. Her objections to it are clearest in her discussion of the climactic scene of the play, Act 4, scene 5. Here Petruchio and Kate argue over whether it is night or day, whether they see the sun or moon above them. When Petruchio threatens to punish Kate once again for her contrariness, Kate suddenly decides to let it be "moon or sun or what you please. / And if you please to call it a rush-candle, / Henceforth I vow it shall be so for me" (13–15). There follows this dialogue, as Petruchio presses his advantage:

> *Petruchio.*   I say it is the moon.
> *Kate.*   I know it is the moon.
> *Petruchio.*   Nay, then you lie. It is the blessèd sun.
> *Kate.*   Then God be blessed, it is the blessèd sun.
>   But sun it is not when you say it is not,
>   And the moon changes even as your mind.

[2]Ibid., p. 99.

What you will have it named, even that it is,
And so it shall be so for Katherine.

(16–22)

Kate has learned to maintain her independence through ironic exaggeration; if Petruchio says it is the moon, Kate *knows* it is the moon. When she cries "Then God be blessed, it is the blessèd sun," her thankfulness is partly sincere. She feels blessed at having finally learned how to keep a pocket of freedom for herself within the limits of Petruchio's dominion over her. But as Kahn points out, Kate's solution is no solution at all. "Her only way of maintaining her inner freedom," says Kahn, "is by outwardly denying it, which thrusts her into a schizoid existence. . . . Furthermore, to hold that she maintains her freedom in words is to posit a distinction without a difference, for whether she remains spiritually independent of Petruchio or sincerely believes in his superiority, her outward behavior must be . . . that of the perfect Griselda, a model for all women."[3] Although the play presents Kate's capitulation as a gesture without consequence to her soul, it cannot seem so to a feminist reader. The battle of the sexes as a theme for comedy is inherently sexist. The battle is only funny to those who assume that the status quo is the natural order of things and likely to prevail. To the rest of us, Kate's compromise is distressing.

Perhaps Shakespeare himself was also dissatisfied with the resolution to *The Taming of the Shrew*, for after this play he abandons both the shrew and the feminist challenge for the comic heroine and the challenge of the green world. C. L. Barber's distinction between satirical and saturnalian comedy may be helpful here. Satirical comedy, he says, "tends to deal with relations between social classes and aberrations in movements between them. Saturnalian comedy is satiric only incidentally; its clarification comes with movement between poles of restraint and release in everybody's experience."[4] The shrew is a figure of satire

[3]Ibid., p. 97.
[4]C. L. Barber, *Shakespeare's Festive Comedy: A Study of Dramatic Form in Its Relation to Social Custom* (Princeton, N.J.: Princeton University Press, 1959), p. 8.

and the comic heroine of saturnalia. The shrew is an aberration in the social order. At the end of the shrew comedy, "relations between social classes"—in this case the classes of men and women—are returned to the status quo. When the shrew challenges the social order, it reasserts itself in response; the comic heroine, by contrast, comes into her own when and where the social order may be taken for granted. The shrew is a representative of specific class interests rising against the power structure, whereas the comic heroine represents something beyond definition by class altogether, something that offers "release in *everybody's* experience." The comic heroine has a more general significance than the shrew, who is a local, political disturbance only.

Satirical comedy has a kind of righting moment: disorder is introduced into a society that rights itself like a balance toy that has been pulled over. The pleasure comes from seeing the center of gravity rejoin the center of resistance so that equilibrium is reestablished. But in saturnalian comedy the pleasure comes from a temporary release, as it were, from the laws of gravity altogether. The return to normalcy is implicit, but it does not provide the energy that drives the play. In *The Taming of the Shrew*, where the Other is a figure of satire, the return to normalcy is the goal throughout, and every action is directed toward it. In *As You Like It* and *Twelfth Night*, however, where the Other is saturnalian, our expectations of a return are muted or suspended during much of the action. We are occupied with the festivity or disorder, by the alternatives to the status quo, more than with the journey by which we return to it.

KAREN NEWMAN

Missing Frames and Female Spectacles

Kate's final speech is "an imaginary or formal solution to unresolvable social contradictions," but that appearance of resolution is an "ideological mirage."[1] On the level of plot, as many readers have noted, if one shrew is tamed, two more reveal themselves. Bianca and the widow refuse to do their husbands' bidding, thereby undoing the sense of closure Kate's "acquiescence" produces. By articulating the contradiction manifested in the scene's formal organization and its social "content"—between the "headstrong women," now Bianca and the widow who refuse their duty, and Kate and her praise of women's submission—the seeming resolution of the play's ending is exploded and its *heterogeneity* rather than its unity is foregrounded. But can transgression of the law of women's silence be subversive? It has become a theoretical commonplace to argue that transgression presupposes norms or taboos. Therefore, the "female dramatizable" is perhaps no more than a release mechanism, a means of managing troubled gender relations. By transgressing the law of women's silence, but far from subverting it, the *Shrew* reconfirms the law, if we remember that Kate, Bianca, and the widow remain the object of the audience's gaze, specular images, represented female bodies on display, as on the cucking stool or in the cart, the traditional punishments for prosti-

From Karen Newman, "Renaissance Family Politics and Shakespeare's *The Taming of the Shrew*," *English Literary Renaissance* 16 (1986): 86–100. Used with permission of the publishers.
[1]Frederic Jameson, *The Political Unconscious* (1981), pp. 79, 56.

tutes and scolds. Representation contains female rebellion. And because the play has no final framing scene, no return to Sly, it could be argued that its artifice is relaxed, that the final scene is experienced naturalistically. The missing frame allows the audience to forget that Petruchio's taming of Kate is presented as a fiction.

Yet even with its missing frame and containment of woman through spectacle, the *Shrew* finally deconstructs its own mimetic effect if we remember the bisexual aspect of the representation of women on the Elizabethan and Jacobean stage. Kate would have been played by a boy whose transvestism ... emblematically embodied the sexual contradictions manifest both in the play and Elizabethan culture. The very indeterminateness of the actor's sexuality, of the woman/man's body, the supplementarity of its titillating homoerotic play (Sly's desire for the page boy disguised as a woman, Petruchio's "Come Kate, we'll to bed"), foregrounds its artifice and therefore subverts the play's patriarchal master narrative by exposing it as neither natural nor divinely ordained, but culturally constructed.

CAMILLE WELLS SLIGHTS

From Shakespeare's Comic Commonwealths

The understanding and cooperation between Kate and
Petruchio in the last act has prompted several of the play's
most perceptive critics to comment on their creation of a
separate world, what Marianne Novy calls "a private
world, a joke that the rest of the characters miss" or what
J. Dennis Huston calls "a select society, which includes
themselves, the playwright, and perhaps a few members of
his audience."[1] I believe that this emphasis on an exclusive
community in collusion against the rest of the world
assumes a twentieth-century opposition between public
and private worlds that distorts the play's conceptual and
structural dynamics.[2] Unlike Christopher Sly, who remains
suspended in his dream of aristocratic splendor, Kate
returns to her old environment.[3]

From Camille Wells Slights, *Shakespeare's Comic Commonwealths* (University of Toronto Press, 1993), pp. 50–54. Reprinted by permission of University of Toronto Press Incorporated.

[1]Marianne L. Novy, *Love's Argument: Gender Relations in Shakespeare* (Chapel Hill: University of North Carolina Press, 1984), p. 61; J. Dennis Huston, *Shakespeare's Comedies of Play* (New York: Columbia University Press, 1981), p. 64.

[2]In early modern England the family was usually thought of as the fundamental social unit rather than as a refuge from society. See Susan Amussen, "Gender, Family and the Social Order, 1560–1725," pp. 196–217, in *Order and Disorder in Early Modern England*, ed. Anthony Fletcher and John Stevenson (Cambridge: Cambridge University Press, 1985), and Amussen, *An Ordered Society: Gender and Class in Early Modern England* (Oxford: Basil Blackwell, 1988).

[3]In *The Taming of a Shrew*, which most scholars now see as a bad quarto or memorial reconstruction of *The Taming of the Shrew*, Sly falls asleep after commenting on the play several times and in an epilogue awakes in his own clothes and interprets his experience as a dream. Some scholars have argued that Shakespeare intended *The Taming of the Shrew* to include similar scenes and have proposed various explanations for their loss. Other hypotheses are that Shakespeare deliberately dropped Sly from later scenes for artistic reasons or that Sly's expanded role is an unauthorized addition by those responsible

The action rises to a climax in Act 3 with the farcical violence of Petruchio rescuing his bride from her family and friends, but neither Kate nor Petruchio expresses any wish to remain isolated in Petruchio's country house. Acts 4 and 5 dramatize Kate's gradual reintegration into society. Certainly the play works against Norbert Elias's thesis that the civilizing process depends on the coercive power of a strong central government:[4] The basis of Kate's transformation is the self-understanding she develops in her relationship with her husband. But her domestication is complete only when it is made public. Hortensio assures Petruchio that "the field is won" (4.5.23) as soon as Kate yields to him over what to call the sun, but Petruchio arranges a series of increasingly public demonstrations of Kate's new civility. The incident with Vincentio adds a stranger to the audience that already includes Hortensio and the servants. Next, Petruchio demands a kiss in the public street. Finally, Kate wins the wager on whose wife is most obedient before the assembled group of family and friends. Her education culminates, then, not in achieving intimacy with Petruchio but in winning recognition and approval from the social group. The pattern of interrupted feast, solitary fast, and celebratory feast marks the stages of her separation from and return to society. Significantly her final speech explaining the rationale of her obedience is not a private act of submission to Petruchio but a public demonstration of her full acceptance of her position as Petruchio's wife and a public reprimand of the Widow and Bianca for their failures "to serve, love, and obey" (5.2.164) their husbands.

Kate's demonstration of obedience is presented as a victory, not a humiliation. Her offer to place her hand under Petruchio's foot acknowledges her subordination in a hierarchical relationship, but the gesture also expresses gratitude at being cherished and pride at fulfilling her husband's

---

for *The Taming of a Shrew*. For a discussion of the relationship of the texts see Brian Morris's Introduction to the Arden edition (London: Methuen, 1981), pp. 12–50.

[4]Norbert Elias, *The Civilizing Process*, trans. Edmund Jephcott, 2 vols. (Oxford: Basil Blackwell, 1978; 1982).

desires. Petruchio certainly demands that Katherina submit to his will, but we know, as she does, that he won't step on her hand. Shakespeare, then, does not ironically subvert the patriarchal power structure portrayed in *The Taming of the Shrew*. As David Underdown has demonstrated, in the period between 1560 and 1640 a perceived threat to patriarchal order from unruly women produced a widespread fascination with literary shrews as well as a marked increase in legal proceedings against assertive women.[5] The representation of Kate's domestication as a paradigm of the civilizing process responds to that cultural anxiety by affirming women's subordination. Readings of Kate's endorsement of patriarchy as ironic are, I think, unconvincing.[6] Unlike Petruchio's claim that Kate is "My horse, my ox, my ass, my anything" (3.2.232), which is qualified by the farcical context, Kate's exposition of wifely submission stands unqualified and unrefuted. Similarly, in *The Comedy of Errors* the Abbess's lecture to Adriana on how a nagging wife can drive a man mad (5.1.68–86) is consonant with the view of marriage in the play as a whole. Neither play is designed merely to teach uppity women their places. Both suggest that husbands and wives should be subject to each other in love, but both also endorse a hierarchical view of marriage in which wives owe obedience to husbands that husbands do not owe wives.

As tempting as it is to explain away Kate's final speech, such revisionism deflects needed attention from the patriarchal ideology the play enacts. As Lynda Boose convincingly argues, "the impulse to rewrite the more oppressively patriarchal material in this play serves the very ideologies about gender that it makes less visible by making less

[5]David Underdown, "The Taming of the Scold: The Enforcement of Patriarchal Authority in Early Modern England," in Fletcher and Stevenson, pp. 116–36, and Underdown, *Revel, Riot, and Rebellion: Popular Politics and Culture in England, 1603–1660* (Oxford: Clarendon Press, 1985), pp. 38–40.
[6]On the development of the ironic reading of Kate's speech see Robert Heilman, "The *Taming* Untamed, or the Return of the Shrew," *Modern Language Quarterly* 27 (1966): 147–61. Linda Woodbridge presents a sensible critique of ahistorical attempts to exonerate Shakespeare from the charge of sexism in *The Taming of the Shrew* in *Women and the English Renaissance: Literature and the Nature of Womankind, 1540–1620* (Urbana: University of Illinois Press, 1984), pp. 221–22.

offensive."[7] Similarly, to ignore the play's consistent exclusion of physical brutality also obstructs the feminist project of writing the history of the construction of gender in Western society. While endorsing women's subordination within patriarchal marriage, *The Taming of the Shrew* mitigates the violence used to control unruly women in the real world and in the shrew-taming literary tradition. Although sparring verbally with Katherina excites Petruchio in their pre-marital battle of the sexes, his goal is "peace ... love, and quiet life" (5.2.108), and he puts a stop to the violence she initiates. His use of physical and economic force to deprive Katherina temporarily of food and sleep is relatively mild compared with the horrifying brutalities of actual social practice and with the sadism of earlier versions of the shrew story.[8] For example, in contrast to the hero of *A meery Jeste of a Shrewde and curste Wyfe lapped in Morrelles skin,* who subjects his bride to a brutal sexual initiation, Petruchio on their wedding night lectures Kate on continence. Not only do the methods employed in Petruchio's taming school appear humane in the context of a society that tortured women judged to be scolds with cucking stools and scold's bridles, the play also demystifies the patriarchal authority it confirms. Discussions of unruly women in the years around 1600 usually represent female insubordination as a perversion of natural order and a symptom of an incipient breakdown of all social order. In contrast, Kate's shrewishness is a danger to no one but herself. Although Kate invokes the familiar analogy between familial and political order in her final speech, her subjection to Petruchio is presented, not as an inevitable alignment with the natural relations between men and women, but as the result of protracted negotiations between two people, anticipating Locke's theory of a contractual basis for marriage rather than re-inscribing the family as the divinely instituted origin of political power.[9]

---

[7]Lynda E. Boose, "Scolding Brides and Bridling Scolds: Taming the Woman's Unruly Member," *Shakespeare Quarterly* 42 (1991): 181–82.

[8]For the literary tradition, see Woodbridge, 201–07; for historical practices of controlling women, see Underdown, "The Taming of the Scold," and Boose, 179–213.

[9]On the analogy between familial and political power, and on Locke's undermining of the organic theory of patriarchal power, see Amussen, *An Ordered Society*, pp. 37–66.

Kate's exposition of a wife's duties is general and normative rather than personal, but she justifies wifely obedience on the basis, not of the religious sanctity of the conventional sexual hierarchy, but of its justice and convenience. The only inherent superiority she attributes to men is their greater physical strength, and she describes a wife's duties of "love, fair looks, and true obedience" (5.2.153) as just recompense to a husband who endures "painful labor" to care for her (149).[10]

The Taming of the Shrew offers Kate and Bianca no alternative to the limited choice between spinsterhood and patriarchal marriage. In the context of contemporary discussions of domestic relations, it supports the ideal of marriage based on mutual love within the framework of masculine authority.[11] Petruchio's announced desire for a rich wife and Baptista's offer of his youngest daughter to the highest bidder allude unmistakably to the practice among the propertied classes of arranging marriages on an economic basis, and the play explicitly subordinates these financial motives to the emotional responses of the female characters. Petruchio's success consists not in winning a rich wife but in winning the love and obedience of a shrewish one and is proved not by Kate's humiliation but by her triumph. Her prompt response when Petruchio sends for her and her long final speech demonstrate to the community she lives in and to the audience that she is no longer wild but self-assured, self-controlled, and considerate—a civilized woman who understands human relationships as a balance of duties and privileges. By her

[10]See John C. Bean, "Comic Structure and the Humanizing of Kate in The *Taming of the Shrew*" in *The Woman's Part: Feminist Criticism of Shakespeare*, ed. Carolyn Ruth Swift Lenz, Gayle Green, and Carol Thomas Neely (Urbana: University of Illinois Press, 1980), pp. 65–78, especially pp. 68–71; Juliet Dusinberre, *Shakespeare and the Nature of Women* (London: Macmillan, 1975), pp. 78–79; Morris, pp. 148–49; and Novy, pp. 58–60.

[11]Some historians attribute a growing emphasis on marriage as an affective rather than an economic relationship to the influence of Puritan ideas of spiritual equality. See Stone, *The Family, Sex and Marriage, 1500–1800*. Others stress that the ideal of marriage based on love appears throughout the period. See, for example, Ralph A. Houlbrooke, *The English Family, 1450–1700* (London: Longman, 1984). Ann Jennalie Cook, whose useful study of marriage in Shakespeare's society appeared after I had completed this book, provides references on this controversy. *Making a Match: Courtship in Shakespeare and His Society* (Princeton: Princeton University Press, 1991), p. 13.

public submission to her husband and her dominance over the Widow and Bianca, she simultaneously acknowledges her dependence and asserts her personal worth. Kate, in short, achieves what she has always wanted: a dominant place as a valued member of society.

The comedy's happy ending embodies the achievement of mutual love and understanding recommended by the proponents of companionate marriage who insist also on husbands' authority over their wives. *The Taming of the Shrew* is distinctive, not in its unresolved tension between mutuality and inequality, but in its uncompromising acknowledgment of the demand that women choose their own subordination. The play exposes the inequities and potential brutality of male power, the patriarchal attitudes and institutions only temporarily disguised by courtship rhetoric such as Lucentio's, and the voluntary subjection required of women by love within a framework of gender inequality. At the same time it shows men and women achieving happiness by actively asserting control over those structures. By the last scene all the major characters have been able to fulfill their personal desires through their relationships with each other. Petruchio has a rich and spirited wife as well as "peace . . . and love, and quiet life, / . . . and right supremacy" (108–9). Lucentio has Bianca, and Bianca has parental approval for the husband she has chosen for herself; moreover, she is still learning her lessons as she pleases. Baptista and Vincentio have seen their children married to their social equals, with appropriate financial settlements. Even Gremio and Hortensio, who lose Bianca to Lucentio, have the satisfaction of watching their successful rival's discomfort with his wife. In spite of—or better, because of—the tensions and rivalries of personal relationships, the conclusion of *The Taming of the Shrew* presents us with an image of a society that conforms to all the members' individual desires. And the supreme example of eating his cake and having it too is Shakespeare: By transforming the traditional shrew story of a struggle for domestic mastery into a process of domestication, he manages to satirize the absurdities of social convention while simultaneously celebrating the human capacity to shape society to express individual values. By presenting Kate's transformation in a play-within-a-play, he also allows the unsettling implication that this happy reconciliation of individual freedom with repressive communal values is possible only in a work of art.

SYLVAN BARNET

The Taming of the Shrew
on Stage and Screen

The last scene is altogether disgusting to modern sensibility. No man with any decency of feeling can sit it out in the company of a woman without being extremely ashamed of the lord-of-creation moral implied in the wager and the speech put into the woman's own mouth.

—GEORGE BERNARD SHAW (1897)

The speech in question (5.2.136–79) is given in full on pages 108–109, but a brief reminder of the context, and a brief extract, can be given here. Three men have made a bet on whether their wives will come to them on command. Kate comes when called but the other two wives resist. When they finally appear, Kate gives them a long lecture, part of which runs thus:

Thy husband is thy lord, thy life, thy keeper,
Thy head, thy sovereign—one that cares for thee. . . .
Such duty as the subject owes the prince,
Even such a woman oweth to her husband. . . ,
Then vail your stomachs, for it is no boot,
And place your hands below your husband's foot,
In token of which duty, if he please,
My hand is ready, may it do him ease.

Among the famous players who have spoken Kate's lines are Edith Evans, Peggy Ashcroft, Lynn Fontanne, Claire Booth Luce, Katharine Hepburn, Elizabeth Taylor, Vanessa Redgrave, and Meryl Streep. And Laurence

Olivier. (Yes, Laurence Olivier, when at the age of fifteen he played Kate at Stratford in an all-male production of *The Taming of the Shrew*.)

Performers have, of course, delivered the speech in various ways. Some have played it straight, assuming that the words mean just what they say. Some (such as Mary Pickford in a film version) have given a wink to the audience, thereby indicating that they are going along with an act so as to delude their big baby of a husband into believing that he rules the roost whereas in fact *they* are really in charge. Others, when they placed their hand beneath their husband's foot in apparent submission, have suddenly jerked their hand upward and have tipped the complacent oaf from his chair, again to show that they are in charge. It is perhaps hardly necessary to add that these signs of mastery are not found in productions before the twentieth century.

The Taming of the Shrew has never been regarded as one of Shakespeare's greatest plays, but it has had a long and prosperous stage history. Whether it will continue to delight spectators who live in an age that has learned something from the women's movement is uncertain, but some feminist critics—Germaine Greer, for instance—have given the play their approval, and it apparently continues to delight audiences.

Of the earliest performances, in the late sixteenth century and the early seventeenth, we know almost nothing except that the play was popular enough to engender a sort of theatrical reply, John Fletcher's *The Woman's Prize, or The Tamer Tamed* (c. 1611), in which Petruchio, now a widower, marries again and is tamed by his new wife. *The Taming of the Shrew* was staged at court in 1633, and was reported to have been "liked," but that is about all we have for the first half of the seventeenth century. From 1642 to 1660 the theaters were closed by act of Parliament, but with the return to the throne of Charles II, drama was revived. *The Taming of the Shrew,* however, did not appear on the stage in its original form; like most other early plays, it was drastically adapted to suit a new taste. John (?) Lacy rewrote it entirely in prose, omitting the induction and turning Shakespeare's Grumio into the chief character, whom he called Sauny, probably a form of Sandy (from Alexander). This version, titled *Sauny the Scott: or The Taming of the Shrew*—performed at least as early as 1667, though not published until 1698—continued on the stage for about two centuries. Crude though some of Shakespeare's play is, *Sauny* is infinitely cruder. To take a single example: Petruchio, proposing to Margaret (Kate is called Margaret in this version), says, "Hold, get me a stick there, Sauny. By this, deny to promise before your father, I'll not leave you a whole rib. I'll make you do't and be glad on't." On the other hand, Lacy reduced to two lines the wife's long speech on subordination, perhaps a sign that even in the late seventeenth century the speech was regarded as hard to take.

What competition *Sauny* had from the late seventeenth century to the middle of the nineteenth came not from Shakespeare's original but from other adaptations, the most enduring of which was David Garrick's *Catharine and Petruchio* (published 1756). Garrick's play is closer to Shakespeare's than is *Sauny,* but he omits the Sly induction and the Lucentio subplot (Bianca is already married to Hortensio), omits many other passages of dialogue, transfers some speeches from deleted characters to the survivors, revises other lines, creates some of his own—including a brief passage at the end, in which Petruchio says he will "doff the lordly husband"—and condenses the play into three acts. Shakespeare's text is about 2,650 lines, Garrick's—even with the added dialogue— runs only to about 1,000 lines. Still, compared with Lacy's version, Garrick's short three-act play was fairly close to Shakespeare; it was highly popular for a century, and even after Shakespeare's play was restored to the stage in 1844, Garrick's was occasionally performed—and preferred.

Shakespeare's own play was first restored on 16 March 1844, when Benjamin Webster and J. R. Planché staged it in London in what was thought to be the Elizabethan style. Webster (1797–1882) was an English actor, dramatist, and manager of the Haymarket Theatre in London; Planché

(1796–1880), an Englishman of Huguenot descent, was a dramatist, musician, and an antiquary with a keen and highly scholarly interest in the history of costume. Despite reviews of their production, one of which even includes an illustration of the stage, it is a bit unclear exactly how they staged the play, but apparently they used no scenery other than some portable furniture, two screens, and a painted curtain at the rear. Actors entered and exited through a split in this curtain. The locale of each scene (e.g., "*In a public place in Padua*," or "*A room in Baptista's house*," or "*A public road*") was indicated by a placard fastened to the rear curtain. The actors changed the placards as they exited from one scene, and thus introduced the next scene. The only change of scenery was the shift from a view of the exterior of an inn (painted on the rear curtain) to a view of the Lord's room in which the visiting troupe performs. The front curtain fell only at the end of the play. Planché used Elizabethan costumes, and given his great knowledge of the subject, they were accurate. This attempt to imitate Elizabethan staging, it should be noted, took place almost forty years before William Poel's far better known staging of *Hamlet* in what was thought to be an Elizabethan manner. Webster and Planché—like Poel—did not go all the way; that is, they did not use boys to play the female parts, but even so, the production was an amazing departure from mid-nineteenth-century theater practice, which relied heavily on illusionistic scenery.

Webster and Planché revised *The Shrew* again in 1847. In both productions they used the induction—indeed, it was the induction that prompted Planché to the experiment of staging the play in the Elizabethan manner, for he took seriously the idea that the story of Baptista and his two daughters is a play performed, by a group of traveling players visiting a Lord's house, for the entertainment of the Lord who plays a trick on the drunken tinker. Given the absence of a written epilogue, at the end of the play-within-the play the actors bowed to the Lord, and at a sign from the Lord, a servant carried out the sleeping tinker. Reviewers were divided in their responses; some praised its "beautiful simplicity," others ridiculed its underlying idea as pedantic, asserting that if one were to forgo visual effects of the modern theater one might as well simply stay home and read the play. Shakespeare, it was said, would eagerly have used nineteenth-century stage machinery if it had been available to him. One review trounced not only the performance but also the author, saying that long ago it had been justly decided that Garrick's *Catharine and Petruchio* was superior to Shakespeare's *The Taming of the Shrew*. Planché's own verdict on his experiment, however, was unambiguous: "The revival was eminently successful, incontestably proving that a good play, well acted, will carry the audience along with it, unassisted by scenery; and in this case also, remember, it was a comedy in five acts, without the curtain once falling during its performance."

The Webster-Planché revival of *The Taming of the Shrew* did not, however, permanently restore the original play. Garrick's *Catharine and Petruchio* was occasionally revived in the next few decades, but it was finally driven from the stage by Augustin Daly's presentation of Shakespeare's play in 1887. Daly (1839–1899), an American dramatist and manager, first produced *The Taming of the Shrew* in New York, with two of America's most highly regarded performers, John Drew and Ada Rehan. Although *Catharine and Petruchio* had been acted in Philadelphia as early as 1766, Shakespeare's own play was not done in America until Daly gave it. The production was immensely successful; in 1888 Daly gave it in London and in Stratford-upon-Avon, and it remained in his repertory. Although he purified some of the language—for example he deleted such words as "lechery" and "belly," and the stuff about wasps and tails in 2.1.210–16— telescoped some of the scenes, and kept a few of Garrick's additions—including Petruchio's remark that he will "doff the lordly husband"—his version is, on the whole, faithful to Shakespeare. He even retained the induction, which is seen only occasionally today. But his use of elaborate scenery, common in the period, required some telescoping or rearrangement of scenes so that the massive sets would not have to be set up, struck, and set up again. Thus, Daly made one scene—set in Petruchio's country house—out of Shakespeare's 4.1, 4.3, and 4.5. That is, by removing 4.2 (which takes place in Baptista's house) and 4.4 (in front of Baptista's house), he played the "taming" in Petruchio's house as a single scene. The other two scenes of the fourth act, scenes 2 and 4, dealing with Tranio and Lucentio, i.e., with what is commonly regarded as the subplot of the play, Daly ran together, giving them before the newly made long scene in Petruchio's country house.

   Mention has already been made of William Poel, who in the later nineteenth century advocated staging the plays in the Elizabethan manner, that is, without the cumbersome scenery whose erection and removal required intervals between scenes, or required rearrangement of scenes. In 1913 Martin Harvey, the English actor-manager, consulted with Poel and produced *The Taming of the Shrew* in a "neutral" locale, that is, a locale that became Baptista's house, or Petruchio's house, or whatever, by means of the dialogue and a few props brought in by the itinerant players who, at the Lord's request, perform the story of Kate and Petruchio. The players entered from the rear of the stage; Sly watched them from a bench at the very front of the apron. The background, at the start, was a tapestry (really a painting of a tapestry) depicting a landscape; this tapestry then parted, revealing white curtains with decorative medallions to indicate the Lord's room with its erotic pictures (Induction, 2.49ff.). Harvey has described the staging of the piece:

> Any change of scene was suggested by the actors themselves, who moved into this hall either such screens as could be found in the house of the princely host crudely to suggest a street, or else some trellis-work covered with leaves cut from the neighboring garden to represent a leafy lane; or again, some of the Lord's own hangings were let down from the ceiling of the hall for interior scenery.

Strictly speaking, the itinerant players did not always use only what might be found in a lord's house; a table was let down from above to indicate Petruchio's house. But Harvey's point and his purpose are clear enough. He

wanted to keep the play moving, and he wanted to emphasize the idea that the play, with its two wooing plots, is a
theatrical performance, not a bit of real life. By emphasizing the play as a play-within-a-play, performed for the
Lord by a traveling company, the offensiveness of the
taming plot was reduced; it was only a play, not life but
theater.

On the other hand, an occasional production seeks to
emphasize the reality of the story by doing it in modern
dress. H. K. Ayliff in 1925 and Barry Jackson in 1928 used
modern dress, though Barry Jackson's expressed reason
was to help the players to approach the play freshly,
freeing it from encrusted conventions. The most famous
production of the twentieth century, however, that of
Alfred Lunt and Lynn Fontanne in 1935–36 and again in
1940, was not in modern dress. In fact, the theatrical elements were played up, insuring that the play seemed
remote from real life. Thus an actor occasionally missed
his cues so that another actor would loudly repeat the cue
line. Among the many outrageous bits of business—the
production is said to have resembled a three-ring circus—
the one that seems to have evoked the most comment is
Petruchio's skipping rope with a string of sausages. But
one other point should be made in connection with this
production. Despite the emphasis on farce, which helped
to distance or make unreal and therefore presumably inof-
fensive the story of the taming, Lunt did convey (under his
antics) a sense of love for Kate. G. B. Stern, in *And Did He
Stop and Speak to You*, clearly sets forth this point:

> *The Taming of the Shrew*, being a rampageous comedy-farce,
> absolves us from a moral need to "make allowances" for Petru-
> chio's methods of taming; but when Alfred played the part, by
> another silent revealing moment that I shall never forget, he let us
> in on the man's deep reluctance to assume such brutal insensitivity:
> it happened at the end of one of those mannerless brawls between
> the pair, where one might have assumed (and perhaps Shakespeare
> meant us to assume) that the bully only cared about getting his way
> by shouting and stamping like a madman; but after Kate the Shrew
> had swept off, crying from thwarted rage at having met her master,

Petruchio suddenly collapsed from sheer weariness and leaned exhausted against the door . . . , by his complete surrender conveying how hatefully the masquerade had gone against the grain, and that he loved Kate, really loved her, but in carrying on in this abominable fashion until she capitulated lay their only hope of ultimate happiness.

One other point should be made about the Lunt-Fontanne production: Lunt and Fontanne, who performed together in many plays, were known as a loving husband and wife, and audiences must have more or less kept this in mind while they watched a performance. That is, the potentially offensive elements in the play must have been softened, in the audience's mind, by an awareness that the two figures "really" were in love. (Other husband-wife teams to perform the play successfully were Frank and Constance Benson, Oscar Asche and Lily Brayton, E. H. Sothern and Julia Marlowe, and in a film, Richard Burton and Elizabeth Taylor.)

Before turning to film and television versions, we can look very briefly at what seem to have been the two most interesting recent stage productions, both of 1978. In New York's Central Park, Joseph Papp directed Meryl Streep and Raul Julia, in a production that did not seek to evade the difficulties (for a modern audience) of Kate's speech on obedience in the fifth act. The production was true to the text—Streep's Kate was shrewish, and Julia's Petruchio was dominating—but the personal charm of the two leading performers insured that the audience was never alienated. Such a passage as Petruchio's "She is my goods, my chattels; she is my house, / My household stuff, my field, my barn, / My horse, my ox, my ass, my anything" drew boos, but good-natured ones. In an interview in *The New York Times* Streep said she had no trouble delivering the big speech in the last act. The man whom she had loved, John Cazale (who played Alfredo in *The Godfather*), had recently died. Two years earlier, in *Measure for Measure*, Cazale had played the lustful Angelo, to Streep's virgin Isabella. At that time, Streep suggested, she and Cazale found their love in a sort of Kate-Petruchio relation. At one point in the interview Streep said, "What I'm saying is, I'll do *anything* for this man. . . . Why is selflessness here wrong? Service is the only thing that's important about love. Everybody is worrying about 'losing yourself'—all this narcissism. Duty. We can't stand that idea now either. It has the real ugly slave-driving connotation. But duty might be a suit of armor you put on to fight for your love."

The second important recent production was Michael Bogdanov's at Stratford-upon-Avon. It began with a quarrel in the audience; a drunken member of the audience upbraided a female attendant, shouting something to the effect that "no bloody woman is going to tell me what to do." (You have already seen the connection with the rest of the play. The drunk was Sly, who later became Petruchio, and the theater employee became Kate.) The drunk leaped onto the stage and began tearing down the set, wings, and drop flats showing a perspective view of a street in Renaissance Padua. Such scenery was indeed out of place and old-fashioned for the Royal Shakespeare Company. The havoc he wreaked revealed a more typical RSC set: metal frames and a catwalk. The implication was that the play is not some museum piece from the Renaissance but is something relevant to our own time. The drunk—Sly—then collapsed, the lights dimmed and then rose to reveal (to the accompaniment of hunting horns) the Lord and his huntsmen in modern red hunting outfits. As the play proceeded, Sly became Petruchio—in this role, he entered on a motorbike, and all in all behaved like a drunken ruffian. Apparently the director wished to emphasize the brutality of the story, beginning with the angry behavior in the audience, continuing with the Lord's hunting party (a pelt was tossed onto the drunken Sly), and running throughout the rest of the play. Unlike most productions, there was little or no slapstick comedy; the brutality for the most part was merely brutal, not funny, and Kate's big speech on submission was uttered flatly, or (according to some reviewers) with a touch of sarcasm. The sound of hunting horns at the end of the play connected with the beginning, apparently to emphasize the cruelty of a story in which men treat women like animals.

Two film versions of *The Taming of the Shrew* are historically important, one with Mary Pickford and Douglas Fairbanks (1929), the other with Elizabeth Taylor and Richard Burton (1966); the first of these versions is scarcely accessible and we will say little about it. The text is chiefly an abridgment of Garrick's abridgment; this version uses only about five hundred of Shakespeare's lines, and only a handful of the lines that Garrick added to Shakespeare. It omits the induction with Sly, beginning instead with a Punch and Judy show (the puppets look like Petruchio and Kate) presented in a public square. We witness their fighting, then the camera pulls back, moves down the street, and we encounter Petruchio coming to town. Putting aside its merits and the fact that it is the first talkie made of a play by Shakespeare, the film is important for a reason that has already been mentioned: at the end of her speech preaching obedience, Kate winks to the women. She then sits on Petruchio's lap, but the poor fellow doesn't know that his wife is merely indulging him in his fantasy of male supremacy; everyone sings merrily, the camera pulls back for a long shot, and the scene fades out.

Zeffirelli's 1966 film is much better known, and is often screened in courses in Shakespeare. As is usual in Zeffirelli's works, there is a great deal of bustling. Zeffirelli omits the induction and replaces it with some business of his own invention: a solemn service is interrupted by the sound of cannon, and masked figures appear, suggesting that what follows is part of a saturnalia. Kate and Petruchio fall in love almost as soon as they see each other, but they fight like maniacs. For example, early in the film Petruchio swings from the ground to an upper level, pursues Kate across rooftops, falls through a roof into a pile of wool, pins Kate down, and vows to marry her. Before the film is over, windows have been smashed, plates have been thrown, servants have been chased—and indeed, at the end, after Kate gives her lecture on obedience, Kate slips away, thus requiring Petruchio to set out on yet another chase.

In addition to omitting the Sly induction, this film greatly reduces the Bianca-Lucentio subplot and amplifies the vigor of Kate and Petruchio, seeing in these two lovers an energy that sets them against the hypocrites and fools who surround them. Unfortunately, the vigor is often tedious; Petruchio is a drunken brute (it has been said that Burton was playing himself) who engages in lots of hearty, self-satisfied laughter. But as with the Lunt-Fontanne production, probably the viewer keeps in mind the fact that the two chief characters are married, and such an awareness softens and supposedly makes acceptable the coarseness. It should be mentioned, too, that Petruchio not only changes Kate but also changes himself, from a boor to a somewhat genial, civilized person.

Passing over Cole Porter's musical of 1948, *Kiss Me Kate,* which uses the story but is not really a version of Shakespeare's play, we can, finally, look briefly at what today may be the best-known version of the play, the BBC television production directed by Jonathan Miller, which starred John Cleese of *Monty Python* fame. A greater contrast with the Zeffirelli production is scarcely imaginable, for Cleese—an unfunny Petruchio—played down the farcical and physical elements. Briefly, as Miller explains in an interview in *Shakespeare Quarterly,* Summer 1981, he saw the play as one "about the setting up of a sober household and the necessity for marital obedience in order to maintain it." Petruchio, in Miller's view, is not a dashing cavalier but a sober puritan; one of the most important lines in the play, according to Miller, is Petruchio's "To me she's married, not unto my clothes." Of this line (3.2.117) Miller says, "That is the great line which expressed Calvinism. The idea that you are, in fact, naked before the eye of God, and that that is the way you come before the eye of your partner." In Miller's view, Kate is shrewish because her father has withheld his love from her; Petruchio does not so much *tame* Kate as *teach* her or *treat* her, by holding a mirror to her. Miller cut the Christopher Sly material—strange, since the BBC usually makes only very small cuts—and at the end added, over the credits, Psalm 128, about the orderliness of the family ("How blest is he that fears the Lord, and walketh in his way"), while the characters all jointly sing a part song, i.e., the characters harmoniously reconcile their voices. A bold if not unassailable interpretation, it offers a welcome contrast to the usual farcical productions.

Bibliographic Note: For information concerning performances, see the books by Coursen, Haring-Smith, and Holderness cited in Section 11, *The Taming of the Shrew*, of the Suggested References.

Suggested References

The number of possible references is vast and grows alarmingly. (The *Shakespeare Quarterly* devotes one issue each year to a list of the previous year's work, and *Shakespeare Survey*—an annual publication—includes a substantial review of biographical, critical, and textual studies, as well as a survey of performances.) The vast bibliography is best approached through James Harner, *The World Shakespeare Bibliography on CD-Rom: 1900–Present.* The first release, in 1996, included more than 12,000 annotated items from 1990–93, plus references to several thousand book reviews, productions, films, and audio recordings. The plan is to update the publication annually, moving forward one year and backward three years. Thus, the second issue (1997), with 24,700 entries, and another 35,000 or so references to reviews, newspaper pieces, and so on, covered 1987–94.

Though no works are indispensable, those listed below have been found especially helpful. The arrangement is as follows:

1. Shakespeare's Times
2. Shakespeare's Life
3. Shakespeare's Theater
4. Shakespeare on Stage and Screen
5. Miscellaneous Reference Works
6. Shakespeare's Plays: General Studies
7. The Comedies
8. The Romances
9. The Tragedies
10. The Histories
11. *The Taming of the Shrew*

The titles in the first five sections are accompanied by brief explanatory annotations.

1. Shakespeare's Times

Andrews, John F., ed. *William Shakespeare: His World, His Work, His Influence*, 3 vols. (1985). Sixty articles, dealing not only with such subjects as "The State," "The Church," "Law," "Science, Magic, and Folklore," but also with the plays and poems themselves and Shakespeare's influence (e.g., translations, films, reputation)

Byrne, Muriel St. Clare. *Elizabethan Life in Town and Country* (8th ed., 1970). Chapters on manners, beliefs, education, etc., with illustrations.

Dollimore, John, and Alan Sinfield, eds. *Political Shakespeare: New Essays in Cultural Materialism* (1985). Essays on such topics as the subordination of women and colonialism, presented in connection with some of Shakespeare's plays.

Greenblatt, Stephen. *Representing the English Renaissance* (1988). New Historicist essays, especially on connections between political and aesthetic matters, statecraft and stagecraft.

Joseph, B. L. *Shakespeare's Eden: the Commonwealth of England 1558–1629* (1971). An account of the social, political, economic, and cultural life of England.

Kernan, Alvin. *Shakespeare, the King's Playwright: Theater in the Stuart Court 1603–1613* (1995). The social setting and the politics of the court of James I, in relation to *Hamlet, Measure for Measure, Macbeth, King Lear, Antony and Cleopatra, Coriolanus*, and *The Tempest*.

Montrose, Louis. *The Purpose of Playing: Shakespeare and the Cultural Politics of the Elizabethan Theatre* (1996). A poststructuralist view, discussing the professional theater "within the ideological and material frameworks of Elizabethan culture and society," with an extended analysis of *A Midsummer Night's Dream*.

Mullaney, Steven. *The Place of the Stage: License, Play, and Power in Renaissance England* (1988). New Historicist analysis, arguing that popular drama became a cultural institution "only by . . . taking up a place on the margins of society."

Schoenbaum, S. *Shakespeare: The Globe and the World*

(1979). A readable, abundantly illustrated introductory book on the world of the Elizabethans.

Shakespeare's England, 2 vols. (1916). A large collection of scholarly essays on a wide variety of topics, e.g., astrology, costume, gardening, horsemanship, with special attention to Shakespeare's references to these topics.

2. Shakespeare's Life

Andrews, John F., ed. *William Shakespeare: His World, His Work, His Influence,* 3 vols. (1985). See the description above.

Bentley, Gerald E. *Shakespeare: A Biographical Handbook* (1961). The facts about Shakespeare, with virtually no conjecture intermingled.

Chambers, E. K. *William Shakespeare: A Study of Facts and Problems,* 2 vols. (1930). The fullest collection of data.

Fraser, Russell. *Young Shakespeare* (1988). A highly readable account that simultaneously considers Shakespeare's life and Shakespeare's art.

———. *Shakespeare: The Later Years* (1992).

Schoenbaum, S. *Shakespeare's Lives* (1970). A review of the evidence and an examination of many biographies, including those of Baconians and other heretics.

———. *William Shakespeare: A Compact Documentary Life* (1977). An abbreviated version, in a smaller format, of the next title. The compact version reproduces some fifty documents in reduced form. A readable presentation of all that the documents tell us about Shakespeare.

———. *William Shakespeare: A Documentary Life* (1975). A large-format book setting forth the biography with facsimiles of more than two hundred documents, and with transcriptions and commentaries.

3. Shakespeare's Theater

Astington, John H., ed. *The Development of Shakespeare's Theater* (1992). Eight specialized essays on theatrical companies, playing spaces, and performance.

Beckerman, Bernard. *Shakespeare at the Globe, 1599–1609* (1962). On the playhouse and on Elizabethan dramaturgy, acting, and staging.

Bentley, Gerald E. *The Profession of Dramatist in Shakespeare's Time* (1971). An account of the dramatist's status in the Elizabethan period.

———. *The Profession of Player in Shakespeare's Time, 1590–1642* (1984). An account of the status of members of London companies (sharers, hired men, apprentices, managers) and a discussion of conditions when they toured.

Berry, Herbert. *Shakespeare's Playhouses* (1987). Usefully emphasizes how little we know about the construction of Elizabethan theaters.

Brown, John Russell. *Shakespeare's Plays in Performance* (1966). A speculative and practical analysis relevant to all of the plays, but with emphasis on *The Merchant of Venice, Richard II, Hamlet, Romeo and Juliet,* and *Twelfth Night.*

———. *William Shakespeare: Writing for Performance* (1996). A discussion aimed at helping readers to develop theatrically conscious habits of reading.

Chambers, E. K. *The Elizabethan Stage,* 4 vols. (1945). A major reference work on theaters, theatrical companies, and staging at court.

Cook, Ann Jennalie. *The Privileged Playgoers of Shakespeare's London, 1576–1642* (1981). Sees Shakespeare's audience as wealthier, more middle-class, and more intellectual than Harbage (below) does.

Dessen, Alan C. *Elizabethan Drama and the Viewer's Eye* (1977). On how certain scenes may have looked to spectators in an Elizabethan theater.

Gurr, Andrew. *Playgoing in Shakespeare's London* (1987). Something of a middle ground between Cook (above) and Harbage (below).

———. *The Shakespearean Stage, 1579–1642* (2nd ed., 1980). On the acting companies, the actors, the playhouses, the stages, and the audiences.

Harbage, Alfred. *Shakespeare's Audience* (1941). A study of the size and nature of the theatrical public, emphasizing the representativeness of its working class and middle-class audience.

Hodges, C. Walter. *The Globe Restored* (1968). A conjectural restoration, with lucid drawings.

Hosley, Richard. "The Playhouses," in *The Revels History of Drama in English*, vol. 3, general editors Clifford Leech and T. W. Craik (1975). An essay of a hundred pages on the physical aspects of the playhouses.

Howard, Jane E. "Crossdressing, the Theatre, and Gender Struggle in Early Modern England," *Shakespeare Quarterly* 39 (1988): 418–40. Judicious comments on the effects of boys playing female roles.

Orrell, John. *The Human Stage: English Theatre Design, 1567–1640* (1988). Argues that the public, private, and court playhouses are less indebted to popular structures (e.g., innyards and bear-baiting pits) than to banqueting halls and to Renaissance conceptions of Roman amphitheaters.

Slater, Ann Pasternak. *Shakespeare the Director* (1982). An analysis of theatrical effects (e.g., kissing, kneeling) in stage directions and dialogue.

Styan, J. L. *Shakespeare's Stagecraft* (1967). An introduction to Shakespeare's visual and aural stagecraft, with chapters on such topics as acting conventions, stage groupings, and speech.

Thompson, Peter. *Shakespeare's Professional Career* (1992). An examination of patronage and related theatrical conditions.

———. *Shakespeare's Theatre* (1983). A discussion of how plays were staged in Shakespeare's time.

4. Shakespeare on Stage and Screen

Bate, Jonathan, and Russell Jackson, eds. *Shakespeare: An Illustrated Stage History* (1996). Highly readable essays on stage productions from the Renaissance to the present.

Berry, Ralph. *Changing Styles in Shakespeare* (1981). Discusses productions of six plays (*Coriolanus, Hamlet, Henry V, Measure for Measure, The Tempest,* and *Twelfth Night*) on the English stage, chiefly 1950–1980.

————. *On Directing Shakespeare: Interviews with Contemporary Directors* (1989). An enlarged edition of a book first published in 1977, this version includes the seven interviews from the early 1970s and adds five interviews conducted in 1988.

Brockbank, Philip, ed. *Players of Shakespeare: Essays in Shakespearean Performance* (1985). Comments by twelve actors, reporting their experiences with roles. See also the entry for Russell Jackson (below).

Bulman, J. C., and H. R. Coursen, eds. *Shakespeare on Television* (1988). An anthology of general and theoretical essays, essays on individual productions, and shorter reviews, with a bibliography and a videography listing cassettes that may be rented.

Coursen, H. P. *Watching Shakespeare on Television* (1993). Analyses not only of TV versions but also of films and videotapes of stage presentations that are shown on television.

Davies, Anthony, and Stanley Wells, eds. *Shakespeare and the Moving Image: The Plays on Film and Television* (1994). General essays (e.g., on the comedies) as well as essays devoted entirely to *Hamlet, King Lear*, and *Macbeth*.

Dawson, Anthony B. *Watching Shakespeare: A Playgoer's Guide* (1988). About half of the plays are discussed, chiefly in terms of decisions that actors and directors make in putting the works onto the stage.

Dessen, Alan. *Elizabethan Stage Conventions and Modern Interpretations* (1984). On interpreting conventions such as the representation of light and darkness and stage violence (duels, battles).

Donaldson, Peter. *Shakespearean Films/Shakespearean Directors* (1990). Postmodernist analyses, drawing on Freudianism, Feminism, Deconstruction, and Queer Theory.

Jackson, Russell, and Robert Smallwood, eds. *Players of Shakespeare 2: Further Essays in Shakespearean Performance by Players with the Royal Shakespeare Company* (1988). Fourteen actors discuss their roles in productions between 1982 and 1987.

————. *Players of Shakespeare 3: Further Essays in Shake-*

spearean Performance by Players with the Royal Shakespeare Company (1993). Comments by thirteen performers.

Jorgens, Jack. *Shakespeare on Film* (1977). Fairly detailed studies of eighteen films, preceded by an introductory chapter addressing such issues as music, and whether to "open" the play by including scenes of landscape.

Kennedy, Dennis. *Looking at Shakespeare: A Visual History of Twentieth-Century Performance* (1993). Lucid descriptions (with 170 photographs) of European, British, and American performances.

Leiter, Samuel L. *Shakespeare Around the Globe: A Guide to Notable Postwar Revivals* (1986). For each play there are about two pages of introductory comments, then discussions (about five hundred words per production) of ten or so productions, and finally bibliographic references.

McMurty, Jo. *Shakespeare Films in the Classroom* (1994). Useful evaluations of the chief films most likely to be shown in undergraduate courses.

Rothwell, Kenneth, and Annabelle Henkin Melzer. *Shakespeare on Screen: An International Filmography and Videography* (1990). A reference guide to several hundred films and videos produced between 1899 and 1989, including spinoffs such as musicals and dance versions.

Sprague, Arthur Colby. *Shakespeare and the Actors* (1944). Detailed discussions of stage business (gestures, etc.) over the years.

Willis, Susan. *The BBC Shakespeare Plays: Making the Televised Canon* (1991). A history of the series, with interviews and production diaries for some plays.

5. Miscellaneous Reference Works

Abbott, E. A. *A Shakespearean Grammar* (new edition, 1877). An examination of differences between Elizabethan and modern grammar.

Allen, Michael J. B., and Kenneth Muir, eds. *Shakespeare's Plays in Quarto* (1981). One volume containing facsimiles of the plays issued in small format before they were collected in the First Folio of 1623.

Bevington, David. *Shakespeare* (1978). A short guide to hundreds of important writings on the subject.

Blake, Norman. *Shakespeare's Language: An Introduction* (1983). On vocabulary, parts of speech, and word order.

Bullough, Geoffrey. *Narrative and Dramatic Sources of Shakespeare*, 8 vols. (1957–75). A collection of many of the books Shakespeare drew on, with judicious comments.

Campbell, Oscar James, and Edward G. Quinn, eds. *The Reader's Encyclopedia of Shakespeare* (1966). Old, but still the most useful single reference work on Shakespeare.

Cercignani, Fausto. *Shakespeare's Works and Elizabethan Pronunciation* (1981). Considered the best work on the topic, but remains controversial.

Dent, R. W. *Shakespeare's Proverbial Language: An Index* (1981). An index of proverbs, with an introduction concerning a form Shakespeare frequently drew on.

Greg, W. W. *The Shakespeare First Folio* (1955). A detailed yet readable history of the first collection (1623) of Shakespeare's plays.

Harner, James. *The World Shakespeare Bibliography*. See headnote to Suggested References.

Hosley, Richard. *Shakespeare's Holinshed* (1968). Valuable presentation of one of Shakespeare's major sources.

Kökeritz, Helge. *Shakespeare's Names* (1959). A guide to pronouncing some 1,800 names appearing in Shakespeare.

———. *Shakespeare's Pronunciation* (1953). Contains much information about puns and rhymes, but see Cercignani (above).

Muir, Kenneth. *The Sources of Shakespeare's Plays* (1978). An account of Shakespeare's use of his reading. It covers all the plays, in chronological order.

Miriam Joseph, Sister. *Shakespeare's Use of the Arts of Language* (1947). A study of Shakespeare's use of rhetorical devices, reprinted in part as *Rhetoric in Shakespeare's Time* (1962).

The Norton Facsimile: The First Folio of Shakespeare's Plays (1968). A handsome and accurate facsimile of the first collection (1623) of Shakespeare's plays, with a valuable introduction by Charlton Hinman.

Onions, C. T. *A Shakespeare Glossary*, rev. and enlarged by

R. D. Eagleson (1986). Definitions of words (or senses of words) now obsolete.

Partridge, Eric. *Shakespeare's Bawdy*, rev. ed. (1955). Relatively brief dictionary of bawdy words; useful, but see Williams, below.

Shakespeare Quarterly. See headnote to Suggested References.

Shakespeare Survey. See headnote to Suggested References.

Spevack, Marvin. *The Harvard Concordance to Shakespeare* (1973). An index to Shakespeare's words.

Vickers, Brian. *Appropriating Shakespeare: Contemporary Critical Quarrels* (1993). A survey—chiefly hostile—of recent schools of criticism.

Wells, Stanley, ed. *Shakespeare: A Bibliographical Guide* (new edition, 1990). Nineteen chapters (some devoted to single plays, others devoted to groups of related plays) on recent scholarship on the life and all of the works.

Williams, Gordon. *A Dictionary of Sexual Language and Imagery in Shakespearean and Stuart Literature*, 3 vols. (1994). Extended discussions of words and passages; much fuller than Partridge, cited above.

6. Shakespeare's Plays: General Studies

Bamber, Linda. *Comic Women, Tragic Men: A Study of Gender and Genre in Shakespeare* (1982).

Barnet, Sylvan. *A Short Guide to Shakespeare* (1974).

Callaghan, Dympna, Lorraine Helms, and Jyotsna Singh. *The Weyward Sisters: Shakespeare and Feminist Politics* (1994).

Clemen, Wolfgang H. *The Development of Shakespeare's Imagery* (1951).

Cook, Ann Jennalie. *Making a Match: Courtship in Shakespeare and His Society* (1991).

Dollimore, Jonathan, and Alan Sinfield. *Political Shakespeare: New Essays in Cultural Materialism* (1985).

Dusinberre, Juliet. *Shakespeare and the Nature of Women* (1975).

Granville-Barker, Harley. *Prefaces to Shakespeare*, 2 vols. (1946–47; volume 1 contains essays on *Hamlet, King*

Lear, Merchant of Venice, Antony and Cleopatra, and *Cymbeline*; volume 2 contains essays on *Othello, Coriolanus, Julius Caesar, Romeo and Juliet, Love's Labor's Lost*).

————. *More Prefaces to Shakespeare* (1974; essays on *Twelfth Night, A Midsummer Night's Dream, The Winter's Tale, Macbeth*).

Harbage, Alfred. *William Shakespeare: A Reader's Guide* (1963).

Howard, Jean E. *Shakespeare's Art of Orchestration: Stage Technique and Audience Response* (1984).

Jones, Emrys. *Scenic Form in Shakespeare* (1971).

Lenz, Carolyn Ruth Swift, Gayle Greene, and Carol Thomas Neely, eds. *The Woman's Part: Feminist Criticism of Shakespeare* (1980).

Novy, Marianne. *Love's Argument: Gender Relations in Shakespeare* (1984).

Rose, Mark. *Shakespearean Design* (1972).

Scragg, Leah. *Discovering Shakespeare's Meaning* (1994).

————. *Shakespeare's "Mouldy Tales": Recurrent Plot Motifs in Shakespearean Drama* (1992).

Traub, Valerie. *Desire and Anxiety: Circulations of Sexuality in Shakespearean Drama* (1992).

Traversi, D. A. *An Approach to Shakespeare,* 2 vols. (3rd rev. ed, 1968–69).

Vickers, Brian. *The Artistry of Shakespeare's Prose* (1968).

Wells, Stanley. *Shakespeare: A Dramatic Life* (1994).

Wright, George T. *Shakespeare's Metrical Art* (1988).

7. The Comedies

Barber, C. L. *Shakespeare's Festive Comedy* (1959; discusses *Love's Labor's Lost, A Midsummer Night's Dream, The Merchant of Venice, As You Like It, Twelfth Night*).

Barton, Anne. *The Names of Comedy* (1990).

Berry, Ralph. *Shakespeare's Comedy: Explorations in Form* (1972).

Bradbury, Malcolm, and David Palmer, eds. *Shakespearean Comedy* (1972).

Bryant, J. A., Jr. *Shakespeare and the Uses of Comedy* (1986).

Carroll, William. *The Metamorphoses of Shakespearean Comedy* (1985).

Champion, Larry S. *The Evolution of Shakespeare's Comedy* (1970).

Evans, Bertrand. *Shakespeare's Comedies* (1960).

Frye, Northrop. *Shakespearean Comedy and Romance* (1965).

Leggatt, Alexander. *Shakespeare's Comedy of Love* (1974).

Miola, Robert S. *Shakespeare and Classical Comedy: The Influence of Plautus and Terence* (1994).

Nevo, Ruth. *Comic Transformations in Shakespeare* (1980).

Ornstein, Robert. *Shakespeare's Comedies: From Roman Farce to Romantic Mystery* (1986).

Richman, David. *Laughter, Pain, and Wonder: Shakespeare's Comedies and the Audience in the Theater* (1990).

Salingar, Leo. *Shakespeare and the Traditions of Comedy* (1974).

Slights, Camille Wells. *Shakespeare's Comic Commonwealths* (1993).

Waller, Gary, ed. *Shakespeare's Comedies* (1991).

Westlund, Joseph. *Shakespeare's Reparative Comedies: A Psychoanalytic View of the Middle Plays* (1984).

Williamson, Marilyn. *The Patriarchy of Shakespeare's Comedies* (1986).

8. The Romances (*Pericles, Cymbeline, The Winter's Tale, The Tempest, The Two Noble Kinsmen*)

Adams, Robert M. *Shakespeare: The Four Romances* (1989).

Felperin, Howard. *Shakespearean Romance* (1972).

Frye, Northrop. *A Natural Perspective: The Development of Shakespearean Comedy and Romance* (1965).

Mowat, Barbara. *The Dramaturgy of Shakespeare's Romances* (1976).

Warren, Roger. *Staging Shakespeare's Late Plays* (1990).

Young, David. *The Heart's Forest: A Study of Shakespeare's Pastoral Plays* (1972).

9. The Tragedies

Bradley, A. C. *Shakespearean Tragedy* (1904).

Brooke, Nicholas. *Shakespeare's Early Tragedies* (1968).

Champion, Larry. *Shakespeare's Tragic Perspective* (1976).

Drakakis, John, ed. *Shakespearean Tragedy* (1992).

Evans, Bertrand. *Shakespeare's Tragic Practice* (1979).

Everett, Barbara. *Young Hamlet: Essays on Shakespeare's Tragedies* (1989).

Foakes, R. A. *Hamlet Versus Lear: Cultural Politics and Shakespeare's Art* (1993).

Frye, Northrop. *Fools of Time: Studies in Shakespearean Tragedy* (1967).

Harbage, Alfred, ed. *Shakespeare: The Tragedies* (1964).

Mack, Maynard. *Everybody's Shakespeare: Reflections Chiefly on the Tragedies* (1993).

McAlindon, T. *Shakespeare's Tragic Cosmos* (1991).

Miola, Robert S. *Shakespeare and Classical Tragedy: The Influence of Seneca* (1992).

——. *Shakespeare's Rome* (1983).

Nevo, Ruth. *Tragic Form in Shakespeare* (1972).

Rackin, Phyllis. *Shakespeare's Tragedies* (1978).

Rose, Mark, ed. *Shakespeare's Early Tragedies: A Collection of Critical Essays* (1995).

Rosen, William. *Shakespeare and the Craft of Tragedy* (1960).

Snyder, Susan. *The Comic Matrix of Shakespeare's Tragedies* (1979).

Wofford, Susanne. *Shakespeare's Late Tragedies: A Collection of Critical Essays* (1996).

Young, David. *The Action to the Word: Structure and Style in Shakespearean Tragedy* (1990).

——. *Shakespeare's Middle Tragedies: A Collection of Critical Essays* (1993).

10. The Histories

Blanpied, John W. *Time and the Artist in Shakespeare's English Histories* (1983).

Campbell, Lily B. *Shakespeare's "Histories": Mirrors of Elizabethan Policy* (1947).

Champion, Larry S. *Perspective in Shakespeare's English Histories* (1980).

Hodgdon, Barbara. *The End Crowns All: Closure and Contradiction in Shakespeare's History* (1991).

Holderness, Graham. *Shakespeare Recycled: The Making of Historical Drama* (1992).

——, ed. *Shakespeare's History Plays: "Richard II" to "Henry V"* (1992).

Leggatt, Alexander. *Shakespeare's Political Drama: The History Plays and the Roman Plays* (1988).

Ornstein, Robert. *A Kingdom for a Stage: The Achievement of Shakespeare's History Plays* (1972).

Rackin, Phyllis. *Stages of History: Shakespeare's English Chronicles* (1990).

Saccio, Peter. *Shakespeare's English Kings: History, Chronicle, and Drama* (1977).

Tillyard, E. M. W. *Shakespeare's History Plays* (1944).

Velz, John W., ed. *Shakespeare's English Histories: A Quest for Form and Genre* (1996).

11. *The Taming of the Shrew*

In addition to the titles listed above in Section 7, The Comedies, see the following:

Aspinall, Dana E. *The Taming of the Shrew: Critical Essays* (2002).

Bean, John C. "Comic Structure and the Humanizing of Kate in *The Taming of the Shrew*." *The Woman's Part: Feminist Criticism of Shakespeare*. Eds. Carolyn Ruth Lenz, Gayle Greene, and Carol Thomas Neely (1980), pp. 65–78.

Boose, Linda. "*The Taming of the Shrew*: Good Husbandry, and Enclosure." *Shakespeare Reread*. Ed. Russ McDonald (1994), pp. 193–225.

Burns, Margie. "The Ending of *The Shrew*." *Shakespeare Studies* 18 (1986): 41–64.

Coursen, H. R. *Shakespearean Performance as Interpretation* (1992).

Dusinberre, Juliet. *"The Taming of the Shrew:* Women, Acting and Power." *Studies in the Literary Imagination* 26 (1993): 67–84.

Haring-Smith, Tori. *From Farce to Metadrama: A Stage History of "The Taming of the Shrew," 1594–1983* (1983).

Hodgdon, Barbara, ed. *The Taming of the Shrew* (2010).

Holderness, Graham. *The Taming of the Shrew [Shakespeare in Performance]* (1989).

Huston, J. Dennis. *Shakespeare's Comedies of Play* (1981).

Loos, Pamela, ed. *The Taming of the Shrew* (2008) [critical essays].

Newman, Karen. *Fashioning Femininity and English Renaissance Drama* (1991).

Saccio, Peter. "Shrewd and Kindly Farce." *Shakespeare Survey* 37 (1984): 33–40.

Tillyard, E. M. W. *Shakespeare's Early Comedies* (1965).